What Kind of University?

SRHE and Open University Press Imprint
General Editor: Heather Eggins

Current titles include:

Catherine Bargh, Peter Scott and David Smith: *Governing Universities*
Ronald Barnett: *Improving Higher Education: Total Quality Care*
Ronald Barnett: *The Idea of Higher Education*
Ronald Barnett: *The Limits of Competence*
Ronald Barnett: *Higher Education: A Critical Business*
John Biggs: *Teaching for Quality Learning at University*
David Boud *et al.* (eds): *Using Experience for Learning*
Etienne Bourgeois *et al.*: *The Adult University*
John Brennan *et al.* (eds): *What Kind of University?*
Angela Brew (ed.): *Directions in Staff Development*
Anne Brockbank and Ian McGill: *Facilitating Reflective Learning in Higher Education*
Ann Brooks: *Academic Women*
Sally Brown and Angela Glasner (eds): *Assessment Matters in Higher Education*
Frank Coffield and Bill Williamson (eds): *Repositioning Higher Education*
John Cowan: *On Becoming an Innovative University Teacher*
Heather Eggins (ed.): *Women as Leaders and Managers in Higher Education*
Gillian Evans: *Calling Academia to Account*
David Farnham (ed.): *Managing Academic Staff in Changing University Systems*
Sinclair Goodlad: *The Quest for Quality*
Harry Gray (ed.): *Universities and the Creation of Wealth*
Diana Green (ed.): *What is Quality in Higher Education?*
Elaine Martin: *Changing Academic Work*
Robin Middlehurst: *Leading Academics*
Sarah Neal: *The Making of Equal Opportunities Policies in Universities*
David Palfreyman and David Warner (eds): *Higher Education and the Law*
John Pratt: *The Polytechnic Experiment*
Michael Prosser and Keith Trigwell: *Understanding Learning and Teaching*
Yoni Ryan and Ortrun Zuber-Skerritt: *Supervising Postgraduates from Non-English speaking Backgrounds*
Tom Schuller (ed.): *The Changing University?*
Peter Scott: *The Meanings of Mass Higher Education*
Peter Scott (ed.): *The Globalization of Higher Education*
Harold Silver and Pamela Silver: *Students*
Anthony Smith and Frank Webster (eds): *The Postmodern University?*
Imogen Taylor: *Developing Learning in Professional Education*
Susan Toohey: *Designing Courses for Higher Education*
Paul R. Trowler: *Academics Responding to Change*
David Warner and Elaine Crosthwaite (eds): *Human Resource Management in Higher and Further Education*
David Warner and Charles Leonard: *The Income Generation Handbook* (Second Edition)
David Warner and David Palfreyman (eds): *Higher Education Management*
Graham Webb: *Understanding Staff Development*
Sue Wheeler and Jan Birtle: *A Handbook for Personal Tutors*

What Kind of University?

International Perspectives on Knowledge, Participation and Governance

Edited by
John Brennan, Jutta Fedrowitz,
Mary Huber and Tarla Shah

The Society for Research into Higher Education
& Open University Press

Published by SRHE and
Open University Press
Celtic Court
22 Ballmoor
Buckingham
MK18 1XW

email: enquiries@openup.co.uk
world wide web: http://www.openup.co.uk

and
325 Chestnut Street
Philadelphia, PA 19106, USA

First published 1999

ISBN 0 335 20429 5 (hbk)

A catalogue record of this book is available from the British Library

Library of Congress Cataloging-in-Publication Data
What kind of university? / edited by John Brennan ... [et al.].
      p.   cm.
   Includes bibliographical references and index.
   ISBN 0-335-20429-5
   1. Education, Higher—Aims and objectives.   2. Education, Higher—Curricula.
3. College students.   4. Universities and colleges—Administration—Case studies.
I. Brennan, J. L. (John Leslie), 1947–
LB2922.2.W43   1999
378—dc21   98-55540
                                                                                                    CIP

Copy-edited and typeset by The Running Head Limited, London and Cambridge
Printed in Great Britain by St Edmundsbury Press, Bury St Edmunds, Suffolk

Contents

The Editors and Contributors

Joel E. Anderson is Provost and Vice Chancellor for Academic Affairs at the University of Arkansas at Little Rock, USA.

A. W. (Tony) Bates is the Director of Distance Education and Technology at the University of British Columbia, Canada.

Li Bennich-Björkman is Assistant Professor at the Department of Government at the University of Uppsala, Sweden.

Harry F. de Boer is Research Associate at the Centre for Higher Education Policy Studies, University of Twente in The Netherlands.

John Brennan is Director of the Centre for Higher Education Research and Information (QSC), Open University, UK.

Steve Cannon is Secretary of the University of Aberdeen, UK. He was previously Secretary of the Scottish Higher Education Funding Council, UK.

John Daniel is the Vice-Chancellor of the Open University, UK.

Peter Darvas is an education economist in the Social and Human Development Sector Unit (Europe and Central Asia Region) at the World Bank. He was Director of the Higher Education Support Programme at the Open Society Institute, Hungary.

David D. Dill is Professor of Public Policy Analysis and Education at the University of North Carolina at Chapel Hill, USA.

Janet Gail Donald is Professor and Director of the Graduate Programme in Cognition and Instruction at the Centre for University Teaching and Learning, McGill University, Canada.

Jutta Fedrowitz is Programme Manager at the Centre for Higher Education Development of the Bertelsmann Foundation, Germany.

Michael Gibbons is the Secretary General at the Association of Commonwealth Universities, UK.

Brenda M. Gourley is Vice Chancellor of the University of Natal, South Africa.

Mary Huber is Senior Fellow and Director of Planning and Policy Reports, Carnegie Foundation for the Advancement of Teaching, USA.

D. Bruce Johnstone is Professor of Higher and Comparative Education at the State University of New York at Buffalo, USA.

Sybe B. Jongeling is the Director of the Office of Research and Development at Edith Cowan University, Australia.

Brian P. Nedwek is Dean of the College of Liberal Arts at the University of Detroit Mercy, USA.

Juan-Francisco Perellon is Assistant Diplomé and Research Fellow at the Institut des Sciences Sociales et Pédagogiques, Université de Lausanne, Switzerland.

Karl S. Pister is Chancellor Emeritus, Office of the President, UC Santa Cruz, University of California, USA.

Tarla Shah is Projects and Development Officer in the Centre for Higher Education Research and Information (QSC), Open University, UK.

Lee Shulman is President of the Carnegie Foundation for the Advancement of Teaching, USA.

John Sizer is the Chief Executive of the Scottish Higher Education Funding Council, UK.

Jan de Vuyst is Director of Social Services at the Catholic University of Leuven, Belgium.

Foreword

The problem with the future is it ain't what it used to be.

(Anonymous sage)

We don't predict the future; we invent it.

(Silicon Valley aphorism)

Predicting the future is always a risky enterprise. Economists have been embarrassed doing it. Prophets have been stoned (or worse!) for it. And historians have long since given it up entirely. Why, then, would scores of otherwise intelligent and prudent leaders in the world of higher education have gathered together in London to explore the future of the university? In part, one might argue, because their jobs depend on their skill in anticipating how the institutions they inhabit will change in the coming decades. More likely, because they truly believe that they are already engaged in changing the world of their prophecies.

The partners in this enterprise were the Centre for Higher Education Research and Information (QSC) of the Open University in the UK, the Carnegie Foundation for the Advancement of Teaching in the US, the Centre for Higher Education Policy Studies of the University of Twente in The Netherlands, and CHE Centre for Higher Education Development in Germany. Each partner contributed its own favourite thematic ideas. For example, for the Open University it was a combination of technology, distance learning (and hence both regionalization and internationalization) and increasing access for non-traditional students. For the Carnegie Foundation, it was the changing roles of the professorate, especially in connection with teaching, and the need to craft forms of graduate education to prepare a new generation of faculty to play those roles.

The structure of this volume reflects the general categories within which the present was analysed and the future foretold. Three major topics defined the content of the presentations and discussions. The first topic was the curriculum: what will count as important knowledge in the future, how will it be organized, and how will it be taught? We have seen universities evolve from a focus on the classical *trivium* and *quadrivium* to fluid institutions where many kinds of knowledge – liberal and professional, general and specialized, religious and secular, theoretical and practical – vie for space in the classroom and the catalogue. What knowledge is worth most? What knowledge is most worth teaching? What websites are most worth linking to one's own?

The second major topic asked who will be the university's students. How will access to and participation in the worlds of higher education be accomplished? We are no longer in the world of fifteenth-century Oxford, where 13-year-old college students reside in supervised quarters called 'colleges', coached by hired tutors to pass the examinations conducted by the university. In contemporary community colleges in the United States, students who are retirees in their 70s are sitting next to adolescents looking ahead to a career. Our institutions are no longer restricted to the children of the very rich and privileged. They have become increasingly open, both as a result of public policy and changing social norms, as well as following dramatic changes in the 'delivery' of higher education.

The largest number of chapters is devoted to the third general topic: issues of governance. How are the management and organization of institutions likely to change, both as a function of differences among nations and national systems, as well as changes in conceptions and technologies of management? That the largest number of contributions deal with issues of governance should not surprise us. Scholars of higher education have a long history of attending to important social and organizational contexts of higher education. Now it is time to give equal attention to the teaching, learning and personal interactions that occur within the institutions' walls.

Two powerful themes pervaded the discussions of these major topics. The first was the recognition that these were indeed international issues. Higher education, like the economy, has become global. The second theme was clearly technology. Perhaps because our London host was the Open University with its formidable technological resources and inventions, perhaps because of the manner in which the participants were selected, but more likely because computer-mediated technologies of instruction and assessment have already become ubiquitous, conversations about technology dominated both the formal and informal work of the conference.

The form and international scope of this meeting is as interesting as its substance. Why should pedagogical questions of curriculum, teaching, learning and instructional design be addressed at a conference whose sponsorship spans the Atlantic, and whose participants inhabit the globe? There was doubtless a time when such questions were quite properly perceived as fundamentally local ones. A university was a local or regional institution, whose activities were of interest primarily to its immediate neighbours. It would have been absurd to suggest that its quite local efforts would have a significant impact on its nation's future, much less have any consequences beyond national borders.

This local conception of universities dissolved dramatically in the twentieth-century's romance with scholarship in general and science in particular. We have learned that knowledge itself leaps across national boundaries. The work of scholars needs no passports, and worries not over expired visas. University scholars became true citizens of the world, recognized and honoured for their accomplishments by colleagues everywhere.

But what was traditionally the status of the investigations of scholars has now also become characteristic of their teaching functions as well. Research readily crosses frontiers, and Internet communications among researchers instantaneously cross oceans, deserts and hemispheres. The epiphany of this conference and this volume is the recognition that university teaching has now joined university research as an international, technologically mediated matter of central interest. We at the Carnegie Foundation for the Advancement of Teaching are embarked on a continuing programme of research and dissemination to develop a true scholarship of teaching, and to aid its global development.

There is something entrancing about the Year 2000. It represents a threshold, a demarcation, a historical watershed on the other side of which beckons a new millennium of opportunities and challenges for higher education. This volume offers a rich array of anticipations and designs, along with nightmares and anxieties. From John Daniel's delightful account of his personal odyssey as a 'scholar-gypsy' innovating instructionally in the United Kingdom, Canada and France to Bruce Johnstone's discerning evaluation of the most likely fates of today's revolutionary visions, this volume instructs and enlightens. It proclaims loudly that, whatever their other critical roles in the society, the world's universities will continue to teach. They will teach an ever-growing population of students, in a wildly multiplying range of areas, using technologies as old as the personal tutorial and as new as the interactive website. Universities are among the oldest institutions in the world. They are not about to disappear. Instead, they are adapting to the new demands and expectations of their communities as they commit themselves to the advancement of teaching.

Lee S. Shulman
President, Carnegie Foundation for the Advancement of Teaching

Introductions

1

What Kind of University?

John Brennan

In 1992, 34 new universities were created in the United Kingdom. These were far from being new institutions. Several of them had existed for over a century in a variety of guises as colleges of technology, of teaching, of commerce, of art and design and so on. Over the years, these institutions had merged with other institutions (and sometimes demerged again), changed their function, grown and, above all, had changed their names. Most of these changes reflected local needs (and politics) of the time. They were local institutions, owned by local government, recruiting from the locality, serving local employment needs. Many of the students studied part-time, combining education with employment.

For the last 20 years of their pre-university existence, most of these institutions were designated polytechnics – formed at the end of the 1960s from a series of mergers of existing colleges. During their polytechnic lifetimes, these institutions grew massively: they concentrated their growth on degree work – in which they were a major innovative force in British higher education – they developed their research, they recruited their students nationally. In short, they began to compete with the existing universities.

When Owens College, later to become the Victoria University of Manchester, was formed in 1851, it found a number of pre-existing colleges which, over a hundred years and almost as many mergers later, were to become its larger neighbour as Manchester Metropolitan University. Institutions which had existed side by side for more than a century were now both universities. But what kind of universities?

This was a question being asked during the first half of the 1990s in the UK as the public, employers, students and the academic profession itself sought to come to terms with a mass university system – as they had been doing for some time. Such understanding as there was of that mass higher education system rested on the binary division between the universities and the polytechnics. People might not have been very sure about what the polytechnics actually were, or how they differed from universities, but the existence of the polytechnics preserved an idea of what universities were that was reasonably homogeneous, unambiguous, ancient and prestigious. The binary division helped 'make sense' of the mass, diverse system of higher education that the UK, in common with most other western countries, was creating during the second half of the twentieth century. The creation of the polytechnics allowed the public conception of the universities to remain largely unchanged.

A mass system of universities raised a whole new set of questions. Were all universities the same? Were their degrees equivalent? Were the new ones any good? Were universities essentially to be viewed in hierarchical terms, as basically similar institutions differing primarily in prestige and reputation, with the ancient universities of Oxford and Cambridge at the top and the newest of the new universities bringing up the rear? Or were they best seen as diverse institutions with distinctive missions and clientele, each seeking excellence in its own way, each deserving of reputation in its own terms?

Such questions continue to be asked. The institutions themselves attempt to position themselves within a competitive higher education market place where an improved share of state resources is the sought-after prize for most. Informal categorizations and alliances between 'research-intensive' universities and between 'modern' universities suggest that the institutions do not see themselves as 'all the same'. The state continues to establish an increasingly complex machinery providing not just accountability for state funding but also public information about institutions and their academic programmes, information that is evaluative as well as descriptive. The message is not just that universities are different from each other but that some are better than others.

It was in this context of confusion and questioning about the nature of universities in the UK that the idea of organizing an international conference on the future of universities originated. It was initially going to be entitled 'What is a university?' The question appeared to be appropriate to the UK context with so many newly created universities. However, as the UK organizers developed the conception of the conference with their partners in Germany, The Netherlands and the United States, it became evident that this formulation did not work universally. The Germans retained a unitary and essentially Humboldtian conception of what a university was which made the question uninteresting. The Americans regarded heterogeneity among university institutions as so natural and familiar that the question appeared to invite only philosophical introspection rather than practical engagement with the real world. Thus, after a brief flirtation with 'What are universities?', a conference title of 'What kind of university?' was eventually agreed upon.

The idea was to organize an internal debate among the university community internationally about the kinds of university that are emerging in different parts of the world, about the conditions that shape and constrain their nature, about the features that they share in common and about the main faultlines that define their differences. The conference was not intended to be the occasion when the voices of governments and industry might be heard, vital though their messages might be for the future of the universities. Nor was it to be a platform for debate about higher education in general, locating the universities in a wider and even more diverse set of higher educational institutional forms.

The conference was to be the vehicle for the expression of university perspectives on universities.

The much quoted observation by Clark Kerr that universities are among the oldest forms of social institutions (Kerr, 1963), while true, is somewhat misleading. Most actual universities are very new institutions. A high proportion of them were created in the second half of the twentieth century. Thus, although its history may be important to an understanding of an individual institution, there is a danger of overstating the significance of the antiquity of the institutional type. And most individual universities have very short histories.

In asking the question 'What kind of university?', the aim is to be future orientated rather than historical. What kinds of university are likely to emerge in the twenty-first century? What kinds of university will be needed in different parts of the world? Will all kinds of university be able to survive in the next century or will change and adaptation be necessary for survival? And how might change and adaptation best be achieved? To these general questions must be added quite specific choices which individual universities, to a greater or lesser extent, are having to make at the present time. How institutions make these choices will determine the kinds of universities they will become.

The first set of choices concerns knowledge and curricula. The increasing specialization and differentiation of knowledge, the growth of interdisciplinarity, the relationship between propositional 'disciplinary' knowledge and experiential 'work-based' knowledge, the growing demands of employment, all pose questions about the forms of knowledge that are to be recognized in universities and how they should be organized into curricula and departmental structures. Such choices have to be exercised in the recognition that the university's 'monopolistic' position in the production and transmission of knowledge is being challenged.

A second set of choices concerns access and participation. The expansion of higher education from 'elite' to 'mass' participation increases the diversity of users – both of students (in terms of age, gender, ethnic, social and educational backgrounds) and other 'stakeholders' (for example employers, social and community groups). What are the needs and demands of these users? Which of them will be met by universities and which by other forms of educational institutions? And what are the consequences for the university of the access of 'new' kinds of students?

A third set of choices concerns teaching and learning. Existing approaches to teaching and learning in universities are being questioned as a result of expansion and resource pressures. New possibilities are resulting from the use of educational technologies. What are the implications of the adoption of new technologies for the learning experiences of students, the teaching and research roles of staff, and the ways universities are organized and resourced?

A fourth set of choices concerns decision making and accountability. Traditional forms of management and decision making in universities are being questioned as a result of pressures towards greater societal accountability and responsiveness. How much autonomy will be appropriate at the levels of the individual institution, the faculty, the department, the individual staff member? What sorts of decisions will be the preserve of the state? What will be left to markets? Will universities increasingly need to have professional managers and administrators? On what criteria will universities be judged? And will these criteria increasingly be set by those outside the university?

There are of course many additional questions that can be asked of the modern university. Questions about the role of research underpin several of the issues mentioned above. Other questions concern staffing, quality assurance, planning and the management of change. Labour market features and the likely employment opportunities for graduates present another set of determining factors for the kinds of university of the future.

To a greater or lesser extent, implicitly or explicitly, these sorts of questions are being debated in universities all over the world. If the questions are broadly similar – although with very different emphases in different places – the answers to them are likely to be rather different. Answers will reflect local conditions: of economy, of politics, of social structure. Answers will also reflect culture, tradition and history, both of the individual university and the society in which it is located. But equally, the answers surely have to be similar enough to sustain a conception of 'university' which is recognizable universally, whatever differences of detail. It has been suggested that the only possible answer to the question of 'What kind of university?' is 'all kinds'. But unless some limitation is allowed and understood, the answer might equally be 'no kind'.

Coming to terms with the *diversity* of the modern university may be the key to understanding it. But diversity can be viewed from many different vantage points, both within and outside higher education. The elegant and justly famous Carnegie Classification of US institutions has helped the academic profession in the United States to understand itself (Carnegie Council, 1987). Peter Scott (1995) attempted a categorization of the recently diversified British system in his *Meanings of Mass Higher Education*. But public understandings of their institutions may be much cruder. Whatever the current title, mission or reality of a higher education institution, to the man or woman in the street it may still be the 'poly' or the 'tech' or its local equivalent. How much does public understanding of universities matter and what factors determine it?

There is no shortage of dimensions on which the diversity of the modern university can be described. In many parts of the world, a distinction between state and private is important, determining social and educational function as well as reflecting the funding source. Yet increasing diversity of funding may represent the future for most universities, giving us the 'entrepreneurial university' as a distinctive and ubiquitous form for the twenty-first century (Clark, 1998).

Diversity can also be explored in terms of mission – local $v.$ national, teaching $v.$ research, open access $v.$ elite, etc. – although the difficulty of knowing whether institutional realities accord with institutional mission is often considerable. Diversity in terms of educational technologies is a fast-growing trend, posing for some people questions about quality and standards. However, in many countries the key to understanding diversity lies in understanding hierarchy, and in particular in understanding and distinguishing between the social and the educational underpinnings of hierarchy.

The work of the French sociologist, Pierre Bourdieu, is an elegant testimony to the processes by which elite educational institutions in France serve crucially to reproduce existing social hierarchies in that country (Bourdieu, 1996). Few would doubt the credibility of a similar analysis of the role of the public schools and the universities of Oxford and Cambridge in British society. It would, of course, be a very partial understanding of what such institutions were about to see that as their only role. But the questions remain: how much diversity is also hierarchy, and how much hierarchy is social rather than educational in its source?

Like it or not, universities are typically differentiated in terms of prestige, with antiquity and research reputation being its primary determinants. The claims of some universities to be 'innovative', 'relevant', 'excellent in teaching', 'community focused', 'business focused', or whatever, make little serious impression on well-established institutional hierarchies. The situation is perhaps not helped by the fact that the people who write or speak at international conferences about higher education tend to come from the research/high status end of it. We speak most convincingly about what we know first hand.

Universities exist in local, national and international contexts. In how many countries do increasingly diverse university institutions constitute a coherent and integrated *system* of higher education serving all of society? How far is mobility within the system possible, irrespective of entry and exit points? Or is diversity of universities a source of social divisiveness? Do different social groups tend to use their 'own' academic institutions whose certification serves to confirm (rather than to transform) their social status and life chances?

The increasing diversity of universities is undeniable. In the second chapter of this Introduction, John Daniel charts a 'personal odyssey' through the diversity of a number of institutions in which he has studied and worked. Yet such is the pace of change in many individual universities that a comparable odyssey could have been achieved in some institutions by staying put. Questions of what is to be taught and learned in universities, of who is to get access to universities, and of who is to control universities and by what means are the themes addressed in Parts 1, 2 and 3. In considering the future of the university, the contributors to Part 4 address the book's central question of 'What kind of university?' In so doing, they may also be posing the question of 'What kind of society?'

References

Bourdieu, P. (1996) *The State Nobility: Elite Schools in the Field of Power*. Cambridge: Polity Press.

Carnegie Council of Policy Studies in Higher Education (1987) *A Classification of Institutions of Higher Education*. San Francisco, CA: Jossey-Bass.

Clark, B. R. (1998) *Creating Entrepreneurial Universities: Organisational Pathways of Transformation*. Oxford: Pergamon.

Kerr, C. (1963) *The Uses of the University*. Cambridge, MA: Harvard University Press.

Scott, P. (1995) *The Meanings of Mass Higher Education*. Buckingham: SRHE and Open University Press.

2

Reflections of a Scholar-Gypsy

John Daniel

Introduction

I have more to contribute to the theme of this book as a reflective practitioner of university leadership than as a scholar of higher education. Inspired by a favourite poem of Matthew Arnold, I have chosen the title 'Reflections of a Scholar-Gypsy'. In a wonderfully stimulating career, I have worked in a considerable diversity of universities. Every few years I arrived in a new institution and had to ask myself, 'What kind of university is this?'

I must not overdo the analogy between my nomadic career and Matthew Arnold's account of the Scholar-Gypsy, but let me begin with a key verse of the poem:

> Come, let me read the oft-read tale again!
> The story of the Oxford scholar poor,
> Of pregnant parts and quick inventive brain,
> Who, tired of knocking at preferment's door,
> One summer-morn forsook
> His friends, and went to learn the gypsy lore,
> And roamed the world with that wild brotherhood,
> And came, as most men deemed, to little good,
> But came to Oxford and his friends no more.

The poem goes on to tell how his former friends would occasionally catch sight of the Scholar-Gypsy in the country around Oxford. On one occasion they asked him about his way of life. To quote the poem:

> Whereat he answered, that the gypsy-crew,
> His mates, had arts to rule as they desired
> The workings of men's brains,
> And they can bind them to what thoughts they will.
> 'And I,' he said, 'the secret of their art,
> When fully learned will to the world impart;
> But it needs Heaven-sent moments for this skill!'

I have had the privilege, in my wanderings as a scholar-gypsy, of learning part of the secret of the most important new academic art of our generation. I shall return to that, but first, let me look back on my own academic odyssey and note some of the defining moments in my search for the kind of university that could inspire me. The Scholar-Gypsy said that the acquisition of an important skill requires 'heaven-sent moments'. Ernie Boyer and John Kelly would both have agreed with that.

In my associations with eight universities in five political jurisdictions I have had the good fortune to experience diversity on many dimensions. I have worked in three English-language universities, three French-language universities and two bilingual universities. I have experienced academe ancient and modern; urban and regional; on campus and at a distance. I once had academic responsibility for the world's smallest university, which was how the *Guinness Book of Records* described the Collège universitaire de Hearst in Northern Ontario. Now I head a very large university. The Open University is five thousand times bigger than the Collège de Hearst.

I shall examine the warp and weft of this rich academic tapestry with reference to four themes: knowledge and curricula; access and participation; teaching and learning; decision making and accountability.

Oxford

I began my academic career studying metallurgy at Oxford University. The real affinity of undergraduates at Oxford is with their college – the University is just a vague concept. My college was St Edmund Hall, one of Oxford's oldest foundations. It had been created by students, some of whom had allegedly been thrown out of the University of Paris, as an environment in which they could learn from resident scholars. Edmund Rich, later canonized as Saint Edmund, taught on the site in the 1190s. The medieval university of those days was a rather unstructured group of masters and scholars. Historically the word 'university' had nothing to do with grand notions of the universe or the universality of learning. It simply meant the group, this society of masters and students.
According to Haskins (1923: 2),

> The contrast between those earliest universities and those of today is . . . broad and striking . . . The medieval university had no libraries, laboratories, or museums, no endowment or buildings of its own; it could not possibly have met the requirements of the Carnegie Foundation! . . . The medieval university . . . was fundamentally a society of students.

Today modern technology is re-creating universities which, like those medieval halls, have few of the attributes of material existence that dominate today's campuses. Indeed, the most modern universities, such the Open University, resemble in their essence the early University of Oxford more than other academic models that have come and gone between.
One aspect of that resemblance is a shift of power back to the students. The

union of students that defined the medieval university had the task of keeping the rents of student lodgings low. It did this by using the credible threat of moving the whole university to another city. Another task was to keep the professors in line. This was not difficult because the masters lived wholly from the fees of their pupils. At Bologna the professor had to live under a minute set of regulations which guaranteed value for money to his students. A professor might not be absent without leave, even a single day, and if he wished to leave town he had to make a deposit to ensure his return. Such a regime gives a whole new meaning to our term 'student discipline'.

Chaucer does not say whether the Clerk of Oxenford, the academic who took part in the pilgrimage recorded in *The Canterbury Tales*, had to pay a deposit to ensure his return to Oxford. But Chaucer did give us a timeless academic job description when he wrote of the Clerk of Oxenford, 'And gladly wolde he lerne and gladly teche.' I like that for two reasons. First, both learning and teaching are done gladly – there was joy in academe in those early days. Second, learning comes before teaching.

Chaucer reflects a tradition that I felt as an undergraduate. I found Oxford a joyous place to learn, partly because the teaching was relatively meagre. Lectures were optional and unimportant – although I much enjoyed dropping in on lectures in poetry and art history that had nothing to do with my own programme. Personally, I never found the much-vaunted tutorials very useful either. Those one-on-one or one-on-two meetings between teacher and student may work well in other disciplines, but I did not find them helpful in the natural sciences. What was invaluable was the weekly assignment of essays to write.

A key point about the Oxford curriculum of my day was that part of the student's task was to discover what it was. Had a statement of objectives for my degree course in metallurgy existed – which it did not – it would have run something like this. 'In three years' time you will be examined on metallurgy, physical chemistry and inorganic chemistry. It is up to you to work out what is important in those disciplines, and we will help you do that by setting you an essay topic every week.'

I liked this approach, which meant you could plan your social and academic life over three years. It introduced me to distance education. The library was not very distant, but it was there, rather than in face-to-face encounters, that I worked out the intellectual structure of metallurgy. Not for nothing do Oxford students talk about reading their subject rather than studying it.

The other values I absorbed at Oxford were those of community and conversation. At St Edmund Hall the notion of academic community was real. Canon John Kelly, who was then Principal of the Hall, was one of the great Oxford college heads of all time. St Edmund Hall is numerically a large college but it has a very small quadrangle. Nearly every day John Kelly would spend an hour, around lunch time, simply wandering around the quad and chatting with students.

That, coupled with the Hall's considerable success at intercollegiate sport, created a great sense of community. Kelly's example encouraged students to develop the habit of conversation with each other. We were all studying different disciplines, so the conversations were intellectual in the best sense. The communication between Open University students on our computer conferencing systems resembles those Oxford discussions more than anything I have experienced elsewhere.

Paris

From Oxford I moved to the University of Paris to study for a Doctorat d'État. It was an odd move for a science student with only high-school French to make in those days, so why did I go? The reasons were ignoble as much as noble. My Oxford tutor thought I should do a doctorate. I was not sure I wanted to spend the best years of my life in that way, but if I did I wanted to focus on research. The fourth year of my Oxford programme had been a full-time research project and thesis. I had no desire to do more coursework, which PhD programmes in most of the English-speaking world required.

I could have stayed at Oxford, but the sense of community and ease of conversation across disciplines that I had so much enjoyed as an undergraduate did not seem to feature in graduate student life. Paris seemed an attractive option. I could start straight into research, I would have to learn French and, of course, Paris is synonymous with a good time.

So in October 1965 I found myself walking up the Boulevard Saint Michel looking for the École des Mines. What kind of university was this? The hierarchy of reputation was upside down! In Britain to be a university is to be at the top of the educational tree. In France the real prestige was reserved for the *grandes écoles*, places like the École des Mines where I began my work. The universities were for those who did not make it through the competitive entry exams to the *grandes écoles*.

The system was linked together by the professors, who had appointments in several places. Professor Paul Lacombe, who took me under his wing, held posts at the École des Mines, at the science faculty of the University of Paris, and at a Nuclear Technology Institute. That gave his research students the run of these three places too.

I gradually moved my experiments to the university labs, where the facilities were better, and helped feed my family by teaching at the Nuclear Technology Institute. Although a research lab is a perfect place to learn a language, I thought teaching in French would be a challenge. In the event, teaching crystallographic notation to students whose maths was better than mine was the bigger challenge. But I taught them gladly all the same.

In 1968 traditional forms of management and decision making in French universities were questioned by cobblestones flying over barricades in the Latin Quarter. Those were remarkable days. They generated some wonderful slogans. My favourite graffito was 'je suis marxiste – tendance groucho' (I am a marxist of the Groucho variety). During those May demonstrations we heard a lot about the need for participation in university governance. However, what seemed to be meant was the organized confrontation of interest groups rather than the ideal of a self-governing community of individuals, which I find more attractive.

What difference did the upheaval make? After 1968 people like my own professor were precluded from having posts in several institutions. That may have been desirable, although I had a model supervisor in Professor Paul Lacombe.

My lasting memory is of the day in May 1968 when the banks went on strike. By then there was no public transport and no petrol, so we foreign students already knew that we could not get out of France. We would have to sit out the crisis – but the idea of doing so without money was alarming. That morning Paul Lacombe came to the lab with a full wallet and went round all the foreign students, loaning each of us money until things settled down. The thoughtfulness of that gesture, at a time when students were on the streets yelling about the haughtiness of the academic mandarinate, still impresses me. My kind of university must have room for that kind of personal kindness and trust.

I must also say that while adding my own little brick of research to the wall of knowledge I did have the thrill, when I was in the lab one autumn Saturday afternoon, of a heaven-sent moment of insight into my results that made months of hard slog worthwhile.

Montreal

It was during the fuss in 1968 that I was hired for my first job. A professor from École Polytechnique, the engineering faculty of the University of Montreal, had come to France to recruit academics to his growing department. I had never been to Canada but my wife is from New England and working in a French-language university in North America seemed like a natural move. Because of the strikes my interview took place in the bar at Orly Airport, and after two beers I was hired as an assistant professor at the École Polytechnique. It was not a model of fair selection practice but I thought they made a good decision. A year later our ship docked at the Port of Montreal. What kind of university was I going to?

My first fear, when I did not understand the porter who helped get our bags off the boat, was that it was a kind of university that used a language I did not speak. But that fear proved groundless. Quebec French and France French are in much the same relationship as American English and UK English.

The culture shock was the students. They expected to be taught! They asked questions in class! It was more like a secondary school than any kind of university I knew. Furthermore, because the students did not read English easily and found textbooks from France culturally alien, they expected the faculty to make extensive typewritten teaching notes available for each course. This shock of pedagogical expectations made me decide that if I was to be a university teacher I ought to learn something about education.

I looked for a part-time course that had some intellectual muscle and found an MA in Educational Technology at Sir George Williams University. It was a two-year full-time programme and it took me five years of evening study to get through the coursework. But here was another very different kind of university and I found it exciting. Sir George caters largely to part-time students and is the most ethnically diverse academic community I have experienced.

The Sir George course required a three-month internship in an organization that was using educational technology seriously. This was 1971 and everyone was talking about an amazing innovation in Britain called the Open University. I wrote to them and in the summer of 1972 found myself working as an unpaid visiting lecturer at the Open University headquarters in Milton Keynes. What kind of university was this?

This one really was different. Here was a revolution in higher education. The scale was breathtaking: the OU had only been going for 18 months and already there were 40,000 students. The idealism was inspiring: the staff were totally committed to the idea that people with weak school backgrounds could succeed if they were put in a good learning environment. The team approach to course development was exciting: knowledge was refined through the clash of intellects. The use of media was scintillating: the latent power of television and textual communication was being unlocked. Here was the university of the future. I wanted to join the revolution.

Quebec

My chance came quickly when I returned to Montreal after the internship. The Université du Québec announced that it was looking for a director-general for its new Télé-université, which was to be a local version of the Open University. I applied, was appointed coordinator of educational technology for the new institution, and spent four very exciting years at the Télé-université in Quebec City. What kind of university was this? It attracted brilliant young nationalist intellectuals to its faculty, so the courses broke new ground.

My lasting lesson from the Télé-université is about the governance of innovative projects. The Université du Québec had only been set up in 1969 (along the lines of some of the US state universities) as a network of campuses around the Province. In 1969 something radical was expected. By 1972 the system president, Alphonse Riverin, decided teaching methods on campus were not radical enough. He set up the Télé-université to ginger things up.

The governing body of the Télé-université was made up of representatives from the campuses of the network. But by this stage the new campuses were beginning to settle down and did not want to be gingered up by a new unit at system level.

How self-governing universities respond effectively to change is the single most difficult challenge in university management today. Representative bodies of staff reflect, by definition, the status quo in terms of programmes and methods. Convincing them to make changes that may not be in their short-term interest is a key test of the effectiveness of university leaders. Giving students a strong voice is helpful. Mature students, in particular, usually exhibit a wise combination of conservatism about assessment standards with a readiness to change programmes and methods so that they meet the expectations of the evolving environment.

Athabasca

I experienced strong leadership and the advantages of involving students in university management in my next job. By the late 1970s the Province of Alberta had also created a distance teaching university, Athabasca University. I joined Athabasca as vice-president in 1977 and for the next few years, just as at the Télé-université, had the thrill of managing a university that doubled in size every year.

What kind of university was this? It was different from the Télé-université in an interesting way. The Télé-université followed the Open University in stressing openness and developed a novel if narrow curriculum of high-enrolment courses. Athabasca concentrated more on the distance delivery of a fairly standard curriculum.

For me the remarkable aspects of Athabasca were first, the kind of president we had and second, the unicameral governance structure inspired by the University of Toronto. I did not find the unicameral board particularly effective in its key aim of bringing together financial and academic decisions. However, it did give students a prominent and effective role. One year it was a student, a sergeant in the Calgary City Police, who chaired the board committee that negotiated salaries with the faculty – a splendid return to the approach of the medieval university.

I also worked for a great president. Sam Smith is one of that very small band of people who have held three university presidencies and been successful in each. At Athabasca he thrilled us by making the grand gesture in a crisis. In the late 1970s it became the fashion in Alberta to decentralize government agencies away from Edmonton, the provincial capital. The citizens of the little town of Athabasca saw their chance and lobbied for Athabasca University to be moved there. One day the government announced, without warning, that the University was to be relocated from Edmonton, where it had been since it began, a hundred miles north to Athabasca.

Sam Smith instantly resigned as president. Aside from the discourteous lack of warning, he claimed that the relocation decision violated the principle of university autonomy. I admired his stand. In my view the government had every right to locate a publicly funded university wherever it saw fit. But I like to work with people who have principles, even if I do not agree with all their principles. Ever since General Franco said that Rector Unamuno of the University of Salamanca should be shot for standing up to his regime I feel that university presidents, in the western world at least, have been short on heroism. Sam Smith would deprecate the comparison with Miguel da Unamuno but he made us feel proud.

At Athabasca I continued my own principle of registering as a student. I took a course in management and a remarkable course on the ancient roots of the modern world that took us from the Epic of Gilgamesh to Augustine's City of God and which followed me as I continued on my gypsy wanderings.

Concordia

My next job was as vice-rector, academic of Concordia University – which is what Sir George Williams University had become by merging with Loyola College in 1974.

Concordia, which is a big, downtown university, is the best place in Canada to learn the university leader's trade. It has a unique combination of penury, diversity and the spirit of service. It is always broke because it is an access university with a tradition of serving part-time students that goes back to the nineteenth century. It was an inexpensive operation when the state took over the funding of universities, and historical funding patterns are hard to change. Working at Concordia teaches you that there are some difficult choices concerning access and participation, not least how to make a timetable that accommodates both full-time and part-time students at reasonable cost.

Laurentian

In 1984, after ten years in vice-presidential posts, I was appointed president of Laurentian University in north-eastern Ontario. Laurentian faces interesting choices under each of the four conference themes. One issue is the balance of governance in a system of widely scattered affiliated colleges. It was as chair of the Laurentian Senate that I had academic responsibility for the 30 students at the Collège universitaire de Hearst, the world's smallest university. In winter I flew there over the frozen forests in a small plane, but in summer, with the University mace in the boot of the car, we drove for seven hours to the Hudson's Bay lowlands to conduct a degree ceremony in French.

The most interesting choices at Laurentian are those facing a bilingual institution. Is the concept of a bilingual institution valuable and viable? Should it mean two separate language streams under one roof or individual students taking courses in both languages? These are not simple issues and, like a good academic, I could see both sides of them. However, working in two languages in the same institution was enriching. I also began an associate degree in theology offered by correspondence from one of Laurentian's federated colleges.

Then in 1989, for my first ever sabbatical, I became a full-time student in a programme of international affairs at the National Defense College of Canada. As well as having brilliant visiting lecturers at the College we travelled all over Canada and to 24 other countries. Unfortunately the College has since been closed because it was too costly to the taxpayer. However, the course was a perfect preparation for my next move.

Open

Although my appointments in the 1980s were in conventional universities, I remained active in the international networks of distance education and continued to follow the fortunes of the Open University. It still looked like the world's most exciting university, so when the job of vice-chancellor was advertised, I applied. After seven years in post I can confirm that it is the most exciting university in the world. But what kind of university is it?

It is an open university. I have not yet finished my gypsy wanderings but the Open University is as close as I have come to my kind of university. It embodies the qualities that I now value. They are encapsulated in the simple mission statement of the OU, which is to be open as to people, open as to places, open as to methods and open as to ideas.

It is open to all, without prerequisites. There are 150,000 students in degree credit courses this year and they are there because they want to be. They are learning gladly – at least that is what I hear in speaking individually to thousands of our new graduates at degree ceremonies each year.

It is open as to places. Students study mostly at home, and for 20,000 of them home is outside the UK. Learning at a distance allows students to optimize the use of the study time that they carve out from their obligations to family and work.

Being open as to methods has allowed the OU to develop a teaching system that gives students unbeatable value for money. Costs per student are the lowest in the UK yet the OU ranks tenth out of the 101 British universities in national rankings of teaching quality. It is also unusual in its methods of decision making and accountability. This very modern university practises to a rare degree the medieval forms of collegial government. The Senate, which is the supreme academic decision-making body of the OU, has over a thousand members. These forms of decision making and accountability are a source of strength. Certainly they are a large part of the reason why the devotion shown to the Open University by both its students and its staff are unique in my experience of wandering the academic world.

What about openness to ideas? I believe that OU course teams, which produce courses through the intellectual cut-and-thrust that we associate with research, move forward the scholarship of teaching like nowhere else. A team-produced course inevitably presents a range of viewpoints on academic issues, refuting the accusation of spoon feeding so easily levelled at distance education. The OU gives students great latitude in combining courses within their degrees. Oxford students had to figure out the curriculum, Open University students have to put their curriculum together.

Any university that teaches through technology to students worldwide has to re-create itself continually. The OU is a good place to imagine the kind of university that the next century will need. That has been the object of my recent learning. After I finished my associate degree in theology I decided to complete the MA in Educational Technology that I began at Sir George Williams University in 1971 by completing the dissertation.

What kind of a university is it that allows a student to take 25 years to complete a degree? It is the kind of university that believes in lifelong learning. I hope I have justified its faith in me. I got my MA and then extended the dissertation into my recent book (1996). I gladly learned and gladly tried to teach others as I analysed the contemporary crisis in higher education, reviewed a generation of distance learning, and suggested avenues for the future.

What we know now about the secret of the art of distance learning has already given millions of people of all ages and nationalities the opportunity to learn gladly, to be liberated by the academic mode of thinking and to enjoy heaven-sent moments of understanding. That is my kind of university.

Acknowledgement

In 1993 Ernie Boyer invited me to become a trustee of the Carnegie Foundation. Thus began an enormously stimulating association with some of the leaders of American higher education, above all with Ernie himself. Hearing that wonderful man reflect on education was an inestimable privilege. I dedicate this chapter to the memory of two great academics: Ernie Boyer and John Kelly, former Principal of St Edmund Hall, Oxford, who died in 1997.

References

Daniel, John S. (1996) *Mega-universities and Knowledge Media: Technology Strategies for Higher Education*. London: Kogan Page.
Haskins, Charles H. (1923) *The Rise of Universities*. Ithaca, NY: Cornell University Press.

Part 1

Knowledge and Curricula

The question of what kind of universities the society of the twenty-first century will need is strongly connected with the question of what choices higher education administrators, professors and students will make about knowledge and curricula. Who is to decide what students are going to learn: governments, university departments, representatives of the disciplines, future employers or the students themselves? In this first part of the book new modes of knowledge production are discussed, links between knowledge and learning are defined in Canada, a US researcher argues that academic coherence should be established as a major rule for curricula and new PhD programmes in Australia are described.

Gibbons describes how the production of knowledge is guided by a set of research practices that determine what shall count as new knowledge. The knowledge thus produced has a disciplinary structure because this structure governs the organization and management of universities today. The disciplinary structure provides the framework for the curriculum in science, social science or the humanities. It thus provides the channels along which research output flows and through which young researchers enter the community. Through research, the stock of specialist knowledge grows and transforms the content of disciplines. Because the disciplinary structure is the vital institution connecting research with teaching, the transformation of contents through research also changes the curriculum, alters what is regarded as essential to be taught and introduces both differentiation and more and more specialism. This mode of knowledge production is referred to by Gibbons as Mode 1.

However, Gibbons goes on to argue that, with the increase in the number of research centres, think-tanks and multidisciplinary institutions largely outside the universities – and with the application of new forms of information technology – new research practices are being introduced and the mode of knowledge production is changing. Importantly, it is cutting loose from the disciplinary structure and generating knowledge which, so far, is not institutionalized in the conventional way. This new mode of knowledge production, Mode 2, is characterized by the context of its application, by transdisciplinarity, by heterogeneity and by social accountability. Mode 2 knowledge production is heterarchical and transient. And it involves an expanded system of quality control. Most importantly of all, Mode 2 knowledge is being created and transmitted largely outside of the universities. Can universities adapt to this challenge to their essential heartland: the production and transmission of new knowledge?

Donald focuses on the link between knowlege and learning. This link is provided by academic disciplines which claim authority for developing and evaluating knowledge. Increasing specialization and differentiation have led to a questioning of the role of disciplines in the university. In her contribution, Donald deals with three questions: What is the role of a discipline in the university of the twenty-first century? How can effective learning best be ensured? What steps must universities take to provide students with insight about the nature of learning, and about their intellectual development at university?

Like Gibbons, she notes that knowledge produced at universities has a disciplinary structure. She examines sociological and epistemological models of disciplines in order to describe their effect on the learning environment. Disciplinary differences determine learning goals and gains; knowledge and skills differ according to disciplinary area. In the physical sciences, professors address the integration of knowledge and skills, consider it possible to sequence learning, express belief in the scientific method but are unfamiliar with a critical perspective. In the social sciences, professors acknowledge the potential for sequential learning and consider a critical perspective important, while professors in the humanities object to sequential learning and stress a critical perspective. Professors in the humanities emphasize the development of communication skills, while engineering, mathematics and science teachers emphasize facts, principles and problem solving.

According to Donald, to ensure effective learning, concentrated efforts in two interlinking areas – knowledge base development and the learning of intellectual skills – are required. The long-term goal for universities can be described as providing learning experiences that enable students to develop a repertoire of skills and strategies that are useful for lifelong learning. Donald argucs, therefore, that students must be provided with insight about their disciplines and about the nature of learning at university at the beginning of their studies. Universities have to foster their intellectual development. Only as intellectual centres for a learning society will universities in the twenty-first century continue to have a predominant role as producers and disseminators of knowledge.

Dill considers the contents and the organization of curricula and the extent to which they offer a coherent, integrated academic experience. He proposes a 'rule of coherence' that can be used for evaluating what forms of knowledge should be taught within a university.

The coherence of a curriculum consists of a structured offering of courses and programmes and a sequence of courses which demand the integration of knowledge and learning from different courses. A 'rule of coherence' could be defined as follows: for an academic curriculum to be offered by the university, it must seek to provide a coherent, academic experience for its students. To meet the rule of coherence, an academic curriculum must be able to provide ongoing, summative evidence that its students have had a coherent learning experience.

Dill observes that the direction of developments in many European universities are now towards credit-based modular curricula, featuring progressive forms of assessment. These schemes, if they lead to an elimination of a summative assessment measure, may encourage the academic individualism and curricula atomization that have already emerged in the United States. Similarly, by eliminating information on the performance of a candidate as a whole, modularization may lessen the contribution that external examiners can make to encouraging faculty consideration of curricular coherence. Dill does not believe that modularization per se is necessarily incompatible with educational coherence, but to ensure that coherence is maintained in a modular scheme, progression assessment would need to be combined in some appropriately weighted manner with a required summative assessment for all students.

While the contributions from the UK, USA and Canada focus on modes of knowledge production, the link between disciplines, knowledge and learning, intellectual development and academic and educational coherence, a contribution from Australia considers the ways in which demands from the economy have led to innovations in universities. Jongeling sees growing signs that university autonomy and academic freedom are threatened by such developments. In Australia there is evidence that government pressure is forcing universities to respond to the needs of economy and society, expressed through reduced funding and industry's dissatisfaction with the quality of PhD degrees.

It is this last development that Jongeling examines. Since 1989, more and more professional doctorates have been introduced in Australia. Currently, nearly 30 universities are offering more than 60 professional doctorate programmes in 17 discipline areas. After a report from the Higher Education Council professional PhDs were recommended in the fields of engineering, accounting, law, education and nursing. Most universities have followed this government initiative for more applied research; this was meant to lead to commercial outputs and to the production of graduates with problem-solving skills. A different form of doctoral education had been advocated, to include principles of management, industry-orientated attitudes and personal relationship training. Decisions had to be made concerning the additional costs, forms of supervision, contents and standard of these programmes. By 1997, a number of professional doctorates (such as Doctor of Business Administration, Doctor of Juridical Science, Doctor of Public Health, Doctor of Environmental Design, Doctor of Technology or Doctor of Creative Performance) had been established. Jongeling argues that to achieve an equivalent standard, the same kind of rigour must be included in the professional doctorate as in the PhD.

If anything is clear from the four chapters in Part 1, it is that knowledge, learning and curricula will change in the twenty-first century. It is up to the universities to decide what kind of changes they are prepared to make.

3

Changing Research Practices

Michael Gibbons

Summary

Universities have only recently taken up the mantle of research and organized themselves to produce new knowledge as well as preserving and transmitting it. Research in universities has become a core value. In making this adjustment universities have taken on a function that is bound to change them because the knowledge available to be transmitted is changing all the time. The production of knowledge is guided by a set of research practices that determine, among other things, what shall count as new knowledge. Knowledge thus produced has a disciplinary structure, and it is this structure that governs the organization and management of universities today.

The disciplinary structure not only provides the channels along which research outputs flow: it also provides the framework for the curriculum, whether in science, social science or the humanities. The disciplinary structure is the vital institution that makes it possible to argue that in universities, teaching and research must be connected. Through research, the stock of specialist knowledge grows and transforms the content of disciplines; in time, this changes the curriculum, and alters what is regarded as essential to be taught. Research also contributes to the differentiation of the disciplinary structure, introducing more and more specialisms.

But new research practices are being introduced and the mode of knowledge production is changing in significant ways. We can now distinguish two modes of knowledge production, Mode 1 and Mode 2; each is associated with a distinctive set of research practices. In many areas of scientific advance, knowledge production is cutting loose from the disciplinary structure and generating knowledge which, so far, is not being institutionalized in the conventional way. The numbers of research centres, institutes and think-tanks are multiplying while faculties and departments remain the preferred form for teaching. Universities are confronted with the challenge of how to accommodate these new research practices. At the very least they will have to become more open, porous institutions vis-à-vis the wider community, with 'fewer gates and more revolving doors'.

This development within the research enterprise also presents a challenge to the teaching side of university life. There are now at least two different modes of knowledge production and each can provide a basis for curricular development. What balance should be adopted? In the more open, flexible structures that are carrying research, how will the knowledge produced be absorbed into the curriculum? If it is codified differently, or perhaps not at all, how will it be transmitted? What will transdisciplinary 'curricula' look like? What rules will govern their construction and development? What are the core skills that need to be acquired to function in this mode? These are crucial questions for universities and they have less to do with whether a university is to be a research or a teaching institution than with deciding which modes of knowledge production would benefit from investment of resources.

It is hardly controversial to assert that it is only recently that universities have organized themselves to undertake research. Although individual research activities in universities can be found going back to the nineteenth century and beyond, it is really only since the end of World War II that research – particularly basic research – has been institutionalized in the universities and become one of their core values. Throughout the twentieth century, universities have added the function of generating new knowledge to their previous ones of preserving knowledge and transmitting it.

Disciplinary structures

The research enterprise that has gradually been put in place in universities is guided by a set of research practices, or a system of behavioural and institutional norms, which ensures that results are sound. These research practices set the terms of what counts as knowledge, who is allowed to participate in its production, and how accreditation is organized. These practices have generated what we know as the disciplinary structure of science; this structure, in turn, has come to govern the management and organization of universities today. In particular, it should be noted that the disciplinary structure is specialist. Whether in sciences, the social sciences or the humanities, specialism has been seen as a secure way to advance knowledge.

The disciplinary structure also organizes teaching by providing a framework for the curriculum. The disciplinary structure is the essential link connecting teaching and research and underpinning the argument that in universities they properly belong together. Of course, research not only adds to the stock of specialist knowledge but transforms it as well. The research enterprise is dynamic. Its research practices articulate the disciplinary structure and, over time, change what is regarded as the essential ideas, techniques and methods to be learned.

Changing research practices: Mode 1 and Mode 2

It is a characteristic of the research enterprise to break out of existing cognitive structures. But today the mode of knowledge production is also changing as new research practices are being introduced to cope with the complexities of the research questions that need to be addressed. Two modes of knowledge production – Mode 1 and Mode 2 – can be distinguished, each associated with a distinctive set of research practices.

As I have indicated, most universities make use of a model of knowledge production that has a disciplinary basis. This structure provides the guidelines about what the important problems are, how they should be tackled, who should tackle them, and what should be regarded as a contribution to the field. In brief, the disciplinary structure defines what counts as 'good science'. Because the disciplinary structure has been institutionalized in universities, naturally they have become the primary legitimators of this form of excellence. The currently institutionalized mode of knowledge production is, for the purposes of this chapter, labelled Mode 1. But a new mode of knowledge production may be emerging. The new mode of research production is appearing across the board in the sciences, the social sciences and the humanities. It is labelled Mode 2; knowing its characteristics is essential if we are to understand the role of knowledge and curricula in the universities of the future.

First, let me identify the principal differences between Mode 1 and Mode 2. The term 'Mode 1' refers to a form of knowledge production – a complex of ideas, methods, values and norms – that has grown up to control the diffusion of the Newtonian ideal of mathematical science to more and more fields of enquiry and to ensure its compliance with what is considered sound scientific practice. Mode 1 is meant to summarize in a single phrase the cognitive and social norms which must be followed in the production, legitimation and diffusion of knowledge of this kind. For many, Mode 1 is identical with what is meant by science. Its cognitive and social norms determine what shall count as significant problems, who shall be allowed to practise science and what constitutes good science. Forms of practice that adhere to these rules are by definition 'scientific', while those that break them are not. It is partly for these reasons that, whereas in Mode 1 it is conventional to speak of science and scientists, it has been necessary to use the more general terms 'knowledge' and 'practitioners' when describing Mode 2. This is intended merely to highlight differences, not to suggest that practitioners of Mode 2 are not behaving according to the norms of scientific method.

It is my contention that there is sufficient empirical evidence to indicate that a distinct set of cognitive and social practices is beginning to emerge and that they are different from those that govern Mode 1. The only question may be whether they are sufficiently different to require a new label or whether they can be regarded simply as developments that can be accommodated within existing practices. The final answer to this question depends, in part, on how Mode 1 adapts to changing conditions in the economic and political environment of research.

Changes in practice may provide an empirical starting point. They can be described in terms of a number of attributes that, when taken together, have sufficient coherence to suggest the emergence of a new mode of knowledge production. Analytically, the set of attributes are used to allow the differences between Mode 1 and Mode 2 to be specified. To summarize using terms that will be explored more fully below: in Mode 1 problems are set and solved in a context governed by the largely academic interests of a specific community; by contrast, Mode 2 knowledge is carried out in a context of application. Mode 1 is disciplinary while Mode 2 is transdisciplinary. Mode 1 is characterized by homogeneity; Mode 2, by heterogeneity. Organizationally, Mode 1 is hierarchical and tends to preserve its form, while Mode 2 is more heterarchical and transient. Each employs a different type of quality control. In comparison with Mode 1, Mode 2 is more socially accountable and reflexive. It includes a wider, more temporary and heterogeneous set of practitioners, collaborating on a problem defined in a specific and localized context. As such, it involves a much expanded system of quality control.

Some attributes of knowledge production in Mode 2

Let us now look at some aspects of this new mode (Gibbons *et al.*, 1994). In brief, it is characterized by:

1 knowledge produced in the context of application;
2 transdisciplinarity;
3 heterogeneity and organizational diversity;
4 enhanced social accountability and reflexivity;
5 a more broadly based system of quality control.

Knowledge produced in the context of application

The relevant contrast here is between problem solving that follows the codes of practice relevant to a particular discipline, and problem solving organized around a particular application. In the former, the context is defined in relation to the cognitive and social norms that govern basic research or academic science. Recently this has tended to imply knowledge production carried out in the absence of some practical goal. In Mode 2, by contrast, knowledge results from a broader range of considerations. Such knowledge is intended to be useful to someone whether in industry, government or society more generally; this imperative is present from the beginning. Knowledge thus produced is always produced under an aspect of continuous negotiation, i.e. it will not be produced unless and until the interest of the various actors are included. Such is the context of application.

'Application' in this sense is not product development carried out for industry, and the processes or markets that operate to determine what knowledge is produced are much broader than is normally implied when one speaks about taking ideas to the market place. None the less, knowledge production in Mode 2 is the outcome of a process in which supply and demand factors can be said to operate, but the sources of supply are increasingly diverse, as are the demands for differentiated forms of specialist knowledge. Such processes or markets specify what we mean by the context of application. Because they include much more than commercial considerations, it might be said that in Mode 2 science is in the market but at the same time has also gone beyond it! Knowledge production thus becomes diffused throughout society, being produced in many different sites.

Research carried out in the context of application might be said to characterize a number of disciplines in the applied sciences and engineering, for example chemical engineering, aeronautical engineering or, more recently, computer science. Historically these sciences became established in universities but, strictly speaking, they cannot be called applied sciences, because it was precisely the lack of the relevant science that called them into being. They were genuinely new forms of knowledge – though not necessarily of knowledge production – because they too soon became the sites of disciplinary-based knowledge production in the style of Mode 1. These applied disciplines share with Mode 2 some aspects of the attribute of knowledge produced in the context of application. But in Mode 2 the context is more complex. It is shaped by a more diverse set of intellectual and social demands than was the case in many applied sciences, although it may give rise to genuine basic research.

The development of hypersonic aircraft provides an interesting if somewhat complex example of the processes that can take place in the context of application. The difficulties of taking forward the construction of a hypersonic aircraft perhaps makes it as clear as necessary how inadequate it is to regard the context of application as the regime of applied science, because this science simply is not there. What is more, it cannot get started until certain technological discoveries are made that will structure the scientific domain so that appropriate equations will be not solved but derived. But the structuring of that domain cannot proceed without a whole series of previous judgements as to the shape of a desirable commercial vehicle. It is a good example of the interdependence of theory and design interacting with commercial considerations in order to produce pathbreaking science.

Thus Foray and Gibbons' (1996: 274) analysis of the context of application concludes that

[t]he hypersonic aircraft of the future will of course be a new artefact. This new artefact will not only embody much knowledge scientific and technical but it will also be a new design configuration of that knowledge. Both aspects are important. With regard to knowledge, the existing science and technology do not provide a sufficient base to guide the transition from supersonic to hypersonic velocities . . . As far as hypersonics are concerned

the primary need is for new infratechnologies and instrumentation to allow exploration of the new domain. There is a sense in which these must be available before the research agenda proper can be generated, but the research agenda even at this early stage cannot be constructed independent of the choice of design configuration and that involves interaction with a further range of engineering and commercial expertise. The ultimate mission, after all, is to produce a viable aircraft not merely to elaborate a theory or to produce a schematic design possibility.

In brief, 'discovery' in this 'context' cannot be separated from the particular application that is reflected in the chosen design configuration, which is itself partly a commercial matter.

Transdisciplinarity

Mode 2 does more than assemble a diverse range of specialists to work in teams on problems in a complex applications-orientated environment. To qualify as a specific form of knowledge production it is essential that inquiry be guided by specifiable consensus as to appropriate cognitive and social practice. In Mode 2, the consensus is conditioned by the context of application and evolves with it. The determinants of a potential solution involve the integration of different skills in a framework of action but the consensus may be only temporary, depending on how well it conforms to the requirements set by the specific context of application. In Mode 2 the shape of the final solution will normally be beyond that of any single contributing discipline. It will be transdisciplinary.

Transdisciplinarity has four distinct features. First, it develops a distinct but evolving framework to guide problem-solving efforts. This is generated and sustained in the context of application; it is not developed first and then applied to that context later by a different group of practitioners. The solution does not arise solely, or even mainly, from the application of knowledge that already exists. Although elements of existing knowledge must have entered into it, genuine creativity is involved and the theoretical consensus, once attained, cannot easily be reduced to disciplinary parts.

Second, because the solution comprises both empirical and theoretical components it is undeniably a contribution to knowledge, though not necessarily disciplinary knowledge. Though it has emerged from a particular context of application, transdisciplinary knowledge develops its own distinct theoretical structures, research methods and modes of practice, though they may not be located on the prevalent disciplinary map. The effort is cumulative, though the direction of accumulation may travel in a number of different directions after a major problem has been solved.

Third, unlike Mode 1, where results are communicated through institutional channels, the results are communicated to those who have participated *as* they participate; and so, in a sense, the diffusion of the results is initially accomplished in the process of their production. Subsequent diffusion occurs primarily as the original practitioners move to new problem contexts rather than through reporting results in professional journals or at conferences. Communication links are maintained partly through formal and partly through informal channels.

Fourth, transdisciplinarity is dynamic. It is problem-solving capability on the move. A particular solution can become the cognitive site from which further advances can be made, but where this knowledge will be used next and how it will develop are as difficult to predict as are the possible applications that might arise from discipline-based research. Mode 2 is marked especially (but not exclusively) by the ever closer interaction of knowledge production with a succession of problem contexts. Even though problem contexts are transient, and problem solvers highly mobile, communication networks tend to persist, and the knowledge contained in them is available to enter into further configurations.

Good examples of transdisciplinarity in the context of application can be seen in the development of a new computer architecture. In these cases a diverse set of skills is required, including solid state physics, software engineering, linguistics, psychology, physics, philosophy and, of course, computer science. Experts in these subjects aim to produce knowledge that will be of use. They come together in what has been referred to as a context of application because they are challenged by the problem of the next generation of computer architecture and because they know that whatever the solution found, the next but one generation will begin from it. In a sense they cannot afford to be left out of the conversation. Further, such architectures are not the result of developing theory first and applying it later. Rather, theory must in some sense be as much the outcome of a successfully working computer as an input to its design. Some maintain that in the case of novel computer architectures, the theory, design configuration and relevant software are so intertwined that they emerge at the same time, rather like a new aeroplane that rolls out of a hangar accompanied by a flight simulator precise enough to train the pilots. It is simply too complex to design the aeroplane first and then build a simulator based primarily upon flight test information.

Heterogeneity and organizational diversity

Mode 2 knowledge production demands diverse skills and experience from the people working on it. The composition of a problem-solving team changes over time as requirements evolve. This is not planned or coordinated by any central body. As with Mode 1, challenging problems emerge, if not randomly, then in a way which makes their anticipation very difficult. Accordingly, Mode 2 knowledge production is marked by:

- an increase in the number of potential sites where knowledge can be created; no longer only universities and colleges, but also in the interaction between non-university institutes, research centres, government agencies, industrial laboratories, think-tanks and consultancies;

- the linking of sites together in a variety of ways – electronically, organizationally, socially, informally – through functioning networks of communication;
- the simultaneous differentiation, at these sites, of fields and areas of study into finer and finer specialities. The recombination and reconfiguration of these sub-fields form the bases for new forms of useful knowledge. Over time, knowledge production moves increasingly away from traditional disciplinary activity into new societal contexts.

In Mode 2, flexibility and response time are the crucial factors, and because of this the types of organization used to tackle these problems may vary greatly. New forms of organization have emerged to accommodate the changing and transitory nature of the problems Mode 2 addresses. Characteristically in Mode 2, research groups are less firmly institutionalized; people come together in temporary work teams and networks, which dissolve when a problem is solved or redefined. Members may then reassemble in different groups involving different people, often in different loci, around different problems. The experience gathered in this process creates a competence that becomes highly valued and that is transferred to new contexts. Though problems may be transient and groups short-lived, the organization and communication pattern persists as a matrix from which further groups and networks, dedicated to different problems, will be formed. Mode 2 knowledge is thus created in a great variety of organizations and institutions, including multinational firms, network firms, small hi-tech firms based on a particular technology, government institutions, research universities, laboratories and institutes as well as national and international research programmes. In such environments the patterns of funding exhibit a similar diversity, being assembled from a variety of organizations with a diverse range of requirements and expectations which, in turn, enter into the context of application.

Some of these aspects are illustrated by the Human Genome Project and that part of it concerned with the mapping of human genes.

> The aim of the Human Genome Project, quite simply, is to draw up a catalogue of our entire genetic make-up – the genome. The maps, like geographical maps, can be of varying type and resolution, from large-scale linkage maps of genes in relation to other genes based on frequency of co-inheritance, through various types of physical maps that locate 'landmarks' in the DNA, and eventually to the highest resolution, the sequence of chemical base-pairs which make up the DNA molecule. Proponents of the project claim that it will provide a valuable resource for science and medicine, while opponents have challenged its wisdom in terms of cost, strategy, ethics and the ultimate utility of its results.
>
> (Balmer, 1996b: 534)

But the emergence of a mapping project can only be understood as the outcome of a complex process of negotiation involving a large number of interested parties. Some actors and institutions played a large part while others were less important. The point is that no single person or group was in control dictating the pace and direction of advance. For example, Balmer concludes that

> the HGMP [Human Genome Mapping Project] was not caused by any single factor. The state policies of selectivity and concentration, and value for money were coordinated with the agendas of the MRC and the gene mapping community and their spokespeople. There was no need for different groups to identify with each other's agendas. The project acted as a *boundary object* in this respect, a political entity that *aligned* separate working goals and agendas. Alignment was achieved over a period of time as groups and their agendas were shuffled into and out of the policy arena, or altogether marginalized. As a consequence, money flowed from the state to scientists, and gene mapping under the auspices of a concerted organized programme came to be supported . . . At each stage of the development of the project, however, the contingency of events and the opportunism of the actors cannot be ignored. Brenner and Bodmer may have had some degree of control; the government, ACOST civil servants, and MRC administrators may have had a degree of control. But in sum it was more of an orchestration process, and making the best use of the resources available than a planned strategic, networking process that led to the HGMP in the United Kingdom. In this case, it was rather like having an orchestra where all the players are vying to be the conductor, with no one fully in control and every one ready to improvise.
>
> (Balmer, 1996a: 27–67)

In the case of the Human Genome Project one can observe the role of the context of application under which the overall project was carried forward, and the complex set of negotiations that took place over an extended period of time. There was also a novel form of organization – a boundary object – that acted as a vehicle around which many diverse interests could partially converge, enough to allow funding to flow.

Enhanced social accountability and reflexivity

In recent years, growing public concern about issues to do with the environment, health, communications, privacy and procreation, and so forth, have had the effect of stimulating the growth of knowledge production in Mode 2. Growing awareness about the variety of ways advances in science and technology can affect the public interest has increased the numbers of groups who wish to influence the outcome of the research process. This is reflected in the varied composition of the research teams. Social scientists work alongside natural scientists, engineers, lawyers and businessmen because the nature of the problems requires it. Social accountability permeates the whole knowledge production process. It is reflected not only in the interpretation and diffusion of results but also in the definition of the problem and the setting of research priorities. An expanding number of interest (and so-called 'concerned') groups are demanding representation in setting the policy agenda as well as in the subsequent decision-making process. In Mode 2, sensitivity to the impact of the research is built in from the start. It forms part of the context of application.

Contrary to what one might expect, working in the context of application increases the sensitivity of scientists and technologists to the broader implications of what they are doing. Operating in Mode 2 makes all participants more reflexive. This is because the issues promoting the development of Mode 2 research cannot be specified in scientific and technical terms alone. The research on these types of problems has to incorporate options for the implementation of the solutions; these are bound to touch the values and preferences of different individuals and groups traditionally seen as outside the scientific and technological system. They can now become active agents in the definition and solution of problems as well as in the evaluation of performance. This is expressed partly in terms of the need for greater social accountability, but it also means that the individuals themselves cannot function effectively without reflecting – trying to operate from the standpoint of – all the actors involved. The deepening of understanding that this brings, in turn, has an effect on what is considered worthwhile doing and, hence, on the structure of the research itself. Reflection of the values implied in human aspirations and projects has been a traditional concern of the humanities. As reflexivity within the research process spreads, the humanities too are experiencing an increase in demand for the sorts of knowledge they have to offer.

Some effects of reflexivity and enhanced social accountability can be seen in the outcomes of various fora for the expression of public concern. Of particular interest is the role played by public controversies in the generation of markets for novel knowledge and expertise. Public controversies create meeting places for discussion. Because many diverse actors are involved, these meeting places can be regarded as hybrid fora. Controversies frequently lead to the establishment of inquiries dealing with questions of public policy, regulation and a host of other social and ethical issues. New knowledge is gathered, some of it based on the results of previous scientific research and technological developments that have gradually become the cause of social concern. For example, new forms of knowledge such as risk analysis, technology assessment or the growth of various specialisms in environmental science are responses to public concern about the safety of high-risk buildings, the adverse effects of automobile traffic or the effects of global warming. These controversies help develop markets for alternative technologies and establish foci for new research agendas. This role of public inquiries in generating new research in environmental science has been elaborated by Cambrosio (1992) and his colleagues.

Quality control

Criteria used to assess the quality of the work and the teams researching in Mode 2 differ from those of more traditional, disciplinary science. Quality in Mode 1 is determined essentially through the peer review judgements about the contributions made by individuals. Control is maintained by careful selection of those judged competent to act as peers, which is in part determined by their previous contributions to their discipline. So the peer review process is one in which quality and control mutually reinforce one another. It has both cognitive and social dimensions, in that there is professional control over what problems and techniques are deemed important to work on, as well as who is qualified to pursue their solution. In disciplinary science, peer review operates to channel individuals to work on problems judged to be central to the advance of the discipline. These problems are defined largely in terms of criteria that reflect the intellectual interests and preoccupations of the discipline and its gatekeepers.

In Mode 2 additional criteria are added through the context of application, which now incorporates a diverse range of intellectual interests as well as other social, economic or political ones. As well as the criterion of intellectual interest and its interaction, further questions are posed. Will the solution, if found, be competitive in the market? Will it be cost effective? Will it be socially acceptable? Quality is determined by a wider set of criteria that reflect the broadening social composition of the review system. This implies that 'good science' is more difficult to determine. Since it is no longer limited strictly to the judgements of disciplinary peers, the fear is that control will be weaker and result in lower quality work. Although the quality control process in Mode 2 is more broadly based, it does not follow that because a wider range of expertise is brought to bear on a problem that it will necessarily be of lower quality. It is of a more composite, multidimensional kind.

Commentary

The examples of Mode 2 given above indicate a trend. Although not every attribute appears every time, the contention is that when they appear together they have enough coherence to justify talking about a new mode of knowledge production. The implication for universities is that the research in many important areas is cutting loose from the disciplinary structure and generating knowledge that does not seem to be drawn (so far, at least) to institutionalize itself in university departments and faculties in the conventional way. At times, it often seems that research centres, institutes and 'think-tanks' are multiplying on the periphery of universities while faculties and departments have tended to become the internal locus of teaching provision.

Universities are now confronted with the challenge of how to accommodate these new research practices. Important intellectual problems are emerging in a 'context of application'. The research agenda and the funding of it are now the outcome of a dialogue of researchers and users, regulators, interest groups, etc., and unless that dialogue produces a consensus no research will be done. Research has become a participative exercise involving many actors; experts move less according to the dynamics of their original disciplines and more according to problem interest, which is itself determined by a more complex set of factors than those found *within* disciplines. In this process, universities are only one actor among many. The challenge for them is whether or not they can be sufficiently innovative to remain part of the process of dialogue. This is bound to be difficult in institutions where, up till now, so much status has been invested in the value of individual creativity, as determined by priority in publication.

The frontiers of research are currently following the dynamics of problem interest, and these frontiers are no longer congruent with disciplinary frontiers. Pursuing problem interest means that academics will be required to work in teams, with experts from a wide range of intellectual backgrounds, in a variety of organizational settings. They will contribute solutions that cannot be easily reduced to a recognizable 'disciplinary contribution'. Those who would contribute to research in this mode must adopt a different set of research practices. But if they do they will be 'out of synch' with the existing reward structure of universities. The rubric of survival in academic research has changed from 'publish or perish' to 'partnerships or perish' (Gourley, 1997). How can the existing structure thus be modified?

Universities that wish to be active in Mode 2 research will have to become much more entrepreneurial in the ways they utilize their 'intellectual' capital, and this may mean experimenting with a much broader range of contractual employment arrangements. But, to the extent that universities go down this road, they will be helping to establish two parallel structures within universities: one for teaching and another for research. How will these structures be related to one another? If they are to be related, what would the organization of such universities look like? If research grows and develops in the ways I have suggested – outside disciplinary structures, more in the context of application – how will the results of research be absorbed by the wider academic community and, through them, make their way into the development of new curricula?

In the new, open, more flexible structures that are carrying research, knowledge is codified and transmitted in a different way. Information about the state of the art on a particular question resides less in publications – whether in paper or electronic form – than in the collective memory of the problem-solving teams. But as we have seen, these teams are transient groupings. These teams form and dissolve according to the imperative of problem-solving interest, and the memory of what has been accomplished moves with the relevant experts. It is doubtful if traditional modes of publication will be sufficient to grasp the knowledge and information that is produced in this way. Will it be codified? How can uncodified knowledge be translated in a curriculum? If it is not codified in books and/or papers, how will it be transmitted? What, for example, would a transdisciplinary 'curriculum' look like? How would it be taught and by whom? How can the knowledge produced in the context of application be accessed by those who have not been part of that context, if it belongs primarily in the collective memory of problem-solving teams? Will participation come to replace books? What are the skills required to participate in this mode of knowledge production? How are they to be acquired?

As we have seen, there are now two co-existing modes of knowledge production: Mode 1 and Mode 2. Each can provide a basis for curricular development. What balance should be adopted? The key questions have less to do with deciding whether a university is to be a research or a teaching institution than deciding between which modes of research – and teaching – to invest scarce resources, if, that is, it is still thought desirable to keep a link between teaching and research. These are major questions for any university, and their resolution implies even more institutional diversity than we are currently prepared to contemplate.

References

The ideas developed in this section are drawn from Gibbons, M. *et al.* (1994) *The New Production of Knowledge*. London: Sage Publications.

Balmer, B. (1996a) The political geography of the human genome project, *Perspectives on Science* 4(3): 276–91.

Balmer, B. (1996b) Managing mapping in the human genome project, *Social Studies of Science* 26: 534–47.

Cambrosio, A., Limoges, C. and Hoffman, E. (1992) Expertise as a network: a case study of the controversies over environmental release of genetically engineered organisms, in N. Stehr and R. V. Ericson (eds) *The Culture and Power of Knowledge: Inquiries into Contemporary Societies*. New York and Berlin: Walter de Gruyter.

Foray, D. and Gibbons, M. (1996) Discovery in the context of application, *Technological Forecasting and Social Change*, 53(3): 263–77.

Gourley, B. (1997) Private communication.

4

The Link Between Knowledge and Learning[1]

Janet Gail Donald

As we enter the twenty-first century, fundamental socioeconomic changes are occurring, driven by the need for and utilization of knowledge. In the knowledge era, the construction of and access to information will determine well-being. More specifically, the Internet sends the message that the race is on only for those who have access to the computer keyboard. Not only will both general and specialized knowledge be needed, but so will the skills to acquire and utilize it on a continuous, lifelong basis. Universities are at the centre of this global revolution.

As producers and disseminators of knowledge, universities in the past have operated a virtual monopoly. In the production of knowledge, although universities have had critical competitors – most notably research institutes – their global effect has been limited. The effects of the media, the principal competitor in dissemination, have been constrained because although they have packaged the message, they have not created it, and general access to this information has been limited. Now the Internet allows direct and personal access to knowledge bases in a variety of fields around the world. To date, quality control of knowledge bases on the Internet has been minimal, but they are open and hence can be evaluated. The Internet is a harbinger of radical change in the dissemination and potentially the construction of knowledge. How does the advent of the Internet change the role of the university?

During the twentieth century, the university and its various disciplines have been the main authority for developing and evaluating knowledge. Disciplines have traditionally had this responsibility because by definition they determine the parameters of knowledge and the mode of inquiry that guide learning in a field of studies. The huge increase in the specialization and differentiation of knowledge, coupled with increasing general access to knowledge, have led to a questioning both of the role of disciplines in the university and the university in the larger community. This chapter addresses three questions linking knowledge and learning. First, what is the role of a discipline in the university? What is the relationship of the disciplines to learning? How can effective learning be ensured?

In order to answer these questions, it is necessary to examine more closely disciplines and their knowledge bases, and the nature of learning at the post-secondary level. I will first discuss sociological and epistemological models of disciplines, then the effect of the disciplines on the learning environment, then go on to explore conceptualizations of learning at the post-secondary level, beginning with differences across disciplines in learning goals and proceeding to an analysis of students' conceptions of learning. I will conclude by examining approaches to ensure effective learning.

Sociological models of disciplines

Sociologists and anthropologists studying higher education view knowledge as the commodity of higher education, with universities as social structures for the control of knowledge, and disciplines as a source of segmentation and diversity within the academy (Clark, 1983; Hammack and Heyns, 1992). The earliest model of scholarly disciplines related them on the basis of the order in which they were to be studied. In medieval universities, after completing the trivium (grammar, rhetoric and logic) and the quadrivium (arithmetic, music, geometry and astronomy), students advanced to the faculties of theology, law or medicine. More recent models of disciplines as social entities include Snow's (1964) miscommunicating humanities and scientific cultures, and Becher's (1989) academic tribes tending their territories.

The sociological purpose of a discipline is to provide identity to its members and to control resources. A disciplinary community develops traditions, practices and rules of conduct that integrate it but which also set it apart from others and demand loyalty to the norms of the particular scholarly group. Resource control in the discipline and in the university occurs primarily through knowledge production devices: the organization of research and publications, including peer review mechanisms and professional organizations. Established disciplines – that is, those that defined themselves as scholarly communities early in the history of universities – are more likely to have secure funding sources and procedures and prescribed methods for publishing (for example, a series of journals dealing with different aspects of the discipline) or specific publishers. Disciplines may owe their place in the hierarchy as much to their sociological establishment as to their modes of inquiry and validation processes. In short, the sociology of a discipline affects its epistemology by creating resource conditions, a critical issue in these days of resource-driven decision making in the university.

The relationship between sociology and epistemology in a discipline is rendered more complex because sociological convergence and epistemological coherence do not necessarily correlate. Braxton and Hargens (1996) argue that variation among academic disciplines can be described as a single dimension of the degree of consensus members exhibit on appropriate theoretical orientations, research methods and the relative importance of research questions. However, established disciplines may be sociologically convergent – that is, have long-established and clear procedures governing group behaviour, for example, physics or history – and at the same time be epistemologically convergent (physics) or divergent (history). History, although not characterized by a dominating theoretical structure, is convergent sociologically because historians define themselves as members of a community of scholars (Becher, 1989).

Newer disciplines, particularly the social sciences but also many of the biological fields, may find it more difficult to further their collective interests because they have not gelled as communities. Having a set of diverse communities within the university, with a variety of points of convergence and divergence among them, creates organizational complexity, if not political strife. One respondent in my study of the learning environment commented that the university still operates on a feudal model, with each discipline thinking it could be hermetically sealed and that there is no crossover (Donald, 1997).

The resources under the control of a discipline affect the learning climate. For example, the natural sciences have a well-organized research grants system, which means that a larger percentage of natural science professors are funded and to higher levels than in the social sciences and humanities. The result is that support and incentives are higher in these disciplines. The learning climate in the sciences then becomes buffered, with a higher staff to student ratio, lower teaching loads, and the concurrent possibility of a closer match between teaching and research responsibilities. More generally, as with nations, the distinctions of a discipline may render it mildly xenophobic, less open to other modes of inquiry and hence less critical or capable of monitoring its own behaviour. The sociological attributes of a discipline therefore can have a major effect on learning and on communication across disciplines.

Epistemological models of disciplines

Epistemology is here defined as the theory of the nature and grounds of knowledge, especially with reference to its limits and validity. A widely used classification of knowledge discriminates three levels: knowledge of specifics (terminology and specific facts), knowledge of ways and means of dealing with specifics, and knowledge of universals and abstractions in a field (Bloom, 1956). Knowledge of ways and means of dealing with specifics includes knowledge of conventions, trends and sequences, classifications and categories, criteria by which facts, principles, opinions and conduct are tested or judged, and knowledge of methodology for investigating problems and phenomena. Knowledge of universals and abstractions in a field includes knowledge of principles and generalizations, and of theories and structures that represent a systematic view of a complex phenomenon, problem or field.

Disciplines have traditionally provided homes within the larger learning community because they determine the domain or parameters of knowledge, the theoretical or conceptual structures and the mode of inquiry that guide learning and the construction of knowledge in the domain. A discipline is expected to possess a specialized body of knowledge or theory with a reasonably logical taxonomy so that gaps or incoherencies in knowledge can be recognized (Dressel and Mayhew, 1974). Disciplines are expected to have particular techniques for theory testing and revision and a sense of sequence that enables scholars to predict where they should look next (King and Brownell, 1966; Dressel and Mayhew, 1974).

The production and validation of knowledge within the disciplines raises the question of their epistemology. Some authors have suggested that increasing specialization and accompanying fragmentation within disciplines means that it may no longer make sense to think of a discipline as a coherent domain, but rather as a family that provides local metaphors or models (Leary, 1992). Becher (1989), in *Academic Tribes and Territories*, describes knowledge from the perspective of those engaged in its creation as a badly made patchwork quilt in which the constituent scraps of material are loosely tacked together, untidily overlap, or are omitted entirely, leaving large gaps in the fabric. Becher's metaphor for the developmental incoherence of disciplines is immediately recognizable to those attempting to understand how disciplines affect knowledge construction.

I prefer to describe a discipline as a prototype consisting of a set of typical properties. The most prototypical disciplines, such as physics, will display all of the typical properties, while marginal instances exist with fewer properties (Rosch, 1978; Donald, 1987). Attempts to classify disciplines epistemologically as a first step in understanding them have had moderate success. The most important property used in classification is the extent to which a discipline is logically structured, as defined by the models, the methodology employed to produce the propositions that form the core of a discipline, and the truth criteria by which propositions are assessed (Kuhn, 1970; Toulmin, 1972; Biglan, 1973; Hirst, 1974; Donald, 1986, 1995).

The physical sciences have been described as well-structured, hard or paradigmatic disciplines (Kuhn, 1970; Frederiksen, 1984). A paradigm consists of a logical structure and governing truth criteria that provide maximum direction to scholars in the field (Kuhn, 1970). Another property concerns the parameters or boundaries of the field. Prototypical disciplines restrict the number and kind of phenomena studied. Less prototypical disciplines are not as structured, labelled 'soft' or 'unrestricted'; content and method are more idiosyncratic and the field of phenomena is relatively unlimited (Biglan, 1973; Frederiksen, 1984; Becher, 1989). In less structured disciplines, as in the social sciences and humanities, complexity is regarded as a legitimate aspect of knowledge. The least well-structured areas of study are more often referred to as fields of study, characterized by having ill-defined parameters, lacking a logical structure of knowledge and a generally accepted methodology (Dressel and Mayhew, 1974).

Whether a discipline is pure or applied affects the degree to which and the manner in which it is organized epistemologically. Pure disciplines are more likely to use specific models, while applied areas are more open to environmental complexity, hence eclecticism: the use of the most fitting model or method in a given circumstance. Applied areas of study are sometimes described as fields because the phenomena they study are relatively unrestricted and the methods are frequently taken from several disciplines. In spite of varying degrees of structure, method and territory, it is through the discipline that new knowledge is developed.

The discipline serves as gatekeeper in the validation of new knowledge. In a cross-disciplinary study of validation processes, respondents in representative physical sciences, social sciences and humanities were asked to describe how they validated their work (Donald, 1990, 1995). Differences occurring between groups of disciplines and between pure and applied disciplines suggested that the thinking required to test models in a pure discipline can be more precise because of its bounded or restricted nature. For example, validation in pure disciplines can employ a deductive thought process, with the use of conflicting evidence, counter-examples or alternative explanations. The use of conflicting evidence to validate knowledge was named as important by professors in the pure disciplines studied (physics, psychology and English literature) but was not suggested by professors in matching applied disciplines (engineering, education and applied linguistics).

Similarities across disciplines, most evident in the use of consistency as a criterion for validity, suggested some common meeting grounds. Unexpectedly, the differences across disciplines in the validation processes used were greatest between the social sciences and the humanities. Social science professors (in psychology and education) reported using empirical evidence and conceptual frameworks or models more than humanities professors, who reported greater reliance upon their peers to validate their work. These findings confirm theoretical distinctions made between the social sciences and humanities. Social scientists have been trained to discern and formulate patterns which can be expressed in general terms and can therefore create models that can be tested and verified (Rosenberg, 1979), while the humanities are concerned with phenomena that do not have immediate referents, and thus humanistic truth involves something other than logical or scientific validity (Broudy, 1977).

The effect of disciplines on the learning environment

In the twentieth century, post-secondary educational institutions have, with few exceptions, been organized in departments or programmes according to disciplinary structure. The degree of structure within a discipline and the principal methods of inquiry and validation could be expected to affect the quality of learning, both what is learned and how it is learned. The department (the operationalization of the discipline) is responsible for determining the curriculum and hence for determining the learning objectives of courses and programmes, the kinds of pedagogical and learning strategies utilized, and the methods of evaluation employed. Members of well-structured or prototypical disciplines are more likely to agree on the knowledge structures and modes of inquiry in use. Curricular convergence also means that the disciplinary community can claim a high level of validity, meeting the three major criteria for validity: coherence, consistency and precision (Donald, 1990).

Based on the assumption that a discipline or domain is the perquisite of experts in it, universities have rarely attempted to institute procedures to regulate the curriculum in any discipline. Curriculum is under the jurisdiction of the discipline, preventing review or evaluation by others in the academy. Protected by close association with academic freedom, the right to teach or study a subject without fear of reprisal or hindrance includes choice of course content. The exception to disciplinary control occurs when approval is needed for a new course or programme, but review is cursory except when disciplinary boundaries are breached. Curriculum and learning outcomes are examined on a regular basis in certain fields, usually professional, and then by others in the same field, when programmes undergo review for accreditation.

At a more specific level, course outlines may be filed within a department and may be examined as part of departmental review. However, cross-disciplinary, in-depth curriculum analysis of the vocabulary and methodology of a course or programme does not occur in a normal review process. The effect is to preclude avenues of curriculum development and alignment that might lead to a rationalization of courses and programmes, particularly across disciplines. The assumption of expertise thus tends to prevent cross-disciplinary understanding and development. An additional assumption in some disciplines that there is no longer a canon or the possibility of a paradigm also works against coherence and coordination within and across disciplines.

Specialization within a discipline leads to linkages off-campus rather than in-house, and the Internet is now making off-campus linkages even stronger. One of the respondents in my study on improving the learning environment noted that in most departments, there are usually only one or two persons at the most who share one's research interests, so individual professors cannot talk to a group of colleagues who understand exactly what they are doing (Donald, 1997). Colleagues in their area of specialization are usually off-campus, and are often more readily available on e-mail than members of their own department.

General attempts at curriculum reform show the extent to which disciplines are open to the perspectives and methods of other disciplines. When faculty members in the United States were called upon to participate in curricular change in undergraduate education, the disciplines responded in terms of their disciplinary membership (Lattuca and Stark, 1993). Whether in physical science and mathematics, social sciences or humanities, national taskforces of faculty recommended local variation and autonomy. Emphasis on connectedness with other disciplines was minimal in the physical sciences and increased across disciplines to the point of being assumed in the humanities: another example of restricted versus unrestricted disciplinary tendencies.

In summary, generally speaking, curriculum is not examined outside of the discipline, and cross-disciplinary understanding is limited. In addition, members of the discipline are specialized to the point where they tend to relate off-campus rather than within their programmes. Third, members of disciplines that are well structured and hence have greater curricular convergence, and might therefore serve as models to other disciplines, are less willing to interact with those in other areas. Thus the opportunity in a university to develop curriculum and procedures for ensuring its validity is constrained. But disciplinary differences affect the learning climate more directly.

Disciplinary differences in learning goals and gains

The avowed learning goals in courses in most disciplines include both knowledge and skill development, but the kinds of knowledge and skills differ according to disciplinary area. In the study of curricular reform in undergraduate education, professors in the physical sciences readily addressed the integration of knowledge and skills, considered it possible to sequence learning, expressed belief in the scientific method, but found a critical perspective unfamiliar (Lattuca and Stark, 1993). In the social sciences, professors acknowledged the potential for sequencing learning and considered a critical perspective important, while humanities representatives objected to sequencing learning and stressed a critical perspective. In the social sciences and humanities, oral and written communication skills were deemed important, as were critical reading and lifelong learning. Other studies have shown that professors in the humanities emphasize the development of communication skills, while engineering, mathematics and science teachers emphasize facts, principles and problem solving (Franklin and Theall, 1995). Thus both curricular and learning goals are affected by the disciplinary ethos.

The most extensively used method of evaluating the quality of learning in North America employs students' ratings of what is taught and their satisfaction with it. In a major study (101,710 courses) of disciplinary differences in learning goals and in students' perceptions of what they learn, different kinds of course objectives were emphasized by professors depending upon their discipline (Cashin and Downey, 1995). Students in these courses independently reported making progress in learning what professors in the discipline emphasized. Professors may also present different kinds of scholarly models. Research examining disciplinary differences in responses on student-rating questionnaires shows that although differences in ratings do not tend to occur in course organization or planning, humanities instructors are rated significantly more positively in faculty–student interaction and communication skills than are physical science and mathematics instructors (Marsh, 1984; Centra, 1993).

Differences in favour of the humanities have been shown to extend to overall ratings of the amount learned, the instructor and the course, and course integration (Franklin and Theall, 1995). This is consistent with findings in studies of faculty role differences – most faculty engage in research, but significantly more faculty in the humanities than in the sciences aspire to be good teachers (Milem and Astin, 1994). Taken together, these studies suggest that the learning experience of students in various programmes differs in much more than curriculum. The surrounding disciplinary culture and the specific learning outcomes create distinct learning climates. It is therefore important to examine the perspectives that professors in different disciplinary areas bring to the learning environment.

Physical and life sciences

The sciences tend to provide the most well-structured environment for their members, but it is also a research-driven environment. Furthermore, due to the momentum of discovery, the sciences are the site of greatest differentiation within the university (Kruytbosch, 1992). The most common form of differentiation is into increasing complexity: physics, the most fundamental science, can be apportioned into as many as 18 divisions, from classical mechanics to medical physics (Rothman, 1992). Another form of differentiation is reconfiguration based on empirical evidence. To illustrate, a shift in departmental nomenclature from meteorology to atmospheric and ocean sciences resulted from recognition of interactions between oceanic phenomena such as water temperature and atmospheric events such as hurricanes. A third form of differentiation is the emergence of new disciplines such as computer science from electrical engineering, with additional input from mathematics, logic and psychology.

The biological sciences have tended to differentiate and coalesce in slightly different form as research has led to new points of interest (Mcgregor, 1992). Biologists talk of proliferating disciplines; their departments, recapitulating mitosis, multiply and divide in relatively brief cycles. Medical sciences have differentiated into a set of disciplines, essentially research orientated, that range on a research continuum from pure to applied, and have a history of funding in research institutes. The most general attributes of the physical and life sciences are their continuing growth and differentiation into sub-fields that may or may not later coalesce, and their definition through research. The nature of the research problems that are being investigated drives their disciplinary organization. What effect does this have on learning goals?

Two fields identified in the study of disciplinary differences in learning goals (Cashin and Downey, 1995) – mathematics, because it is foundational to the physical sciences, and biological sciences – serve as examples. The course objectives weighted more highly by professors in mathematics and biological sciences than by professors in other fields were the gaining of factual knowledge and the learning of fundamental principles, generalizations or theories. Students in biological sciences reported making greater progress in gaining factual knowledge than the norm, but students in mathematics reported making less. Students in both fields reported learning fundamental principles, generalizations or theories to the same extent as students in other areas.

Mathematics professors also rated higher than other professors learning to apply course material to improve rational thinking, problem solving, and decision making; students in mathematics rated their progress toward the goal the same as students in other courses. In biological sciences, professors on the whole rated this learning goal less important than the norm, and students rated their progress lower than the norm. Overall in these courses, the most important learning objectives were basal level: gaining factual knowledge and learning fundamental principles, generalizations or theories; students did not report learning greater than the norm except for biological sciences students gaining factual knowledge.

Students reported that the amount of work and the difficulty of the subject matter was greater than the other courses, that they worked harder, and that there were fewer teaching methods involving students. The effect on students' attitudes was that in the mathematics courses, students were slightly more negative toward taking further courses or having positive feelings about the field of study as a result of having taken the course. Biological sciences students' attitudes matched those of students overall. The gist of these results is that the emphasis on knowledge of facts apparent in the physical and life science domains is conveyed into the teaching milieu, but at a cost to students' attitudes and involvement, as Tobias (1990) has affirmed.

Social sciences

The social sciences are not as well structured as the physical sciences, but are closer to them than the humanities in methods and validation processes. Pelikan (1992) points out that as in the physical and biological sciences, knowledge construction in the social sciences proceeds by the collection of data obtained through controlled observation. Although a quest for a unifying theory characterized early development in the social sciences, they too have differentiated and diverged. The institutionalization of the social sciences is relatively recent (the American Economic Association was founded in 1885 and the American Psychological Association in 1892), and internationalization occurred in the latter half of the twentieth century (Scott, 1992). Internationalization led social scientists to recognize that social science knowledge is time- and culture-dependent, which has foreshortened attempts to gain agreement about theoretical perspectives, core methods or concepts.

Learning in the social sciences has likewise been transformed from a generalist approach based on an introductory text that related questions in the field, to a specialized approach in which the serious student can claim a close working knowledge with only a limited sub-area within one specific domain of specialization (Scott, 1992). One of the respondents in my study on the learning environment suggested that the division of labour between disciplines lost sight of the notion of the necessary integration of the parts and the fundamental assumptions that drive the logic of argument. Specialization and fragmentation have contributed to a loss of identity in the social sciences, but a more serious threat has been questioning of the validity of social science research, creating social instability bordering on chaos in some social sciences.

In spite of the turbulence evident in theoretical and methodological debate in the social sciences, there appear to be some consistencies. Sutton (1994) points out that however disturbed some parts of these fields may be by the new scepticisms, relativisms and resistances to authoritative doctrine, there is also the academic ideology of disciplined and critical inquiry which provides a binding sense of shared purpose. Progress in the social sciences, according to Scott (1992), will depend upon debate coloured with tolerance and respect for differences of opinion, in a climate where scholars are free to pursue lines of reasoning and approaches to study to their logical conclusions. What does this mean in terms of the quality of learning in the social sciences?

In the study of disciplinary differences in learning, two social science areas were identified: psychology and education (Cashin and Downey, 1995). The course objectives weighted more highly by psychology professors were similar to those of the mathematics and biological sciences professors: gaining factual knowledge and learning fundamental principles, generalizations or theories. Psychology professors were most different from professors in other disciplines in the greater weight they awarded to discovering the implications of course material for understanding oneself; psychology students concurred, giving greater relative weight to their progress in achieving this learning goal.

Education professors, in accordance with their career orientation, assigned greater importance to developing specific skills, competencies and points of view needed by professionals in the field. Students in education agreed with their professors, but also reported greater progress than others in learning to apply course material to improve rational thinking, problem solving and decision making, in developing oral and written skills and, as for psychology students, in discovering the implications of course material for understanding themselves. Attitudes toward both fields were more positive as a result of students having taken the course than in other courses. These findings are consistent with those of Franklin and Theall (1995), who found that education and social science students rated their instructors as more effective than did students in science and mathematics.

Humanities

Once recognized as the focal point of the university, the onus is now on the humanities to prove their utility and relevance compared to the sciences. A relatively small proportion of government funding for research goes to the humanities, and Weiland (1992) reports that many departments in the humanities are small and are being rationalized or concentrated into area studies. The exploration of particularities, as opposed to generalities, translates for professors in the humanities into welcoming complexity, noting diversity and accepting that many things cannot be proven through replication (Becher, 1989; Austin, 1992). Scholars tend to work independently, professional societies tend to be weaker and publication rates are slower, all making it more difficult for professors to establish a reputation.

At the same time, student demand for the humanities, and their appreciation of them, as shown in elevated ratings of instruction, continues. The humanities address more of students' academic career goals than do the physical and social sciences. According to Rhodes (1994), these include the ability to listen, read and analyse with comprehension, to write and speak with precision and clarity in the expression of disciplined thought, the ability to reason effectively, the ability to engage people of different cultural perspectives, an appreciation of modes of thought and expression of the disciplines, sensitivity toward the ideas, values and goals that have shaped society, and some sense of the moral implications of actions and ideas. The emphasis on personal interpretation that characterizes the humanities – as opposed to an emphasis on public verification and the expansion of knowledge (Snow, 1964) – makes the humanities immediately relevant to the undergraduate.

As an example of the humanities, the learning goals that professors in English language and literature weighted more highly were developing skill in oral and written expression, gaining a broader understanding and appreciation of intellectual-cultural activity, and developing creative capacities (Cashin and Downey, 1995). English language and literature professors attached considerably less importance to gaining factual knowledge and learning fundamental principles than professors in other disciplines. Students in English language and literature programmes reported making greater progress than did other students on average in all the learning objectives. Students judged that their professors stimulated their learning. Humanities courses on the whole are given the highest ratings among disciplines for instructor effectiveness (Franklin and Theall, 1995; Murray and Renaud, 1995).

The differences in learning goals across disciplinary areas are pronounced. Although learning fundamental principles, generalizations or theories (the highest level of knowledge in the Bloom taxonomy) is an important learning goal in all disciplines except English literature, other goals, especially of intellectual skills, vary markedly. According to professors and students, the sciences focus on factual knowledge – the most basic level of knowledge – while in the social sciences and humanities, understanding, creativity and communication skills are important goals that are developed. Is the size of the knowledge base in the physical and life sciences and the rate of change so great that professors and students do not have the opportunity to develop intellectual skills, or does their conceptualization of learning – as knowledge rather than as intellectual development – limit the learning potential?

Approaches to conceptualizing learning

Student learning in the university has been the focus of my programme of research over the past decade. Research shows that students interpret the learning task as their professors describe it. If knowledge is emphasized, students will approach the learning task as one of acquiring knowledge; if thinking is required, students will interpret the task as learning to think. How students conceptualize learning and therefore tend to define their learning task is an important mediating variable in the amount and kind of learning that will occur. We recently examined two approaches to conceptualizing learning, with 120 students from arts, science and engineering programmes enrolled in an English literature course and a physics course in 1995 in a research university.

One approach, based on extensive research undertaken in the United States, investigated students' reasons for attending university (Astin, 1993). The

Table 4.1 Principal components analysis (with varimax rotation) of the importance of students' reasons for deciding to go to university

Component/reason	Loading
Intellectual development (25.4% of variance)	
To develop a meaningful philosophy of life	0.79
To learn more about things that interest me +	0.78
To mature intellectually and develop a sense of judgement +	0.77
To develop a sense of values and to develop habits that will guide my future	0.58
To develop reasoning skills +	0.44
Social openness (13.2% of variance) [more important to arts than physics students]	
To meet new people	0.87
To establish new friendships	0.86
To please my parents	0.51
To establish some clear educational goals and objectives for myself	0.48
General skills (9.6% of variance) [more important to arts students]	
To improve my reading and study skills	0.78
To develop general communication skills	0.65
To improve my writing skills	0.64
To obtain a broad, general education +	0.56
Career preparation (6.7% of variance) [more important to engineering students]	
To acquire specific skills or abilities in preparation for a particular career +	0.85
To prepare myself for graduate or professional school +	0.72
To improve my chances of finding a job + [†]	0.50
Career success (5.7% of variance) [more important to engineering students]	
To be able to make more money	0.72
To discover my career interests	0.65
To improve my chances of finding a job + *	0.59
Non-academic (4.6% of variance)	
I could not find a job —	0.78
There was nothing better to do –	0.67
To get away from home –	0.59

* 'varimax rotation' refers to the rotating of all the variables in the equation to get the greatest clarify of fit
[†] criterion loads on more than one principal component
+ quite important; important;
– somewhat important;
— not at all important

reasons that students considered quite important (+) were concerned primarily with intellectual development and career preparation (Table 4.1) (Donald and Denison, 1997). Programme differences were found for social openness, general skills and career preparation and success. Arts students considered social openness reasons more important in deciding to go to university than did physics students, and awarded greater importance to general skills than either engineering or physics students. Engineering students assigned greater importance to career preparation and career success than students in arts and science. Equally important, students across programmes did not differ in the importance they attached to intellectual development.

A second approach to understanding students' general orientation to learning developed in the work of British and Australian researchers (Entwistle and Tait, 1990; Ramsden, 1992; Biggs, 1993). The term 'orientation' in this research indicates a combination of an approach to studying, style of learning and motivation which is relatively stable across different educational tasks (Ramsden, 1992). A *deep* approach reflects a student's intention to seek personal understanding in an active way, while a *surface* approach reflects the intention to reproduce the content in order to cope with assessment requirements (Entwistle and Tait, 1995). In a *strategic* or *achieving* approach, the student's goal is to be alert to requirements in order to maximize grades. The results of the student orientation research suggest that students who adopt a deep approach to learning experience greater satisfaction in their learning, higher quality outcomes and better grades (Ramsden, 1992).

In our study, arts and science students reported significantly greater deep motivation and strategies than achievement motivation and strategies, which in turn were significantly greater than surface motivation and strategies. The engineering students presented a completely different pattern, with no significant differences between motivations or strategies. They also displayed greater surface motivation and surface strategies and greater achieving motivation than the arts and science students (Table 4.2). The engineering students appeared to have adopted an eclectic or pragmatic stance to studying. The engineering students also displayed a more divergent and complex reaction within the programme group, as those who adopted a deep strategy also adopted an achievement strategy and tended not to adopt a surface strategy.

A comparison of the results for the two approaches to conceptualizing learning shows that students' reasons for attending university and their orientation to studying were consistent in several important ways. The importance of intellectual development correlated significantly with deep motivation and strategy, and to a lesser extent with an achieving strategy (Table 4.3). General skills showed a similar pattern, with more modest correlations. Career preparation and career success correlated with surface motivation and strategy, but also with achieving motivation. Most important for our purposes are (i) the recognition of both intellectual and career preparation goals on the part of students, (ii) the relationship between deep motivation and strategy with intellectual development reasons, and (iii) the relationship between career and surface orientations. An important caution for course and programme planning is the

Table 4.2 Orientation to studying of students in arts, science and engineering programmes

| | English literature course (EL) | | Physics course | | | | | Significance of ANOVA* |
| | n = 66 | | Physics programme (P) n = 29 | | Engineering programme (E) n = 25 | | |
	Mean	SD‡	Mean	SD	Mean	SD	
Motive							
Surface	19.76	5.30	19.11	4.39	23.40	4.55	E > EL, P§
Deep	23.71	4.95	24.69	5.23	22.44	4.60	nsd**
Achieving	20.51	5.08	22.75	4.84	24.76	3.77	E > EL‡
Strategy							
Surface	16.20	5.05	16.97	3.95	20.60	3.70	E > P, EL¶
Deep	22.32	3.80	23.18	4.75	22.16	5.01	nsd
Achieving	20.11	4.90	19.66	5.16	20.80	4.09	nsd

* ANOVA = analysis of variance, i.e. scores on different variables are compared for differences across programmes
‡ SD = standard deviation
** = no significant difference
Note ‡ p = 0.05; § p = 0.01; ¶ p = 0.001

Table 4.3 Correlations between reasons for attending university and orientation to studying

| | Motivation | | | Strategy | | |
	Surface	Deep	Achieving	Surface	Deep	Achieving
Intellectual development	−0.15	0.50¶	0.04	−0.14	0.41¶	0.27§
Social openness	0.28§	0.05	0.17	0.23‡	0.04	0.10
General skills	0.03	0.21‡	0.05	−0.04	0.26§	0.24§
Career preparation	0.37¶	0.12	0.39¶	0.27§	0.21‡	0.23‡
Career success	0.54¶	−0.03	0.32¶	0.39¶	−0.23‡	0.04
Non-academic	0.04	−0.27§	0.02	0.15	−0.10	−0.22‡

variation across programmes within courses; in this study, we found two distinct groups of students with different learning orientations in the same course.

From the results of this research, we can determine that students reflect the overall post-secondary goal of intellectual development, but that their learning orientations match the characteristics of the disciplinary area. Students' learning behaviours thus reflect basic disciplinary differences and consistencies across disciplines. To recapitulate the argument thus far, disciplines play a critical role in determining the parameters of knowledge and the mode of inquiry that guide learning. Disciplines also differ in the emphasis placed on learning goals. In the physical and social sciences, learning fundamental principles, generalizations and theories is important, but in the physical sciences, gaining factual knowledge is a paramount aim, while in the social sciences and humanities, broader intellectual goals and the development of general skills are more important.

One direction for the future that universities are now contemplating is the provision of ever larger knowledge bases, validated by the disciplines, in a technologically supported environment. It would appear that this matches the learning goals in the physical and life sciences, but that the development of the intellectual skills that are the focus of the social sciences and humanities would require another kind of solution. At the same time, there is consistency across the disciplines that students' intellectual development – whether called problem solving or critical thinking, a deep approach or a constructive epistemology – is of the greatest importance. Given this situation, what steps can universities take to provide for effective learning?

Ensuring effective learning

In the twenty-first century, ensuring effective learning in post-secondary education will require concentrated effort in two interlinking precincts: knowledge base development and the learning of intellectual skills. Universities have unique capabilities in responding to these needs. Knowledge base development consists of knowledge construction and knowledge evaluation. What we must first establish is how or the extent to which disciplines can examine their knowledge bases. At what level are knowledge bases best understood: curriculum committees, departments, consortia, learned societies? The broadest approach would be to call upon disciplines to put into place curriculum boards to ensure that the disciplinary knowledge base meets the criteria for scholarship. At the present time, data bases are being set up on the Web in subdisciplinary areas that allow access and feedback: for example, the University of Maryland physics education research group. This idea could be extended to a consortium to provide a network of knowledge bases in specific subdisciplinary areas. Electronic publishing is also moving in this direction.

In universities, ensuring that the knowledge base is available to students and meets disciplinary criteria will require a similar adaptation. One of the academic leaders I interviewed suggested that curriculum review will be the next stage of accountability within universities, following programme review, but still based within individual academic units. This would be accomplished through discussion of common academic floors or minimums of expectation in syllabus review by members of an academic unit. The syllabus would be discussed and approved by faculty colleagues to ensure that students are given a very significant challenge and that each course is a reflection of the field of study; this is intended to bring renewal to the field and allow it to connect to others.

Student learning of intellectual skills requires in the first instance enunciated learning goals that focus on intellectual development. In a study on the identification and acquisition of thinking processes or intellectual skills in post-secondary education, I tested models of thinking in order to develop a comprehensive model of thinking processes. Processes reported in research on critical thinking, problem solving, formal operations and creativity at the post-secondary level in various disciplines were used to produce a working model of thinking processes (Table 4.4). Professors across disciplines were interviewed to ascertain what processes were developed in their course, which were evaluated, which were used by experts in the discipline and which were most important for students to acquire. Students from the courses of the interviewed professors were also interviewed to determine what skills they found most important.

The working model of thinking processes proved useful in identifying the kinds of thinking processes important in the various disciplines and developed in courses. For example, physics professors considered the selection of critical elements and relations important for 'pulling out the guts of the situation' in problem solving, and the development of representation skills was important for getting students both to think in terms of organizing principles and to use those principles. Inference and verification skills were crucial in problem solving (Donald, 1993). Students also identified selection skills and thought descriptive skills important.

Diverse instructional methods were suggested by the professors to develop students' intellectual skills. Although lecturing played an important part, problem-solving groups and assignments (including drills, open-ended projects, the analysis of cases or situations, workshops and tutorials) also played

Table 4.4   A working model of thinking processes in higher education

Description
Identify context, conditions, facts, functions, underlying assumptions, and goals

Selection
Choose relevant information, order it in importance according to its significance, identify important elements and relations

Representation
Recognize organizing principles (laws, methods, rules), organize, illustrate and modify elements and relations

Inference
Draw conclusions from premises or evidence by detecting connections or equivalences between parts, units, components or relations; categorize, order, change perspective, hypothesize

Synthesis
Combine parts to form a whole, elaborate, generate missing links or fill in gaps, develop a course of action

Verification
Confirm accuracy, coherence, consistency, correspondence by comparing alternative outcomes or comparing outcomes to standard; judge validity, use feedback to regulate, adjust, adapt

prominent roles. Instruction that involved students in analysing and hypo-thesizing, in describing and testing, in the professors' views, was essential for developing students' thinking processes. As one psychology professor noted, it is the arguments or inferences in a discipline that must be learned. The long-term goal for universities is, then, to provide learning experiences that enable students to develop a repertoire of skills and strategies that they will be able to use in lifelong learning.

The steps for accomplishing this include providing students at entry to their studies with insight about their disciplines and about the nature of learning at university, aiding them to set academic goals and to articulate their goals in a course (Donald, 1997). The learning climate will be dependent on steps taken by both professors and administrators, and should foster the process of inquiry (in class and across disciplines), making students aware that the learning task requires thinking on their part. It should show them how to do that in the con-text of the course; it should give them a sense of the number of hours of study-ing required to succeed, provide more small-group learning experiences – tutorials, undergraduate research, collaborative learning over an extended period – and give students choice, challenge, control and collaboration in their learning tasks. It should provide students with active learning tasks that improve their attitudes to learning, including participation in group discussion, projects, explaining material to another student.

Universities in the future will continue to have a predominant role as pro-ducers and disseminators of knowledge, but the most central function will be as intellectual centres of a learning society. A particular aim of universities is thus to foster intellectual development. The kind of university that can provide an environment that supports intellectual development in its diverse forms will be making a critically important contribution to the twenty-first century.

Note

1. This chapter is based on research funded by the Social Science and Humanities Research Council of Canada and by les Fonds pour la formation des chercheurs et aide à la recherche du Québec.

References

Astin, A. W. (1993) An empirical typology of college students, *Journal of College Student Development*, 34: 36–46.

Austin, A. E. (1992) Faculty cultures, in B. R. Clark and G. R. Neave (eds) *The Encyclo-pedia of Higher Education* (pp. 1614–23). Oxford: Pergamon Press.

Becher, R. A. (1989) *Academic Tribes and Territories*. Milton Keynes: Open University Press.

Biggs, J. B. (1993) What do inventories of students' learning processes really measure? A theoretical review and clarification, *British Journal of Educational Psychology*, 63: 3–19.

Biglan, A. (1973) The characteristics of subject matter in different academic areas, *Journal of Applied Psychology*, 57(3): 195–203.

Bloom, B. S. (ed.) (1956) *Taxonomy of Educational Objectives*. New York: David McKay.

Braxton, J. M. and Hargens, L. L. (1996) Variation among academic disciplines: analytical frameworks and research, in J. C. Smart (ed.) *Higher Education: Handbook of Theory and Research*, 11 (pp. 1–46). New York: Agathon.

Broudy, H. S. (1977) Types of knowledge and purposes of education, in R. C. Anderson, R. J. Spiro and W. E. Montagne (eds) *Schooling and the Acquisition of Knowledge* (pp. 1–17). Hillsdale, NJ: Lawrence Erlbaum.

Cashin, W. E. and Downey, R. G. (1995) Disciplinary differences in what is taught and in students' perceptions of what they learn and how they are taught, in N. Hativa and M. Marincovich (eds) *Disciplinary Differences in Teaching and Learning in Higher Education*, 64 (pp. 81–92), New Directions for Teaching and Learning. San Francisco, CA: Jossey-Bass.

Centra, J. (1993) *Reflective Faculty Evaluation: Enhancing Teaching and Determining Faculty Effectiveness*. San Francisco, CA: Jossey-Bass.

Clark, B. R. (1983) *The Higher Education System*. Berkeley, CA: University of California Press.

Donald, J. G. (1986) Knowledge and the university curriculum, *Higher Education*, 15(3): 267–82.

Donald, J. G. (1987) Learning schemata: methods of representing cognitive, content and curriculum structures in higher education, *Instructional Science*, 16: 187–211.

Donald, J. G. (1990) University professors' views of knowledge and validation processes, *Journal of Educational Psychology*, 82(2): 242–9.

Donald, J. G. (1993) Professors' and students' conceptualizations of the learning task in physics courses, *Journal of Research on Science Teaching*, 30: 905–18.

Donald, J. G. (1995) Disciplinary differences in knowledge validation, in N. Hativa and M. Marincovich (eds) *Disciplinary Differences in Teaching and Learning in Higher Education*, 64 (pp. 7–17). San Francisco, CA: Jossey-Bass.

Donald, J. G. (1997) *Improving the Environment for Learning: Academic Leaders Talk About What Works*. San Francisco, CA: Jossey-Bass.

Donald, J. G. and Denison, D. B. (1997) Postsecondary students' conceptions of learning. Paper presented at the annual meeting of the Canadian Society for the Study of Higher Education, St. John's, Newfoundland, June.

Dressel, P. and Mayhew, L. (1974) *Higher Education as a Field of Study*. San Francisco, CA: Jossey-Bass.

Entwistle, N. and Tait, H. (1990) Approaches to learning, evaluations of teaching, and preferences for contrasting academic environments, *Higher Education*, 19: 169–94.

Entwistle, N. and Tait, H. (1995) Approaches to studying and perceptions of the learning environment across disciplines, in N. Hativa and M. Marincovich (eds) *Disciplinary Differences in Teaching and Learning in Higher Education*, 64 (pp. 93–103). San Francisco, CA: Jossey-Bass.

Franklin, J. and Theall, M. (1995) The relationship of disciplinary differences and the value of class preparation time to student ratings of teaching, in N. Hativa and M. Marincovich (eds) *Disciplinary Differences in Teaching and Learning in Higher Education*, 64 (pp. 41–8), New Directions for Teaching and Learning. San Francisco, CA: Jossey-Bass.

Frederiksen, N. (1984) Implications of cognitive theory for instruction in problem solving, *Review of Educational Research*, 54(3): 363–407.

Hammack, F. M. and Heyns, B. (1992) Microsociology, in B. R. Clark and G. R. Neave (eds) *The Encyclopedia of Higher Education* (pp. 1871–84). Oxford: Pergamon Press.

Hirst, P. (1974) *Knowledge and the Curriculum: A Collection of Philosophical Papers*. London: Routledge and Kegan Paul.

King, A. and Brownell, J. (1966) *The Curriculum and the Disciplines of Knowledge*. New York: John Wiley.

Kruytbosch, C. (1992) Academic disciplines: physical sciences, in B. R. Clark and G. R. Neave (eds) *The Encyclopedia of Higher Education* (pp. 2329–31). Oxford: Pergamon Press.

Kuhn, T. S. (1970) *The Structure of Scientific Revolutions*. Chicago: University of Chicago Press.

Lattuca, L. R. and Stark, J. S. (1993) Modifying the major: extemporaneous thoughts from ten disciplines. Paper presented at the annual meeting of the Association for the Study of Higher Education, Pittsburgh, PA, November.

Leary, D. E. (1992) Psychology, in B. R. Clark and G. R. Neave (eds) *The Encyclopedia of Higher Education* (pp. 2136–50). Oxford: Pergamon Press.

Marsh, H. W. (1984) Students' evaluations of university teaching: dimensionality, reliability, validity, potential biases and utility, *Journal of Educational Psychology*, 76: 707–54.

Mcgregor, H. C. (1992) Biological sciences: introduction, in B. R. Clark and G. R. Neave (eds) *The Encyclopedia of Higher Education* (pp. 2181–3). Oxford: Pergamon Press.

Milem, J. F. and Astin, H. S. (1994) Scientists as teachers: a look at their culture, their roles, and their pedagogy. Paper presented at the annual meeting of the American Educational Research Association, New Orleans, LA, April.

Murray, H. G. and Renaud, R. D. (1995) Disciplinary differences in classroom teaching behaviors, in N. Hativa and M. Marincovich (eds) *Disciplinary Differences in Teaching and Learning in Higher Education*, 64 (pp. 31–9), New Directions for Teaching and Learning. San Francisco, CA: Jossey-Bass.

Pelikan, J. (1992) *The Idea of the University: A Reexamination*. New Haven, CT: Yale University Press.

Ramsden, P. (1992) *Learning to Teach in Higher Education*. London: Routledge.

Rhodes, F. H. T. (1994) The place of teaching in the research university, in J. R. Cole, E. G. Barber and S. R. Graubard (eds) *The Research University in a Time of Discontent* (pp. 179–89). Baltimore, MD: The Johns Hopkins University Press.

Rosch, E. (1978) Principles of categorization, in E. Rosch and B. B. Lloyd (eds) *Cognition and Categorization* (pp. 27–48). Hillsdale, NJ: Lawrence Erlbaum.

Rosenberg, C. (1979) Towards an ecology of knowledge: on discipline, context, and history, in A. Oleson and J. Voss (eds) *The Organization of Knowledge in Modern America, 1860–1920* (pp. 440–55). Baltimore, MD: The Johns Hopkins University Press.

Rothman, M. A. (1992) Physics in higher education, in B. R. Clark and G. R. Neave (eds) *The Encyclopedia of Higher Education* (pp. 2388–98). Oxford: Pergamon Press.

Scott, R. A. (1992) Social sciences: introduction, in B. R. Clark and G. R. Neave (eds) *The Encyclopedia of Higher Education* (pp. 2071–80). Oxford: Pergamon Press.

Snow, C. P. (1964) *The Two Cultures and the Scientific Revolution. And a Second Look*. Cambridge: Cambridge University Press.

Sutton, F. X. (1994) The distinction and durability of American research universities, in J. R. Cole, E. G. Barber and S. R. Graubard (eds) *The Research University in a Time of Discontent* (pp. 309–32). Baltimore, MD: The Johns Hopkins University Press.

Tobias, S. (1990) *They're Not Dumb, They're Different; Stalking the Second Tier*. Tucson, AZ: Research Corporation.

Toulmin, S. (1972) *Human Understanding*, Vol. 1. Oxford: Clarendon Press.

Weiland, J. S. (1992) Humanities: introduction, in B. R. Clark and G. R. Neave (eds) *The Encyclopedia of Higher Education* (pp. 1981–9). Oxford: Pergamon Press.

5

Student Learning and Academic Choice: The Rule of Coherence

David D. Dill

Introduction

One of the effects of 'massification' and 'knowledge expansion' on higher education has been a proliferation in the number of academic fields and curricula.[1] Providing participation in higher education to a much larger proportion of the traditional age group, as well as to non-traditional populations, has increased demand for more vocationally orientated academic programmes in fields such as business. Correspondingly, knowledge developments in the traditional disciplines (as well as the evolution of new interdisciplinary fields such as molecular biology, public policy and ethnic studies) have led to the rapid expansion of academic programmes in universities throughout the world (Clark, 1996).[2] The resulting proliferation in academic curricula conflicts with growing societal pressure for universities to rationalize their academic offerings and to improve the quality of teaching and learning. The declining unit of resource for academic programmes in almost all countries (with government reductions of per-student support for higher education, and the intrusion of external mechanisms for assuring the quality of teaching and learning) is forcing all universities to make difficult academic choices. Which new academic curricula can the university support? And correspondingly, which traditional curricula will grow, and which must decline, or close? These critical academic choices will be a dominant concern for academic governance in the years to come (Cole, 1994).

Historically, in most countries these choices were guided by the regulations of state ministries of education, by the conventions and norms of the traditional academic disciplines or professions, by the cultural inheritance of the particular country, by market demand, or by some combination of these factors. One of the effects of increased academic specialization and differentiation is that these traditional institutions are no longer influential in controlling the development of academic curricula. The first three of these institutions are now in flux in most countries: educational ministries are increasingly delegating difficult programmatic choices to universities; many new programmes such as those in molecular biology, cognitive psychology or feminist studies are effect-ively interdisciplinary, and disciplinary traditions and norms are no longer an effective rule for choice in these cases; and the increasing diversity of students and cultures within nation-states is eroding the traditional belief in the concept of curricula as received culture. These changes have led to academic 'cultural wars' over the nature and content of the curriculum and to a growing reliance upon market demand as a basis for choice between curricula. Increasingly, uni-versities must develop their own procedures for choosing among potential aca-demic curricula. What academic rules can be used as basis for such choices?

In the arguments that follow a 'rule of coherence' is proposed that can be used in evaluating what forms of knowledge should be taught within a univer-sity. The rule of coherence is based upon research suggesting that an important predictor of student learning in higher education is the extent to which an aca-demic curriculum offers a coherent, integrated academic experience. Applica-tion of a rule of coherence necessarily involves a 'measure of coherence' with which the members of a university can evaluate whether a curriculum possesses sufficient integration to foster effective student learning. In the sections that follow the rationale for a rule of coherence as a basis for academic choice, and the strengths and weakness of a measure of coherence in universities will be examined.

Institutions and the valued attributes of academic curricula

The curricular choices that academics make are influenced by the institutional frameworks within which they work. By 'institutions' is meant the humanly devised constraints that shape academic behaviour, including the formal regu-lations of educational ministries, the informal values and norms of the many academic professions, and the policies of individual universities (North, 1990). These collected institutional rules constrain the way that the academic game is played. The institutions of academic life, however, like those of politics, eco-nomics, and sports, evolve over time, altering the incentives for academic action. In a time of great turbulence, such as the present period of higher edu-cation reform, traditional institutional structures may encourage the prolifer-ation of academic curricula in ways that serve academic self-interest, but are unproductive for students and society as a whole. In this new context there is a need to attend to institutional reform as a means of reconnecting academic behaviour with the public interest.

Institutions are particularly influential on the costs of exchange (North, 1990). Universities, even those not directly subject to market forces, are engaged in the exchange of academic knowledge for financial resources. In the case of state-controlled higher education, governments exchange financial support for student places in academic curricula. In the case of market-orientated higher education, students or their families exchange a sum of money for an academic education. Implicit in this exchange is the assumption that an academic curriculum offers socially valued attributes, which may be defined as human capital in the form of knowledge, skills and values. Part of the cost of exchange, to the government and/or to the individual, therefore, is the time and money invested in validating the existence of these valued attributes of academic curricula.[3] The difficulty and cost of ascertaining these attributes has varied over time. Towards the end of the eighteenth century, academic and religious norms emphasizing a unity of knowledge created a remarkably homogeneous curriculum among the universities of western Europe and the American colonies (Kimball, 1986). As late as 1831, five faculty members were sufficient to cover all the areas of knowledge at the University of North Carolina, and all admitted students met the same detailed standards of knowledge competency at admission and pursued an identical academic programme for four years (Powell, 1972). Thus the uncertainty involved in judging the valued attributes of a university education prior to the nineteenth century was lessened by the institution of common and rigorously enforced norms among the academic community.

The academic norms of the nineteenth and twentieth centuries, which shaped the emergence of the modern university, emphasized the temporal nature of truth, and created opportunities for increased academic specialization (Dill, 1992a). In continental Europe, state ministries of education emerged to play an often conservative role in the approval of new academic programmes, maintaining the curriculum in a traditional form that was generally unresponsive to market demands. In England the small size of the elitist university sector and the powerful normative influence of Cambridge, Oxford and the University of London constrained the development of academic fields and reinforced an academic 'gold standard': the single-subject honours degree in the traditional disciplines. In the US system of higher education, government always played less of a role in regulating academic curricula. Instead, market demand, the informal norms and values of the academic disciplines and the academic rules of the universities themselves were the principal institutions shaping the nature of academic curricula. In the decentralized US system, market demand has historically played a more influential role than in the state-controlled systems of Europe, or the normatively bounded system of the UK. As a result, US higher education has long been noted for its programmatic innovation, if not proliferation (Ben-David, 1972).

In the modern era of mass systems of higher education, the combined demand of new student clienteles and the international growth in the number and variety of disciplines, specialties and inter- or multi-disciplinary subjects, has led to a proliferation of academic curricula that on a worldwide scale appears to be essentially uncontrollable (Clark, 1996). At the same time, governments in many countries have grown concerned that central control of curricula has become too costly, stifling academic innovation and related economic and social developments. Therefore control over academic programme choices in continental Europe has increasingly been devolved to the university level (Huisman, 1996). Massification has also introduced into universities student populations with more varied academic preparation and ambitions, leading to demands for different (often more applied and vocationally orientated) academic programmes (Nowotny, 1995). Thus the regulatory controls of government over the content of academic curricula have been loosened at a time of rapid university expansion.

Massification and the institutions of academic life: the US experience

The US experience with higher education expansion pre-dated that of Europe and the UK by more than a generation, thereby suggesting some of the possible effects of massification on the institutions that govern academic behaviour. There is emerging evidence in the US system that the combination of massification and academic specialization is leading to academic curricula that are more atomized and to faculty life that is more isolated, both within academic fields and within universities. Consensus on what should be taught within academic curricula, or what constitutes an academic curriculum at the university level, appears increasingly difficult to obtain. Whether the focus is on the norms and sanctions of the academic professions, the policies of universities or the rules of relevant departments, the evidence seems to suggest institutions are being created that encourage collective disengagement and individual autonomy.

Surveys on the views of faculty members in different disciplines (Lattuca and Stark, 1994) suggest declining normative influence from the various academic professions on the content of academic programmes. In many disciplines faculty members did not easily agree on definitions of curricular content, nor were they in agreement that specified sequences of learning content were appropriate for students. Even in professional fields such as business and engineering, where faculty members reported the highest perceived consensus on the nature of academic knowledge, they also reported that defining the content of the professional courses was one of their most serious curriculum tensions. In several disciplines, faculty members expressed the belief that the field's diversity precluded achieving a consensus on what students should know.

Recent studies on university-level rules for influencing the structure and coherence of academic curricula reveal a similar loss of consensus. For example, an influential early report on the integrity of the college curriculum argued:

> The curriculum has given way to a market place philosophy: it is a supermarket where students are shopping and professors are merchants of learning. Fads and fashions, the demands of popularity and success, enter where wisdom and experience should prevail. Does it make sense for a college to offer a thousand courses to a student who will only take thirty-six?
>
> The market place philosophy refuses to establish common expectations and norms . . . [T]he institutional course requirements . . . lack a rationale

and cohesion or, even worse, are almost lacking altogether. Electives are being used to fatten majors, and diminish breadth. It is as if no one cares, so long as the store stays open.

(Zemsky, 1989: 39)

Empirical studies of the catalogues of selective universities and of the transcripts of enrolled students have revealed little structure and coherence in the undergraduate general educational curriculum common in the US system (Zemsky, 1989; National Association of Scholars, 1996).[4] As Massy and Zemsky (1994: 2) observe:

there has been an incipient destructuring – or deconstructing – of the undergraduate curriculum over the last two decades that has resulted in fewer required courses, less emphasis on taking courses in ordered sequence, and greater reliance on students to develop their own sense of how the various bits and pieces of knowledge they acquire in the classroom fit together into a coherent picture.

But the decline of curricular coherence is also suggested by research on the content of the subject major or area of concentration of US students. One indicator of structure is the existence of senior theses and comprehensive examinations in the curricula of subject fields. Such requirements foster coherence in students' learning by requiring the integration or analysis of a body of knowledge broader or deeper than that provided in a single course. A study of the curricula requirements over time of the 50 most selective US universities revealed a continuing decline in mandatory requirements for such comprehensive assessments, from 66 per cent of the surveyed universities in 1939, to 56 per cent in 1964, to 12 per cent in 1993 (National Association of Scholars, 1996). Casual empiricism suggests a similar problem of declining coherence even at the level of the PhD, where achieving faculty agreement on the contents of the traditional comprehensive exams has become increasingly difficult in many fields.

Field research at the departmental level in US universities (Massy *et al.*, 1994) has also revealed a pattern of 'hollowed collegiality' in which departments nominally appear to act collectively, but avoid those specific collaborative activities that might lead to real improvements in curricular cohesion. For example, faculty members readily reported informal meetings to share research findings, collective procedures for determining faculty promotion and tenure, and consensus decision making on what particular courses should be offered each term and who should teach them. But:

Despite these trappings of collegiality, respondents told us they seldom led to the more substantial discussions necessary to improve undergraduate education, or to the sense of collective responsibility needed to make departmental efforts more effective. These vestiges of collegiality serve faculty convenience but dodge fundamental questions of task. This is especially the case, and is regrettable, with respect to student learning: collegiality remains thwarted with regard to faculty engagement with issues of curricular structure, pedagogical alternatives, and student assessment.

(Massy *et al.*, 1994: 19)

A major contributor to this hollowed collegiality was an observed pattern of fragmented communication within departments in which traditions of individual autonomy and academic specialization have led to atomization and isolation among faculty members. Faculty members not only do much of their teaching alone, but because disciplinary sub-fields are defined quite narrowly, many faculty members find it almost impossible to discuss their teaching with one another.

The increasing specialization of academic curricula makes assessing their valued characteristics more crucial if governments and consumers are to enter into exchanges of resources for academic programmes with a minimum of uncertainty. But the declining influence of the traditional institutions of governmental regulation, professional norms, university policies and departmental controls over academic curricula appear to have increased the costs of exchange. Instead, the evidence of autonomy and individualism suggests potential for opportunism within academe in the form of programmes that accord with the scholarly interests and professional needs of faculty members, but whose contribution to human capital is unknown or costly to verify.

The concept of coherence

Throughout the previous section reference was made to structure and coherence as attributes of academic curricula that are particularly important to those who finance or purchase academic programmes. But the concept of coherence in academic life is controversial. Some would argue that a focus on coherence in academic curricula could stifle innovation and conflict with academic freedom.

Weick (1984: 15) has noted the paradoxical relationship between cohesion and scholarly accuracy in university communities: 'Actions that strengthen the community weaken the scholarship. And actions that strengthen the scholarship weaken the community.' Weick argues that strong social ties limit and potentially bias the portrait of the world that a group develops. Perceptual accuracy, or the validity of knowledge, is enhanced by the 'fineness' of sensing mechanisms, as in the fineness of film grain. Universities therefore place primary emphasis on encouraging the values of academic freedom and individual autonomy in research and teaching. As a consequence, and as already noted, both formal and informal means of coordinating instruction are rare. The academic content of individual courses both across and within programmes is not normally integrated by the faculty, but is 'interpreted' by the student participating in the various classes. Few sanctions exist for faculty members who refuse to cooperate or coordinate their teaching with others.

While Weick usefully suggests the relevance of academic individualism to successful scholarship, the application of the norm of academic freedom and individualism to the function of teaching is overdrawn. Teaching, unlike research, principally involves the transfer of what is known in a subject or field, not what is undiscovered. Even at the most advanced level of teaching, the research doctorate, teaching is meant to provide a synthesis of essential knowledge in a field, symbolized by the traditional comprehensive exam. Furthermore, the emphasis on individualism in academic work ignores the expanding team orientation of modern scientific research, and the necessity of cooperative research and scholarship in multidisciplinary fields and topics. There is increasing, not decreasing, evidence of cooperative arrangements in research (Gibbons, 1995). The individual scholar, while still important and necessary, is becoming less common. Finally, if encouraging coordination and integration in academic curricula inhibited innovative research, or had a 'chilling effect' on free-thinking scholars, then scholarship and research in multidisciplinary fields with carefully integrated academic programmes (such as business, engineering and medicine) would also likely suffer. There are no signs that this is the case. Rather, there is growing evidence that the academic individualism and lack of coherence evident in many academic curricula encourage opportunistic behaviour in which faculty members design their teaching to satisfy their professional self-interest in research and scholarship.

The analysis of those who advocate academic individualism in academic curricula suggests that the primary ethic of university life is the expansion of knowledge. University faculty, however – at least the vast majority who both research and teach – must live the ambiguity of a dual ethic: a commitment to the expansion of knowledge as well as a commitment to the interests of their students (Braxton *et al.*, 1992). This dual ethic of academic life presents a critical dilemma that can be paraphrased in Weick's terms: 'Actions that strengthen the research productivity of individual scholars may weaken the community of learning for students.' Fulfilling the academic profession's ethical commitment to students necessarily involves stressing coherence in academic curricula.

Why is educational coherence an important curricular attribute for students and society? There is emerging, but not yet definitive, evidence to suggest that the quality of an academic curriculum is best conceptualized in a holistic manner as greater than the sum of the activities of individual teachers in separate classrooms (Ewell, 1988; Pascarella and Terenzini, 1991). As Tony Becher (1992: 58) noted in developing a university-based system for the improvement of academic programmes at the University of Sussex,

> the most important consideration in quality assurance must be a holistic rather than an atomistic one, namely the benefits students derive from the totality of their degree programmes, rather than the satisfactoriness or otherwise of their interactions with individual members of staff.

Similarly, systematic research in the United States on teaching and learning consistently reveals that while students' learning of academic content and their cognitive development is related to the quality of individual teaching they receive, it is also significantly associated with the 'academic coherence' of the curriculum. That is, student learning is affected by the pattern and sequence of the courses in which they enrol, by curricular requirements to integrate learning from separate courses, and by the frequency of communication and interaction among faculty members in the curriculum (Pascarella and Terenzini, 1991). Therefore more systematic efforts to improve the quality of learning outcomes often involve collective efforts by faculty members to 'restructure' the curriculum, to redesign course sequences and requirements in order to identify instances where greater academic coherence can be achieved. Hence the criterion of coherence should be given significant weight in university choices about academic curricula.

The rule of coherence

To use educational coherence to help potential candidates choose between academic curricula would require implementation of the following rule: 'For an academic curriculum to be offered by the university, it must seek to provide a coherent, academic experience for its students. To meet the rule of coherence, an academic curriculum must be able to provide a tangible measure of coherence – ongoing, summative, evidence – that its students have had a coherent learning experience.' The clear intent of this rule is to assert the value of student learning as a primary criterion in choosing among the various curricula that may be proposed within a university. The required measure of coherence would provide public evidence of the extent to which the valued attribute of coherence exists within each existing curriculum, and would also provide a basis for collective efforts at curriculum improvement, a condition that does not now exist in many academic curricula.

The emphasis on an explicit measure of coherence is a necessary condition for enforcing the rule. However, it is also essential to fostering exchange by providing needed information on the valued attributes of academic curricula. In the absence of such a measure, there are insufficient incentives for the cooperative activity necessary to produce a curriculum that contributes to human capital. A reasonable question, however, is why such an additional rule and measure is necessary. Why does cooperative activity to increase integrated curricula not now occur?[5] For example, game theory would suggest that individual faculty members already work within a context that should encourage cooperative activity in the design and development of academic curricula. These conditions are (North, 1990): (i) that individuals have repeated dealings with one another; (ii) that individuals possess information on the other players; and (iii) that individuals deal with a small number of other people. Under these conditions cooperative behaviour for joint gain should theoretically occur. But game theorists have also identified an additional condition: that is, the ability to calculate relevant costs and benefits. Thus, if a measure of the benefit to students of the educational coherence of a curriculum is not available, then individual faculty members will base their decision on the amount of time to commit to cooperative activity in teaching and curricula development on the individual costs and benefits to themselves and to the students in their individual classes. Therefore the benefit of cooperating with other faculty members in the design and implementation of more integrated and coherent curricula will receive little or no value. By the same logic, faculty members also have no incentive to invest time and effort in developing or maintaining measures of coherence, therefore existing integrating experiences (such as comprehensive examinations) have steadily declined.

In sum, because of the basic ethic of responsibility for the interests of students, and the empirical evidence supporting the relationship between curricular coherence and student learning, the rule of coherence should be applied in all decisions involving the creation or continuation of an academic curriculum.[6] Given the central importance of student learning to a university, there should be a strong sanction against violations of the rule of coherence. That is, curricula that cannot meet the rule should not be permitted to exist.

The proposed rule and its matching measure raise a number of obvious concerns and questions. These issues will be briefly explored in an interrogative format:

How could the rule of coherence actually be realized by a faculty, by a department, or within a curriculum?

Meeting the rule of coherence would require that each academic programme to be offered by a university would provide evidence of the coherence of its curricula, including a tangible measure by which the degree to which students received a coherent learning experience can be objectively assessed. Curricula that positively correlate with student learning are generally characterized by carefully designed sequences of courses or learning activities and by required integrative learning experiences in which students have an opportunity to consolidate what they have learned by applying it to a central theme or issue in the subject field (Pascarella and Terenzini, 1991). Examples of such integrative learning experiences might include a 'capstone course' taken toward the conclusion of an academic curriculum. This would be designed to help students integrate the knowledge, skills and values taught throughout the curriculum and to apply what they have learned to a representative problem or task. Alternatively, an integrative learning experience might consist of some other unifying activity such as a required research study, independent study, applied project, or summative performance or exhibition, as in the performing or plastic arts.

There are a wide variety of possible measures of coherence: a written, comprehensive examination for all students in a curriculum would be one obvious means. But so too would be a commonly defined portfolio of student work, as long as it provided a summative measure of the learning achieved by a student from his or her overall programme. An alternative measure might be to track data on appropriate student performances embedded within the curriculum, such as the integrative learning experiences just described. The important point is that all students should be assessed in a reliable manner at or near the conclusion of their academic curriculum, that the assessment should be designed to measure the overall academic experience of the students, and that the assessment should provide tangible evidence (written, oral or visual) of the coherence of the students' learning.

The measure of coherence would clearly favour the traditional disciplines, particularly the sciences, over the social sciences, the humanities or emerging interdisciplinary fields.

The traditional linear disciplines of the physical and natural sciences have often been awarded superior status in research funding and academic prestige. The fractionalization of academic subject matter, however, has also occurred in these fields, and though they may be characterized by more structure and sequence than other fields, this is no guarantee that a curriculum in the sciences has superior academic coherence. Academic quality for the learner is a function of the careful design, coordination and integration of learning experiences, combined with the underlying structure of knowledge in a field.[7] In this sense new interdisciplinary curricula in the sciences, social sciences or humanities have as much opportunity to offer cohesive academic experiences as those in the sciences. Similarly, the fact that traditional disciplines in the sciences, social sciences or humanities have historically had precedence as the core of academic programmes does not automatically mean that they are coherently designed academic experiences. Rather than rely on traditional prejudices, or past measures of reputation, the rule of coherence creates a level playing field: all academic curricula will have to meet the rule; all academic curricula will have to produce a measure of coherence.

The existence of a measure of coherence does not in and of itself ensure that a curriculum will be a coherent learning experience for students. How will this judgement be made and enforced?

The essential content of a curriculum and of relevant student learning experiences must necessarily be decided upon by the relevant faculty. But if a tangible measure of cohesion for an academic curriculum exists, then the validity and reliability of the measure as well as the educational coherence of the designed and implemented curriculum can be publicly discussed and reviewed by faculty members with experience in designing coherent curricula from other parts of a university. (For a comparable point about teaching as community property, see Shulman, 1993.) Thus the peer review process for evaluating the coherence of academic curricula in the traditional disciplines may genuinely benefit from the experience of faculty members from the professional schools and vice versa. The importance in such reviews should not be the disciplinary background of the reviewers, but demonstrated experience in designing, implementing and improving coherent educational experiences for students.

Faculty members can become skilled in orchestrating external reviews in a manner that misrepresents the extent of learning in an academic programme. Such opportunism is less feasible when reviews are made by peers from within the same university and when tangible, continuing evidence is available of the educational experience of students. Thus, proposed measures of academic cohesion likely to be unreliable or invalid are apt to be questioned by experienced faculty members from other disciplines. Furthermore, the rule of cohesion would require the accumulation of evidence on student learning over a number of years. Such trend information would permit more thoughtful evaluations to be made of the educational cohesion and value of a curriculum. For example, does the performance of students on the measure of coherence fluctuate widely from year to year? Does the faculty alter the fundamental nature of the measure each year, thus destroying evidence on student learning over time? Is the measure of coherence so basic that there is no observed variation in student performance? etc.[8]

The existence of a measure of cohesion would permit evaluations of the educational quality of a curriculum by members of the university community, by external members of the relevant discipline or field, and by the faculty members of the curriculum itself, who could also use these evaluations to improve their programme.[9]

The imposition of the rule of cohesion on academic curricula may lead to a suppression of academic innovation, because coherence may not be easily defined or measured in new or emerging academic fields.

Reasonably new curricula are frequently proposed in fields where there is promise of educational value, but where the development of the curriculum is a necessary requirement to proving the value-added by the programme. The rule of cohesion should not be used to prevent educational innovation. Obvious adaptations of the rule might include suspending the requirement of a specific measure of coherence for a stated period of time for new curricula, say for up to three years, to provide the faculty the opportunity to work together to develop needed coherence. Ultimately, however, if a curriculum is to continue, or to be evaluated as a successful learning experience for students, it must be required to meet the same standard as existing curricula.

Conclusion

The current institutions of academic life appear to provide insufficient incentives for academic curricula to offer coherent learning experiences for students and thereby produce human capital of value to the broader society. As a consequence, much time and money is expended by governments and consumers in searching for information about the valued attributes of academic curricula. Both this cost and the university investments made in curricula that offer little measurable value in student learning are wasteful for the university and society alike. The adoption by universities of a rule of coherence provides information on attributes valuable to those who support or purchase academic curricula, thereby decreasing the uncertainties involved in exchange. The rule has the further benefit of providing a self-enforcing standard of conduct, producing information to the members of the curricula and the larger academic community that can be used for improving the capacity of curricula to promote student learning.

Academic knowledge is necessarily temporal. The content of any curriculum is subject to change over time as new knowledge is discovered and added to the existing store. The rule of coherence does not require curricular stasis, but it does require continual effort to define the knowledge that should be part of an academic curriculum, and to improve the structure and coherence of student learning experiences. The greatest danger to the contemporary and future university derives not from asserting the value of educational coherence, but rather from stressing values that foster excessive individualism, isolation and fragmentation in teaching and learning. A university that requires all curricula to provide a coherent body of knowledge, to express and debate that knowledge publicly, and to apply that knowledge in the design of academic experiences intended to integrate student learning is a community that meets its ethical obligation to its students.

Notes

1. Before 1850, US universities offered a curriculum consisting of a few basic subjects: classical languages, mathematics, natural and moral philosophy. By 1993, a survey of university faculty by the National Center for Education Statistics offered respondents over 149 alternative disciplinary affiliations, some of them aggregated categories (Braxton and Hargens, 1996).
2. Commenting on the contribution that disciplinary fragmentation makes to the complexity of higher education systems, Clark (1996: 421–2) observed:
   in mathematics, 200,000 new theorems are published each year, periodicals exceed 1,000, and review journals have developed a classification scheme that includes over 4,500 subtopics arranged under 62 major topic areas. In history, the output of literature in the two decades of 1960–1980 was apparently equal in magnitude to all that was published from the time of the Greek historian Thucydides in the fourth century B.C. to the year 1960. In psychology, 45 major specialties appear in the structure of the American Psychological Association, and one of these specialties, social psychology, reports that it is now comprised of 17 subfields . . . In the mid-1990s, those who track the field of chemistry were reporting that 'more articles on chemistry have been published in the past 2 years than throughout history before 1900.' Chemical Abstracts took 31 years to publish its first million abstracts, 18 years for its second million, and less than 2 years for its most recent million. An exponential growth of about 4 to 8 percent annually, with a doubling period of 10 to 15 years, is now seen as characteristic of most branches of science.
3. Those more familiar with the economic approach to institutions will recognize that these are in fact part of the costs of transacting, or transaction costs (see North, 1990).
4. Zemsky (1989) offers thoughtful operational measures of structure and coherence in academic curricula.
5. One reason, already suggested, is that there are obvious incentives for individuals to

68   David D. Dill

invest time and energy in specialized teaching and research activities that will lead to an enhanced scholarly reputation and eventually to monetary remuneration. Therefore US universities have begun to provide various awards, including monetary incentives, to reward good teaching. But these incentives for good teaching do not necessarily stimulate the cooperative behaviour required to increase the educational coherence of the curriculum for students.

6. I am not suggesting that curricular coherence should be the sole criterion in this choice, but that it should be a necessary condition for all curricula. Other universal criteria have been articulated within universities as a basis for choosing among academic programmes. These include centrality to the mission of the university, student demand and cost effectiveness (see, for example, Dill, 1997a).

7. Individuals familiar with the extensive and growing research on the academic disciplines (see also Becher, 1992) may wish to assert that the amount of curricular coherence in a field is a function of the underlying structure of a discipline, and these structures appear inviolable. A recent thorough review of this literature (Braxton and Hargens, 1996), however, suggests that the different dimensions of disciplinary variation advanced in the research all appear to be built upon the common factor of level of consensus among the members of a discipline. Further, several researchers have suggested that the level of consensus in the disciplines has less to do with their intellectual characteristics, and more to do with their social structure (see, for example, Hagstrom, 1965; Fuchs, 1992). As Sir Ralf Dahrendorf (1995) observed with regard to the social sciences, many of the divisions between fields appear to be socially constructed phenomena designed to carve out discrete professional territory. In any event, the reviewed evidence on academic behaviour does not seem to suggest that the development of coherent curricula cannot be actively pursued in all fields, but rather that the institutions currently influencing academic behaviour offer insufficient incentives for such a pursuit.

8. Experienced faculty members might argue that the emphasis on an end-point measure of coherence is not optimal from the standpoint of designing effective curricula. Equally important may be measures of students taken at the beginning, mid-point, or even following the conclusion of a curriculum. I fully concur with this reasoning (see Dill, 1992b). However, a summative measure of the coherence of a programme appears to be a necessary if not sufficient condition for changing the current structure of incentives in universities.

9. The existence of a summative measure of cohesion increases the potential for discovering innovations in teaching and curriculum design that are more effective and efficient. As North (1990) creatively noted, the absence of measures of valued attributes of a product or service increases both transaction and production costs.

References

Becher, T. (1992) Making audit acceptable: a collegial approach to quality assurance, *Higher Education Quarterly*, 46: 47–66.
Ben-David, J. (1972) *American Higher Education*. New York: McGraw-Hill.
Braxton, J. M., Bayer, A. E. and Finkelstein, M. J. (1992) Teaching performance norms in academia, *Research in Higher Education*, 33: 533–69.
Braxton, J. M. and Hargens, L. L. (1996) Variations among academic disciplines: analytical frameworks and research, in J. Smart (ed.) *Higher Education Handbook of Theory and Research*, vol. XI. New York: Agathon Press.

Clark, B. R. (1996) Substantive growth and innovative organization: new categories for higher education research, *Higher Education*, 32: 417–30.

Cole, J. R. (1994) Balancing acts: dilemmas of choice facing research universities, in J. R. Cole, E. G. Barber and S. R. Graubard (eds) *The Research University in a Time of Discontent*. Baltimore, MD: The Johns Hopkins Press.

Dahrendorf, R. (1995) *Whither Social Sciences. The 6th ESRC Annual Lecture*. Swindon: Economic and Social Research Council.

Dill, D. D. (1992a) Academic administration, in B. R. Clark and G. Neave (eds) *The Encyclopedia of Higher Education*. Oxford: Pergamon Press.

Dill, D. D. (1992b) Quality by design: toward a framework for academic quality management, in J. Smart (ed.) *Higher Education Handbook of Theory and Research*, vol. VIII. New York: Agathon Press.

Dill, D. D. (1997a) Focusing institutional mission to provide coherence and integration, in M. W. Peterson, D. D. Dill and L. A. Mets (eds) *Planning and Management for a Changing Environment: A Handbook on Redesigning Postsecondary Institutions*. San Francisco, CA: Jossey-Bass.

Dill, D. D. (1997b) Accreditation, assessment, anarchy? The evolution of academic quality assurance policies in the United States, in J. Brennan, P. DeVries and R. Williams (eds) *Standards and Quality in Higher Education*. London: Jessica Kingsley Publishers.

Ewell, P. (1988) Outcomes, assessment, and academic improvement: in search of usable knowledge, in J. Smart (ed.) *Higher Education Handbook of Theory and Research*, vol. IV. New York: Agathon Press.

Fuchs, S. (1992) *The Professional Quest for Truth: A Social Theory of Science and Knowledge*. Albany, NY: State University of New York Press.

Gibbons, M. (1995) The university as an instrument for the development of science and basic research: the implications of mode 2 science, in D. D. Dill and B. Sporn (eds) *Emerging Patterns of Social Demand and University Reform: Through a Glass Darkly*. Oxford: Pergamon Press.

Hagstrom, W. O. (1965) *The Scientific Community*. New York: Basic Books.

Huisman, J. (1996) Diversity in The Netherlands, in V. L. Meek, L. Goedegebuure, O. Kivinen and R. Rinne (eds) *The Mockers and the Mocked: Comparative Perspectives on Differentiation, Convergence and Diversity in Higher Education*. Oxford: Pergamon Press.

Kimball, B. (1986) *Orators and Philosophers: A History of the Idea of Liberal Education*. New York: Teachers College Press.

Lattuca, L. R. and Stark, J. S. (1994) Will disciplinary perspectives impede curricular reform? *Journal of Higher Education*, 65: 401–26.

Massy, W. F. and Zemsky, R. (1994) Faculty discretionary time: departments and the 'academic ratchet', *Journal of Higher Education*, 65: 1–22.

Massy, W. F., Wilger, A. K. and Colbeck, C. (1994) Overcoming hollowed collegiality, *Change*, 26: 10–20.

National Association of Scholars (1996) *The Dissolution of General Education: 1914–1993*. Princeton, NJ: National Association of Scholars.

North, D. (1990) *Institutions, Institutional Change, and Economic Performance*. Cambridge: Cambridge University Press.

Nowotny, H. (1995) Mass higher education and social mobility: a tenuous link, in D. D. Dill and B. Sporn (eds) *Emerging Patterns of Social Demand and University Reform: Through a Glass Darkly*. Oxford: Pergamon Press.

Pascarella, E. T. and Terenzini, P. T. (1991) *How College Affects Students: Findings and Insights From Twenty Years of Research*. San Francisco, CA: Jossey-Bass.

Powell, W. (1972) *The First State University*. Chapel Hill, NC: University of North Carolina Press.

Shulman, L. S. (1993) Teaching as community property: putting an end to pedagogical solitude, *Change*, 25: 6–7.

Weick, K. E. (1984) Contradictions in a community of scholars: the cohesion–accuracy tradeoff, in J. L. Bess (ed.) *College and University Organization: Insights from the Behavioral Sciences*. New York: New York University Press.

Zemsky, R. (1989) *Structure and Coherence: Measuring the Undergraduate Curriculum*. Washington, DC: Association of American Colleges.

6

PhD or Professional Doctorate –
Is There a Choice?

Sybe B. Jongeling

There is no doubt that university education has changed significantly during the last 20 years. There are growing signs that university autonomy and academic freedom are under threat. This is clearly evidenced by:

- government pressures for universities to be 'more responsive to the economy and the needs of society which supports [them]';
- demands for greater accountability;
- greater relevance to industry needs;
- reduced funding for higher education;
- increased emphasis on attracting funds from business and industry for research;
- industry dissatisfaction with the quality of PhD degrees.

In Australia these factors may have contributed to a rapid development of alternative professional doctorate programmes, different from but equivalent in standing to the traditional PhD. This chapter focuses on the rise of professional doctorates in Australian universities. It addresses the criticism of employers and shows how the content of curricula and modes of teaching can be modified to be more relevant to society. The position is taken that the professional doctorate allows for real, value-added outcomes often not apparent in the traditional PhD programmes, and that the PhD itself is a professional doctorate aimed mainly at those who seek university teaching positions or those who wish to concentrate on pure basic research.

The rise of professional doctorates

The professional doctorate degree is gaining considerable momentum in Australian universities. The first Doctor of Education (EdD) programme was introduced in 1989; this was followed by the gradual introduction during the 1990s of the Doctor of Psychology and Doctor of Clinical Psychology degrees. Both were the direct result of the need for advanced training in clinical practice beyond the two-year Master's degree as required by the profession. Other degrees have since gained prominence. By 1994 21 of the 38 Australian universities offered professional doctorate awards in eight different discipline areas. By 1996 the number of different programmes had doubled (see Figure 6.1). Currently 29 universities are offering 62 professional doctorate programmes in seventeen different discipline areas.

It appears that most universities, both newly created as well as the older, established ones, have acted on the Higher Education Council (1989) *Review of Australian Graduate Studies and Higher Degrees*, which recommended that universities should introduce 'initially through pilot programmes, professional doctoral degrees in the fields of Engineering, Accounting, Law, Education and Nursing' (R3.1: 32).

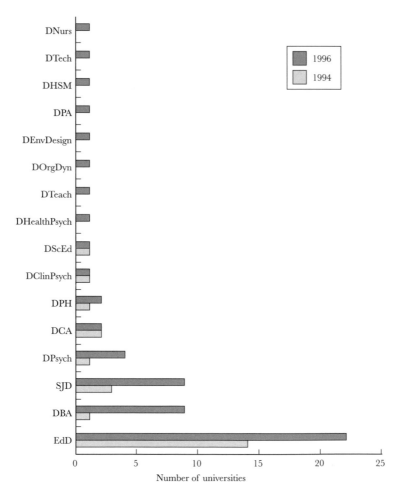

Figure 6.1   Professional doctorates offered at Australian universities in 1994 and 1996
Source: Jongeling (1996)

Table 6.1   Professional doctorate degrees offered at Australian universities 1997

Doctor of Business Administration (DBA),
Doctor of Clinical Psychology (DClinPsych),
Doctor of Creative Arts (DCA),
Doctor of Education (EdD),
Doctor of Environmental Design (DEnvDesign),
Doctor of Health Psychology (DHealthPsych),
Doctor of Health Services Management (DHSM),
Doctor of Juridical Science (SJD),
Doctor of Nursing (DNurs),
Doctor of Organizational Dynamics (DOrgDyn),
Doctor of Psychology (DPsych),
Doctor of Public Administration (DPA),
Doctor of Public Health (DPH),
Doctor of Science Education (DScEd),
Doctor of Teaching (DTeach),
Doctor of Technology (DTech),
and the most recent, Doctor of Creative Performance (DCP).

The current range of professional doctorate programmes on offer is much wider than the recommendation of the Higher Education Council, and interestingly, does not include programmes in engineering and accounting. The most popular programmes are in education, business administration, law, psychology and nursing. Table 6.1 lists the professional doctorate programmes on offer in 1997 at Australian universities.

Government initiatives and legislation

Federal government initiatives for change in doctoral studies had their origin in numerous reports and policy statements made during the late 1980s and early 1990s. They emphasize greater relevance of research in terms of commercial outcomes, industry-focused research training, and responsiveness 'to the economy and the needs of society which support it'. The then Minister for Employment, Education and Training, the Hon. John Dawkins, made it clear that: 'The Government considers that future directions in postgraduate education should better reflect economic and social requirements' (Dawkins, 1987: 69).

In a position paper, the Green Paper, Dawkins (1987: 65) argued that

Research and postgraduate study have a vital role to play in the continuing development of the Australian economy . . . efforts must also be made to increase the interaction between research agencies and with industry, and by the application of research findings to improve Australia's productive capacity.

The subsequent policy statements (Dawkins, 1988) and reports (Strategic Imperatives Committee, 1991) have focused on the need for more applied research leading to commercial outputs and on a greater need for graduates to develop problem-solving skills through 'work-place projects, especially if they can relate to the society and world context' (Strategic Imperatives Committee, 1991: 16).

The increased emphasis on applied research was welcomed by the Industry Commission (1994: C4), which made positive comment that 'Universities have become more involved in applied research and in the commercialization of research results over recent years'; it sees this as an encouraging trend in closer liaison between industry and academia.

Thus, government initiatives and supporting legislation have encouraged closer collaboration between universities and industry. In addition, directed funding towards (i) collaborative research projects with industry, (ii) industry–university postgraduate scholarships, and (iii) the establishment of common-wealth cooperative research centres has driven universities toward applied research on industry-related problems. Within this framework the incentive arose for the development of alternative doctoral degrees more focused toward the needs of industry.

Although government policies have a major influence on the structure and content of university courses, there is a major concern that the frequent changes in government directions have an adverse effect on the morale of staff and the quality of university education. Australia has changed from a Labour (social) government to a Liberal (conservative) government, and there are already signs that the recently established inquiry into higher education (the West Committee) is likely to make, yet again, major changes in tertiary education.

A former Liberal minister of education, Professor Peter Baume, now a member of the West Committee, indicated (Baume 1997: 4) that he doubted 'whether law or medicine or engineering belong to universities'. He sees the place of universities in terms of 'the preparing of students to address issues and problems, to think, to question, to solve problems. In short, it is teaching them to use their minds.' Baume agreed that universities used to perform a vital function as 'repositories of knowledge, guardians of the culture' but he thought now that these functions could be shared. Baume is not impressed with universities 'that drill their students, that train their students, that demand mastery of great amounts of content, unless at the same time they teach themselves and others to think'. With such and other pronouncements made in the press, it appears that radical changes may result from the inquiry.

Dissatisfaction with current PhD programmes

Dissatisfaction with current PhD programmes in Australia has been expressed in several major national reports and in statements made by industry representatives (ASTEC, 1987; Dawkins, 1987; Sekhon, 1989; NBEET, 1992; Cullen, 1993; Industry Commission, 1994; Clark, 1996).

In a study by Sekhon (1989), some eight years ago, it was concluded that, in a technological society, higher education now has become a vital 'determinant of economic development' and that research should be outcome-orientated. Sekhon (1989: 195) indicated that there are marked differences between research at the university and research in industry. He emphasized that 'industrial research is characterized by team effort, by time and financial constraints and by projects which cannot reflect one's own interest'.

The study by Sekhon focused on the quality of PhD education for mathematicians, physicists, engineers and economists leading to positions in applied mathematics in industry. However, the five most important characteristics of PhD graduates identified by the employers interviewed in this study have general significance to the quality of all PhD education. They are:

- effectiveness in problem solving and modelling
- ability to adapt quickly to new problems and challenges
- understanding the realities of industrial environment
- good oral and written communication skills
- motivation toward solving company problems.

(Sekhon, 1989: 197)

Dawkins (1988: 8) also found that employers and industry groups generally prefer students to graduate with a 'broad educational foundation and with well-developed conceptual, analytical and communication skills'. In particular he emphasized that the 'general problem solving skills of inquiry, analysis and synthesis are essential to the building of a flexible, versatile work force able to cope with rapidly changing technology'.

With specific reference to postgraduate training, employers indicated that they would like graduates to have a broad-based PhD education, that they are supervised by staff who have industrial experience, that students should have insights into the practicalities of industry and have proper attitudes toward industry's needs and ways of working. Employers felt that this is best achieved through workplace, part-time or sandwich patterns of attendance and through the selection of research topics from problems faced by the relevant industry (Sekhon, 1989: 203).

One employer, quoted by Sekhon (1989: 204), stated:

> The very nature of the PhD course, unless modified, makes it far from ideal for most applied scientists. They need less research on a highly specialized subject, more coursework in advanced mathematical subjects and much more on the principles of management and on the many areas which will help them to understand human beings better. For in future they will be concerned with people more than books.

Thus, it is advocated that a different form of doctoral education is required which includes principles of management, industry-orientated attitudes, personal relationship training, practical problem solving and a strengthened relationship between industry and higher education institutions.

Seven years later, Clark (1996: 4) indicated that in Australia 'there has been a substantial deterioration in the quality of PhD students for science and technology'. He stated that employers prefer postgraduate appointments from the

UK/USA because they already have had work experience and are therefore better prepared to work in industrial settings. The main weaknesses in PhD training identified by Clark included the following:

- They over-specialize and only know what is needed to get the project done.
- Due to over-specialization students rarely acquire the skills to view issues holistically and synthesize information from wide ranging sources.
- Students have little concept of international best practice or standards, and tend to benchmark only closely related academics.
- Safety awareness is usually poor.
- Few graduates are well trained to effectively plan and execute experimental work and then to analyse it rigorously.
- Many students do not develop good work practices, in areas such as time and deadlines, data, information and project management, and usually progress projects at the rate that suits the task.
- Students are rarely pressured to develop and fine-tune lateral thinking and innovation.
- They are generally weak at using a range of approaches to solve problems, the limitations of conventional logic are evident and more 'out-of-the-box' thinking is required.
- Postgraduates tend to be individuals used to working alone and often find working in a multi-skilled project team difficult.
- They tend to have poorly developed people, leadership, negotiation and communication skills, usually limited to an academic audience.
- Finally, the most important deficiency is the lack of understanding of the importance of teamwork.

(Clark, 1996: 5–6)

Although not advocating an alternative doctoral award, Clark (1996: 8) sees great merit in a restructured PhD programme. He indicates that industry needs postgraduates who have

- highly developed skills to adapt to new areas of activity;
- a reasonably broad practical knowledge;
- familiarity and knowledge of broader literature;
- skills in the scientific method and linkage to the broad context;
- good communication and presentation skills;
- good work practices and collaborative skills.

In addition to the high-level technical skills 'of international standing' specific to the professional field of knowledge, common technical skills required by industry include (Clark, 1996: 8):

- experimental design, modelling and statistics;
- information technology and computer literacy;
- the ability to utilize fundamental and technical knowledge to applied systems;
- occupational health and safety, and hazards analysis;
- good manufacturing practice and good laboratory practice;
- intellectual property management.

These technical skills, according to Clark (1996: 9) must be supported by improved personal competencies including:

- communication skills (oral, written, graphic and listening) to a wide range of audiences including those that do not have the same body of knowledge or depth of knowledge;
- negotiating skills;
- problem-solving and decision-making skills. Ability to tackle and solve a problem utilizing a range of approaches, rather than being limited to a narrow range of techniques;
- project planning;
- team skills and good interpersonal skills to encourage teamwork and manage conflicts;
- better ability to network with external groups to maximize the outcomes of their research efforts.

It seems that despite similar concerns expressed by employers in 1989 and 1996, little change has taken place in Australia in restructuring the traditional PhD. The emphasis in Australia is now more towards offering a range of alternative doctoral awards more relevant to the needs of industry and the professions.

Reasons for establishing professional doctorates

The studies by Howell and Jongeling (1994) and Jongeling (1996) have identi-fied a number of reasons for establishing professional doctorates. Table 6.2 provides an overview of the main reasons identified by academics, employers and professional organizations, for the establishment of professional doctorate programmes in Australian universities.

It appears that some university administrators are reconsidering the content of PhD programmes. In their deliberations a major decision must be made whether to restructure the PhD or whether to develop alternative doctoral degrees more focused to meeting the needs of industry. Is it more appropriate to restructure the PhD, weed out the weaknesses as outlined by Clark (1996) and incorporate 'coursework' activities that will give graduates the skills iden-tified by the professional associations and industry, or is it more beneficial to develop a new range of professional doctorates? It appears that the growing trend is toward alternative doctoral programmes, with specific 'activities' to emphasize the types of skills identified by Clark (1996).

Those universities that have developed genuine coursework doctoral pro-grammes have included a variety of activities requiring close supervision from academic staff and from industry partners. This may well increase the costs of supervision and provide an extra burden on the decreasing university resources. The advantages of the alternative doctoral programme must be greater than the extra costs imposed to make the introduction of such pro-grammes worthwhile.

Table 6.2   Reasons identified by employers and academics for introducing professional doctorate programmes in Australian universities

---

Needs for advanced training
Training of senior managers
Training for leadership
Improving professional practice
Teaching advanced skills
Training mid-career personnel
Staff development

Needs for linking theory and practice
Linking practice with professional knowledge
Practitioners can consolidate, refine and extend the theoretical basis of their profession
Investigating problems related to professional practice
Small projects based on problems arising from practice

Problem-based research
Research directly related to the needs of professional practice
Research directly relevant to the workplace
Practical application of research
Desk-top research rather than data-gathering
Number of minor papers instead of one lengthy thesis

Miscellaneous
Clinical training
Supervised practical experience
Tradition of research-based professional degrees (Harvard, Stanford, MIT, Colombia, Toronto)
Registration requirements of professional associations (e.g. Psychology)

Source: Jongeling (1996: 19)

In the development of professional doctorates the needs of potential employers, professional organizations and academia must be considered critically. Questions that must be asked include:

- Should supervision be similar as for a PhD?
- Is there more work required?
- Do staff receive an increased time allocation?
- Is there joint supervision with industry partner?
- What should be the relationship between industry and university?
- Can professional doctorates supervise professional doctoral students?
- Can professional doctorates supervise PhD students?
- Should there be any restrictions on the proportion of individual research?
- What should the course content be, to be markedly different to the PhD?
- Does the introduction of professional doctorates lower the standard of the PhD?
- Should there be a major thesis and what should be the length?
- Is the content of the thesis based on a single investigation or is it a portfolio of different, smaller, industry-relevant investigations?
- Can the thesis include a collection of refereed papers?

- Must examiners be external, internal or a combination of both?
- Should the doctorate be based on the thesis result only?

The links between coursework and research thesis become critical in the development of professional doctorates. The addition of more coursework units at Master's level or 'advanced' coursework units at 'doctoral' level (whatever that means) does not in itself make the new professional doctorates of 'equivalent standing to the PhD'. To be equivalent, the professional doctorate must include the same kind of rigour as required of the PhD. It must show that the student is capable of working at the pinnacle of his/her profession and that the student will make a 'significant contribution' to both knowledge and practice in regard to the professional context in which the student works. Thus, supervised research training leading to independent research, research skill development, and workplace-related research projects appear to be the hallmark of well-developed professional doctorate degrees.

Professional doctorate or PhD?

Evidence of innovative programmes leading to professional doctorate degrees of high standing are emerging. Such programmes are not focused on the 'advancement of knowledge through individual research' alone, but incorporate a mix of research training, research writing, industry-related research skill development, and workplace-relevant research projects. The professional doctorate in Education (EdD) at Deakin University and the Doctor of Engineering (EngD) at the University of Warwick (UK) are two examples of alternative doctorate programmes designed to meet the challenges posed by Clark (1996) in his critique of current PhD programmes.

Both programmes appear to focus on cooperative/collaborative learning and research. They incorporate adult learning practices and seem to answer the weaknesses identified by Baume in his latest criticism of some university courses. The programmes involve research training activities; in-depth analysis of industry-identified problems leading to industry-related research projects; innovation in the application of knowledge to their relevant profession; critical analysis; and the presentation of a portfolio of completed work. The latter forms the basis for assessment by a team of examiners from both academia and industry. The portfolio must show that the candidate has met specified criteria and competencies to be considered for admission to the award.

A typical portfolio may contain research assignments; submissions; discussion papers; evaluation reports; major dissertation; published refereed papers; papers in professional journals; project papers and reports; conference papers; book reviews; and other media such as CD-ROM, video, photographic materials, working models, designs and technical drawings. In the University of Warwick's EngD portfolio published research reports must also show evidence of competence in:

- expert knowledge of an engineering area;
- project planning, management and control;

- teamwork and leadership;
- oral and written communications;
- searching out relevant information sources;
- seeking optimal but viable solutions to multifaceted problems.

Close cooperation between the university and industry partners can give rise to innovative, alternative doctoral programmes that meet the needs of employers and which are of sufficient rigour to be equivalent to the PhD. Both the professional doctorate and the PhD have a place in the tertiary education system. One may be more relevant to the immediate needs of industry, while the other may be more appropriate for the training of future researchers focusing on basic research. The choice is not simply PhD or professional doctorate. The choice must be based on the perceived needs of the nation and the skills needed to enhance rapidly a country's economic and social development.

References

Australian Science and Technology Council (ASTEC) (1987) *Improving the Research Performance of Australia's Universities and Other Higher Education Institutions.* Canberra: Commonwealth Government Printer.

Baume, P. (1997) Guardian of spirit of inquiry v. 'stamp collectors', *Campus Review*, 7(13): 4.

Clark, J. (1996) Postgraduate skills: a view from industry. Paper presented at the Deans of Graduate Schools meeting, Adelaide, 16 April.

Cullen, D. J. (ed.) (1993) *Quality in PhD Education.* Canberra: The Centre for Educational Development and Academic Methods (CEDAM).

Dawkins, J. S. (1987) *Higher Education: A Policy Discussion Paper.* Canberra: Australian Government Publishing Service.

Dawkins, J. S. (1988) *Higher Education: A Policy Statement.* Canberra: Australian Government Publishing Service.

Higher Education Council (1989) *Review of Australian Graduate Studies and Higher Degrees.* Canberra: Australian Government Printing Service.

Howell, J. and Jongeling, S. B. (1994) Professional doctorate programmes: Australian universities. Paper presented at the Pro Vice-Chancellors (Research) meeting, Australian National University, Canberra, 17–18 August.

Industry Commission (1994) *Research and Development: Volume 1, The Report.* Canberra: Industry Commission.

Jongeling, S. B. (1996) Professional doctorates in Australian universities. Paper presented at the Second Seminar of Deans and Directors of Graduate Studies in Australian Universities, Stamford Plaza Hotel, Adelaide, 17 April.

National Board of Employment, Education and Training (1992) *Towards 2005: A Prospectus for Research and Research Training in the Australian Earth Sciences.* Canberra: Australian Government Publishing Service.

Sekhon, J. G. (1989) PhD education and Australia's industrial future: time to think again, *Higher Education Research and Development*, 8: 191–215.

Strategic Imperatives Committee (1991) *Wealth Creation in Australia.* Sydney: Price Waterhouse.

Part 2

Access and Participation

The role of the university in the reproduction of structures of social inequality has been analysed recently by Pierre Bourdieu in his book *The State Nobility* (1996). Bourdieu's account of the place of higher education in the reproduction of elites in French society could be replicated for most other societies. Yet alongside this deep-rooted role in the transmission of social privilege, universities have also been assigned a more radical and transformative role in extending opportunity and enhancing democratization in the social institutions of modern societies. These two aspects of the university idea sit uneasily alongside each other in most countries of the world.

The growth and diversification of higher education systems has given new prominence to questions of access and participation. Largely financed by state support, who is meant to benefit? Who is expansion intended to serve? That access to a university education continues to be restricted according to social class, ethnicity, gender, geography and so on, is well known. But policies to extend access confront the question of 'access to what?' Answers might be given in terms of a conventional and essentially unitary idea of the university (itself historically and geographically variable, of course); alternatively, answers might be in terms of new non-university forms of higher education (almost universally accorded lower status than their traditional university counterparts); a third alternative is to require a significant re-think of the idea and form of the university. The three chapters in Part 2 of the book all approach questions of access and participation in terms of this third alternative, viewing questions of access as intimately bound up with issues that provide the other concerns of this book: knowledge and curricula, teaching and learning, decision making and accountability.

In her chapter, Brenda Gourley adopts a global view that emphasizes the link between access and diversity in higher education and which sees the issues raised as primarily ethical ones central to the role and justification of the university in the modern world. For Gourley, the ethics of access and participation require nothing less than the transformation of institutions and systems to make them open to all. Moreover, the implications of new educational and communication technologies mean that answers must be global. Purely national frameworks and definitions will no longer be sufficient.

Gourley offers a rallying cry for those who believe that universities matter, not just in developing countries such as her own South Africa, but universally. Access to universities is important only if universities transform the lives of people and their societies. Questions of access, therefore, confront universities with a challenging ethical critique of their very existence. It is hard not to conclude from reading Brenda Gourley's chapter that universities worldwide have fallen hopelessly short of the ethical (and intellectual?) challenge. She quotes Derek Bok's comments about the difficulty of the enterprise and the slowness of progress but agrees with him that 'what is harder to forgive is a refusal even to recognize the problem or to acknowledge a duty to work on it conscientiously' (Bok, 1990: 102).

In Chapter 8, de Vuyst poses definitional questions with profoundly ideological underpinnings: equality, meritocracy, democratization. Like Gourley, he sees a moral dimension to questions of access and participation.

Drawing on his experience of Belgian higher education, de Vuyst emphasizes the need to go beyond developing opportunities for equal access *to* university and to address questions of equality *within* university as well as at the start of a professional career. He considers structural, ideological and funding issues and makes comparisons with social welfare developments in other fields. Also like Gourley, de Vuyst seems pessimistic about the progress likely to be made in addressing access issues. Looking at the university in terms of access and participation, he finds little to celebrate and much for dissatisfaction and critique.

The final chapter in this section is rather more up-beat, even if the cause for celebration is historical rather than present-day. Joel Anderson records the achievements of the land-grant universities established by Lincoln in 1862 as representing a unique achievement in 'taking knowledge out to rural people and helping them to use it to make their lives better'. He sees the approach of 'linking people to research' as an important element of the mission of the urban/metropolitan universities of present-day America.

Concepts of outreach, extension, professional service and applied research are central to both sets of institutions. They involve taking the university out into people's lives; they involve engagement with practical problems; they place service to society as the highest university goal.

Yet the land-grant universities transformed themselves into some of the most successful research universities of the twentieth century. And, according to Anderson, the metropolitan universities face the likelihood of a gradual conversion towards more conventional university priorities, driven by the research values and reward systems of academic cultures and peer groups.

How will universities respond to the challenges of access and participation in the future? Notwithstanding the enormous growth in participation in the second half of the twentieth century, the omens for radical transformation to the benefit of students and society do not seem good. Writing about the development of mass higher education in Britain, Peter Scott (1995) has commented that Britain has developed a mass system while retaining an elite mentality of higher education. It is worth remembering, however, that outside of North America, most of those teaching in institutions of mass higher education were themselves educated in elite systems. Perhaps when the academic generation of graduates from mass higher education comes to have its day, things will be different. If not, if universities continue to find their role in the reproduction, rather than in the transformation of society, then Gourley's warnings of 'a vanishing future if we do not wake up to our ethical duty' might well turn out to be true.

References

Bok, D. (1990) *Universities and the Future of America*. Durham and London: Duke University Press.

Bourdieu, P. (1996) *The State Nobility*. Cambridge: Polity Press.

Scott, P. (1995) *The Meanings of Mass Higher Education*. Buckingham: SRHE and Open University Press.

7

Against the Odds

Brenda M. Gourley

In a well-known Buddhist parable, the Buddha imagines a group of blind men who are asked to identify an elephant. One takes the tail and says it's a rope, another holds a leg and says it's a pillar; another feels the side and says it's a wall, and the one holding the trunk says it's a tube. Depending on which part of Buddhism you grasp, you might identify it as a philosophy, a system of ethics, a contemplative psychotherapy or a religion. While it contains all of these it can no more be reduced to any one of them than an elephant can be reduced to its tail (Batchelor, 1997: 18). The same could be said of universities. To discuss access and participation at universities in isolation from say finance, curriculum or selection would be to discuss the tail, albeit the tail that is wagging the elephant.

Issues about access and participation seem to me to go to the very heart of what societal function a university conceives itself as fulfilling. It is one thing to level the educational terrain but how does this manifest in what Carol Schneider calls the public square or what others have called the civil or public domain? She says that for such issues to be truly embraced we ought to have 'significant and substantial experiences of engaging with diversity issues as preparation for civic engagement and social responsibility' (1997: 38). In this view, access and participation are contained in the sphere of educational diversity, or what one might term second-generation educational rights. This is not to suggest that equity is not still a primary intention of access, but rather that the pursuit of diversity is now generally seen as intrinsic to achieving equity and participation.

I should be clear here that I include in my definition of diversity any manifestations of difference including culture, religion, race, class, gender and ability. The manner of engaging with diversity issues within universities tells you everything you need to know about the way they perceive their relation to society, and their ethos. It is, I would add also, critical to their survival as universities.

Though there may be little resistance to access and diversity as policies of governments and higher education managers, there is yet resistance among academics (who largely maintain what Boyd (1996: 609) calls a 'groundless tolerance'), and in the very structure and ethos of institutions (which remain largely male), to the reform and transformation that might make access and participation more equitable, and socially and economically more valued. Whether driven by economic necessity or democratic principle, the opening of access to universities is at the source not only of organizational and governance questions that now challenge them but equally at the heart of the philosophical and ethical questions that face them. These are questions about the very nature of universities and all of their constituent obligations: the production of knowledge, teaching, research, the nurturing of civic-minded citizens, supplying and revivifying professional ranks, engaging skilfully with policy and society, building economic and communal strength. But I am jumping the gun with this prescription for universities for these may well be things that universities can no longer do (if they ever did) or can only do in part, or even ought not do.

The view that educational attainment has a major influence on a person's life chances lies behind many post-World War II efforts to increase access to universities and to make universities more reflective of the demographies of their catchment areas. Distance education initiatives extended the idea of demographic representativity into a wider domain, a more spherical geography that included people marginalized by occupation, ability, age, class, gender and indeed distance itself. These access experiments also coincided with changes in the labour market accompanying a trend away from goods production to service, and a rise in educational requirements for jobs in key sectors of a developing global economy. Further, an increased orientation toward state-organized and funded welfare created a need for people skilled in applied social sciences. It is important to add that the political mobilization of disenfranchised groups, minorities, and students themselves, was a significant factor in challenging the exclusivity and elitism that characterized the 'western' universities earlier this century. (There are exceptions to this characterization, such as the land-grant colleges in the midwestern United States, where more open access prevailed from their inception in the latter part of the nineteenth century.)

This simplistic description does not take account of great differences between the contexts of institutions themselves or the economies and polities in which they are located. But I think it is safe to say that even countries, like South Africa, that are not quite industrial nations let alone post-industrial ones, largely derive their ideological notion of access and diversity from a more global view, albeit a rather west-derived one. Hence university missions are generally inclined toward a post-industrial world-view even when the local context may still be one of grappling with feudal legacies. In South Africa of course, so newly democratic, access and participation issues stem from a fierce determination to be as democratic as possible and to make our fledgling democracy work. In my university we make a particular point in our selection of students to have both rural and urban, both male and female, as well as aiming to represent demographic realities. In our research budget we specifically tie some allocations to research that focuses on development issues.

Charles Van Onselen, arguably South Africa's pre-eminent historian, has recently suggested that South Africans might be wise to reconceptualize the conventional wisdom that our universities reflect global patterns of massification – that is, that the massive expansion of student intake is essentially a correlative of the demands of industrial and post-industrial societies for new kinds of knowledge and labour. Further, he suggests that the student riots and protests that are pervasive are not just the consequences of adjustment after apartheid but also of a protracted feudalism binding young people in a prolonged commitment to an extended family; they are also the consequence of an unusually large youthful population – possibly half the population are under 20.

According to Van Onselen (1997: 14),

> when these two . . . facts – the preponderance of young people and their social commitment to the extended family – are inserted into a context of acute rural poverty, low economic growth, an unemployment rate of 35 per cent, large scale underemployment, and a rapidly changing education system, there are consequences which extend well beyond the mere quantitative dimensions envisaged in the proposed 'massification' of tertiary education . . . For thousands of black South Africans, access to tertiary education has become the difference between having a roof over your head and being homeless, between being fed half of the year or starving, between owning some clothing and being decked out in rags, and between meeting social commitments by sending home small amounts of cash to your family, or joining the ranks of those who are fully unemployed.

Van Onselen's analysis has met with a range of responses. In particular his suggestion, that the tertiary education sector 'becomes in effect a sponge which the state – perhaps unwittingly – uses to absorb thousands of unemployed youth who still seethe with a revolutionary anger that derives from the injustices of the recent past' (1997: 11), is not popular with the government. Student leaders also object to Van Onselen's characterization, I think, because it undermines at least some of the platforms from which they protest. They characterize themselves as actors not victims. More substantive criticisms of Van Onselen's analysis point to a lack of method or research, especially around regional and institutional variations. Yet I think Van Onselen's arguments do point to a cluster of problems related to access that will continue to beset universities, especially in second and third world countries but indeed wherever there is a tightening of the purse-strings. And whenever public purse-strings are being tightened – it seems everywhere – issues of access will overlap with ones of social welfare.

In their book about the history of open access at the City University of New York (CUNY), *Changing the Odds*, Lavin and Hyllegard (1996: 244) say:

> times of scarcity intensify debates about how resources should be distributed. Those who are more privileged often seek to derogate those who

have less as undeserving of support. In this perception CUNY's effort is treated as if it were a failed welfare entitlement programme left over from the bureaucratically bloated days of the Great Society.

They make the point too that open access unleashes a twin backlash from advocates of 'excellence' and opponents of welfare. They say that

at CUNY, as elsewhere in higher education, the conflict between established groups and newcomers has, to a considerable extent, been packaged in the rhetoric of 'academic standards' rather than in some of the cruder disparagements acceptable earlier in this century. In practice, of course, even though the claims of new groups are judged as academically unworthy and as a threat to standards, the American higher education system has always had places for those with the economic resources to afford tuition, regardless of their academic qualifications.

(p. 208)

And is it not odd that in an information economy where intellectual and knowledge work become more important, universities are struggling as never before for economic survival? How do we marry the growing recognition of the importance of knowledge work to the disillusion with universities that is pervasive in public discourse and mirrored in financial constraints? The litany of complaints about universities noted by Christodoulou in 1988 remains true today. He says,

governments in many countries have grown impatient . . . perceiving universities as expensive and wasteful, stubborn and slow to change, addicted to academic nicety and disdainful of business and industry, inculcating the wrong values in their students, irrelevant and prodigal in much of their research, unable to maintain discipline within their own communities, and over-protective of their rights without addressing their responsibilities . . .

(Christodoulou, 1988: 97)

The macro socioeconomic thrust towards opening and increasing access seems to be thwarted or unsupported at the level of implementation maybe because of an unhealthy co-dependence in the relation between universities and government, and perhaps because of a perceived (and sometimes very real) inability of universities to distinguish themselves as a vanguard of critical thinking devoting their resources to the pressing problems of our world.

Derek Bok (1990: 105) points out that

armed with the security of tenure and the time to study the world with care, professors would appear to have a unique opportunity to act as society's scouts to signal impending problems long before they are visible to others. Yet rarely have members of the academy succeeded in discovering emerging issues and bringing them vividly to the attention of the public. What Rachel Carson did for risks to the environment, Ralph Nader for consumer protection, Michael Harrington for problems of poverty, Betty

Friedan for women's rights, they did as independent critics, not as members of a faculty.

Not only that, but 'most universities continue to do their least impressive work on the very subjects where society's need for greater knowledge and better education is most acute': poverty, violence, war, unemployment, etc. (Bok, 1990: 122).

A diversity of higher education institutions providing different needs and filling distinct niches is so generally accepted and acceptable that it need not be debated here. What is still in the arena of debate is which or who can best do what, and the possibility that entirely new kinds of institutions or trans-institutional allegiances may be necessary to fulfil various tasks. Certainly in Bill Saint's (1997) paper about the revitalization of universities in Africa, he sees institutional linkages as crucial. Yet it seems that despite the ubiquitous agreement for diversity and variety in the institutions and offerings of higher education, there persist binaries or at worst polarities between knowledge production and utilization, between vocational and more 'purist' intellectual spheres, between the notion of servicing economies and polities or servicing knowledge for a more arcane, self-defined purpose ('self-defined' being cloaked in the fuzzy language of academic freedom). Although these issues manifest in different ways in different countries, purism not necessarily being revered above professionalism or vocationalism, they persist. I think it is the fact of that persistence that brings us together to ask 'What kind of university?' Are we uncomfortable perhaps?

Most of us would probably resist the idea that universities could or should be diluted into one of the many kinds of higher education institutions that exist today. Yet unless we find and passionately defend distinguishing characteristics, we may have to look beyond the transformation or dilution of universities to the possibility of their vitiation or at least reconception. And that, it seems to me, may happen despite universities, rather than because of them. It may be that diversity both of institutions and within them, coupled with increasing trends towards individual rather than social responsibility for education, may atomize rather than unify societies. Such a scenario suggests a radical reformulation of who and what constitute *societies*, let alone universities. It is as though the atomization of work allowed by technology will be reflected in the individualization of learning. Indeed, the idea of a learning market in which individuals take responsibility for their own learning is beginning to hold sway over that of a learning society (Edwards, 1995: 188). Castell points to what he calls the rise of 'the network society'. You are either in or out. Your identity (national or otherwise) will have to be found elsewhere. How do universities intervene for the wretched majority of the world's citizens who are out?

What then of the argument for universities remaining the elite institutions – bearers of a particular canon and reproducers of a particular class or meritocracy – that they have been for the major portion of their chronological histories? Archaic as it may seem, this notion of a university continues to prolong our debates about transformation. Even at times when experiments in open access were underwritten by massive state funding they have been met with 'canonical' disapproval and resistance, as though somehow an understood orthodoxy had been transgressed. And though we may dissociate ourselves from this wishful, retrogressive disapproval we are yet its co-conspirators. Where in the world is there a university transformed, one that isn't short of cash and tugged one way by an academic clerisy and other ways by students, governments and economies?

If we do not make some very brave and possibly distasteful decisions, economic imperatives fuelled increasingly by technology will make them for us. The technology explosion has dealt universities, as they are presently conceived, an almost mortal blow. Universities did at least have some kind of strategic advantage as storehouses or repositories of knowledge. No more! The fact is we do not need universities to find out the latest on any topic at all. This is demonstrated very dramatically by the growth in the conference business. Gurus in every field earn large sums of money and support their own research teams without any recourse to universities. They do not need universities to give them jobs and they do not need universities to give them an audience. It is also demonstrated by even a cursory acquaintance with the Internet. *The Economist* (7 January 1994: 38) put it succinctly:

> Soon you will be able to enjoy many of the advantages of a first class education without ever setting foot on a campus. If you want to learn economics you will be able to watch a lecture delivered by a Nobel laureate; if you want to learn geometry you will be able to interact with your computer screen; if you want to do some original research you will be able to summon library-loads of information. Universities, far from responding to these developments, still expect their students to turn up to lectures – a ritual rendered superfluous by Caxton.

Robert B. Reich, writing in 1993, made a similar point in much stronger terms. He claimed that the transformation through which we are living

> will rearrange the politics and economics of the coming century. There will be no national products or technologies, no national corporations, no national industries. There will be no national economies, at least as we have come to understand that concept. All that will remain rooted within national borders are the people who (have agreed to) comprise a nation. Each nation's primary assets will be its citizens' skills and insights. Each nation's primary political task will be to cope with the centrifugal forces of the global economy which tear at the ties binding citizens together – bestowing ever greater wealth on the most skilled and insightful, while consigning the less skilled to a declining standard of living. As borders become ever more meaningless in economic terms, those citizens best positioned to thrive in the world market are tempted to slip the bonds of national allegiance, and by so doing disengage themselves from their less favoured fellows.
>
> (Reich, 1993: 3)

Here are the issues we have to confront. Can universities act as a counter-vailing, democratizing force against the self-interest of the market despite the fact that they will have to be increasingly market-orientated in order to survive? Are we to become servants of our country's economies or nurturers of rounded civically responsible citizens and sites of reflective thinking and policy formu-lation? Will we continue to worry about what makes someone educated or will we perforce lapse into higher education profiteering? What will make us viable economically? Is profitability an appropriate question for educators to ponder?

The collective post-1989 sigh of relief at the fall of closed demand economies has dulled our perception of the hierarchies, distortions, tariffs and unfreedoms that characterize the 'free' market. We have been lulled by amorphous formu-lations that mingle accumulation and participation as though there were a common understanding that the one enhances the other. To dwell on the per-sistence of class inequality, the excluding qualities of the market, the short-comings of meritocracy and the increasing gap between rich and poor is almost heretical despite evidence to the contrary.

In 1996 the United Nations Development Programme (UNDP) released the results of a study showing that in the last 15 years the disparities between rich and poor have, in fact, increased. James Speth from the UNDP is quoted as saying 'if present trends continue, economic disparities between industrial and developing nations will move from inequitable to inhuman' (*Time*, 29 July 1996: 13). It is no coincidence that these same 15 years have also seen massive changes in communication and other technologies. Whatever technology has done for some of us, it has not changed the lives of most of us.

Questioning what lies behind the banner of the 'learning society', Richard Edwards asks:

> what are the boundaries of collective self-interest to which 'we' belong and that 'we' can call 'our' society? Given the heterogeneity and differences of those living within the boundaries of a nation state, who is the 'we' that is referred to in discourses of 'national interest'? Rather than being mem-bers of a single society, we may be part of a heterogenous series of over-lapping and inter-related local, regional, national and international, global societies.
>
> (Edwards, 1995: 188)

Certainly universities like to see themselves as part of an international com-munity, yet how does this help in healing and closing the rifts that characterize the world today?

An underlying assumption of this chapter is that there is an overriding value, an ethical impetus behind the increasing of diversity, access, participation or whatever we may call it. Further, I would say that it is this ethical drive, rather than market or government pressures, that universities need to be concerned with. In this view diversity is necessary because it promotes social justice and is just and compassionate; because it helps make democracy work; because it challenges orthodoxies and stereotypes; because it creates new ways of relat-ing and associating, discovers new circuitries for the mind. In this view then, ethically driven access and diversity are not national political programmes or economic multipliers. An ethical view of access is perforce a global view.

If access is a global ethical issue then we must cover untrodden terrain. Let me tell you about work of the Forum of African Women Educators (FAWE) – a fine example of thinking globally and acting locally. As we discuss the appropriate role of universities, FAWE grapples with the practical difficulty of getting girls into primary and secondary schooling (much less universities) in the majority of sub-Saharan African countries. It is a nineteenth-century battle fought with 1990s technology and vision. It is a battle about access. Girls in Africa are still not widely considered to be fit for anything other than agricultural and domestic tasks, let alone any kind of formal education. Yet a remarkable group of women, from a head office in Kenya, has galvanized the governments and leading educators of 27 African countries to put their energy into making access to formal education a possibility and right for girl children.

This requires a massive dissemination of information across the continent: a continent where quite often you would do as well first to fly to Europe in order to get to a neighbouring country in Africa, and where the postal systems are considerably less reliable than those of the nineteenth century in Europe. Yet technology can cut a swathe through the developmental backlog. I am often intrigued that I can have an e-mail exchange with my FAWE colleagues in many parts of Africa sometimes more readily than I can access first-worlders.

I can only imagine that efficiency breeds complacency in some spheres. I am not suggesting that most countries in Africa are effectively networked. That they are at all, should magnify our vision of access and participation. If we think globally, can we talk about access without talking about girl children in China or Africa? Can we talk about access as a democratizing force, a global one, unless we have a place in it for African or Chinese girls? Can we even talk about access as a democratizing force if we do not first look at our primary and secondary schools as potential templates for diversity?

FAWE's internal discourse about gender, and even sometimes its public discourse, is completely at odds with local narratives and realities in Africa. It is global in the way that their technology is global. Of course, materials development, training and implementation arc adapted to localized discourses but the vision behind them would not sit uncomfortably with debates about gender and diversity at universities in Europe or America.

Much as it challenges the methodology of conventional learning and teaching, technological and virtual capability is altering the tested ways in which we conceive of knowledge transmission and of conventional spatial and physical reality. In South Africa we often speak of the 'geography' of apartheid. We live in a country where years of political manipulation and racial segregation have created striations on physical maps, let alone political ones. Prolonged deprivation in rural areas has led to micro-climatic changes. Erosion has led to topographical alteration. It is no accident that, around the world, the fractures between rich and poor are often described in terms of a division between north and south, or between urban and rural worlds. I think we would also do well to think of the geography of university education and I am not just thinking of South Africa.

Much as I have suggested that access must be considered as part of a democratizing and diversifying package that ought to reflect itself in the public domain, I am also arguing that we must begin to conceive of that domain as global. Or else we will continue to isolate ourselves in a local and nation-state mentality while casting a greedy eye on the possibilities for profit in developing countries, rather as tobacco and pharmaceutical companies cultivate markets for pernicious products that have lost their foothold in the first world.

I have suggested previously, and not very originally considering the scope of distance and open-learning discourse and practice in developed countries, that universities ought to consider the creation of learning centres. In poor countries these could be strategically located in hopeless, violence-torn regions – the spatial equivalent of equity and diversity policies within established institutions. Ethical access means that we need to affirm the unfavoured places of human habitation and endeavour. Learning sites should be the pedagogic equivalent of electrification or road building. But they cannot rest at being installations. Though they may be made possible by technology, allowing students to tap a world library of intellectual riches, they will be as stark as our world at the moment if they do not carry a commitment to a new ethics that puts diversity and access into the mainstream of global critical thinking. In other words, I propose that a serious commitment to the sociopolitical health of our world requires a reassessment of the geographical location of universities. Many scholars and teachers believe that the transmission of wisdom and critical thinking happen through a dialectical process that technology has not yet colonized. I think they are right.

I have talked about FAWE because for me, and I imagine for many girls in Africa, their endeavours raise hope: hope against the odds and access from beyond the furthest boundaries of poverty and exclusion. I have not talked much about users of education in the sense suggested by the theme of 'Choices Concerning Access and Participation', nor about the stakeholders, whether employers or community groups. I have no doubt that knowledge production is growing and diversifying. I have no doubt either that entrepreneurs among us will sell packages of skills and facts, profitably. What I do not see is a more contented or equitable world. It is that absence that I think universities should try to fill, not with complacence or orthodoxy, rather with an ethical and challenging critique of both. 'One can appreciate the difficulty of the enterprise and understand if progress is slow' but, as Derek Bok (1990: 102) argues, 'what is harder to forgive is a refusal even to recognize the problem or to acknowledge a duty to work on it conscientiously.'

I do not really believe that the traditionalists in our midst are the enemies of promise or fortune, nor am I too concerned if universities survive in their archaic form or as retooled enterprises fitted for productivity beyond the millennium. What I would not live with, though, is to find myself defending the gateway to economic, technological or cultural advancement and productivity if it meant that those who go through the gate are not properly equipped to engage with the diversity of cultures and values, race and class, poverty and wealth, despair and beauty, and to live as mediators and interlocutors of difference and disparity. Our doors must be open at the entry point but it is by the attributes of those who leave that we will be valued.

I have not offered much in the way of a template for universities of the future but I hope I have smudged the possibility of them as the cloisters of particular epistemologies or as enterprises solely kitted for the market. We need to dissolve our view of the world as a cluster of discrete things. With a vision of the world as a dynamic interrelated whole we are poised to engage with it afresh. In the words of Batchelor (1997: 22),

> if we cannot imagine forms of life that respond effectively to the situation at hand, we will be limited in what we can do. Instead of finding a voice that speaks to the unique contingencies of our own situation, we repeat the cliches and dogmas of other epochs. Instead of creatively participating in a contemporary culture of awakening, we confine ourselves to preserving those cultures of a vanishing past.

I would add that we will also tack them onto a vanishing future if we do not wake up to our ethical duty.

References

Batchelor, S. (1997) Buddhism without beliefs, *Tricycle*, 7(3): 18–23.

Bok, D. (1990) *Universities and the Future of America*. Durham and London: Duke University Press.

Boyd, D. (1996) Dominance concealed through diversity: implications of inadequate perspectives on cultural pluralism, *Harvard Educational Review*, 66(3): 609–30.

Christodoulou, A. (1988) *New Challenges, New Responses, The Commonwealth of Universities*. London: Association of Commonwealth Universities.

Edwards, R. (1995) Behind the banner: whither the learning society, *Adults Learning*, 6(6): 187–9.

Lavin, D. E. and Hyllegard, D. (1996) *Changing the Odds: Open Admissions and Life Chances of the Disadvantaged*. New Haven, CT: Yale University Press.

Maassen, P. A. M. (1995) Restructuring higher education: major trends and issues. Paper presented at OISE conference on 'Restructuring Postsecondary Education', 27–28 April.

Reich, R. (1993) *The Work of Nations. A Blueprint for the Future*. London: Simon and Schuster.

Saint, W. (1997) *Revitalising Universities in Africa*. Washington, DC: World Bank.

Schneider, C. (1997) From diversity to engaging difference. Paper presented at seminar on 'Curriculum Responses to a Changing National and Global Environment in an African Context', p. 38, 21–23 March. Johannesburg: Centre for Higher Education Transformation.

UNDP (1996) *The Human Development Report*. Oxford: Oxford University Press.

Van Onselen, C. (1997) Closer to home: student unrest and the welfare function, *Focus* 7, Johannesburg: The Helen Suzman Foundation.

8

Making the Educational System More Equal

Jan de Vuyst

The participation paradox

In a column in a Flemish quality newspaper, a columnist speaks about 'the unjustly dying race of those who find the egalitarianization of the educational system to be as yet unfinished, and for whom it must thus remain an obsession' (*De Standaard*, 7 August 1995: 6). At the same time he finds that over a period of seven years, young people's participation in university education in Flanders has increased from 12 to 19 per cent. Such growth did not even occur in the golden years for the movement towards equality, the 1960s and 1970s. This paradox, however, only turns out to be an apparent contradiction: indeed, participation in education is unequally divided, and not in favour of the lower socioprofessional and income groups (Deleeck and Storms, 1989).

How to interpret egalitarianization

The term 'egalitarianization' is far from unequivocal, and has different meanings depending on the purposes it has to serve. In the discussion about the formation of a more egalitarian educational system, the demand for equal opportunities is a very abstract idea, which can be operationalized in very different ways (Wellens, 1982). Education that is based on the principle of equality could be defined as education that gives each individual the opportunity to obtain the highest possible degree in general education and professional skills corresponding to his/her aspirations and talent, i.e. independently of socioeconomic status, race, sex and religion. Equality in this kind of education system is proportional to individual initial possibilities. We must therefore ask ourselves if the flow of students to university higher education is proportional to the intellectual capacity present in society.

The problem of developing a more egalitarian educational system can be seen in the light of several frames of reference. For example, one might look for 'equality of opportunity' and establish that youngsters from a lower socioprofessional level who attend university are percentage-wise outnumbered by those who originate from a higher socioprofessional level. We can also compare the distribution of the category under consideration with the total population and demonstrate that fewer students of a particular environment are at university than could be expected on the basis of that particular population group's size. Such procedures use 'participation indexes'. Another basis for comparison, however, might be the distribution of intellectual capacities across different population groups. One can then speak of social inequality when individuals with equal abilities do not participate equally in higher education ('equal use for equal ability').

Let us look at two views of what equal opportunities might mean. A first system creates different systems of education, for different types of talents and social positions, and formally gives everyone the right to participate in them. Such participation, however, does not have to be promoted. This *meritocratic* or *liberal* view considers a system equal if it has 'equality of opportunity of access'. Hence everyone who proves (through intelligence tests, exam results, etc.) that they have the skills required to follow their chosen study programme enjoys equal chances. Within this conceptual framework, measures such as scholarships, the geographical spread of educational institutes, the provision of study advice and other facilities, are essential.

The *egalitarian* view objects to the meritocratic one because it has not achieved the intended result. Furthermore, the supporters of the egalitarian point of view argue that allegedly 'objective' criteria, such as tests and exams, are influenced by socioeconomic factors. Lastly, they point out that 'equality of opportunity of access' is not identical to 'equality of opportunity of success'. Even if one provides free education with the same curriculum in the same school, the results will be different. According to them, education should create more equality within society, not consolidate or exacerbate the present differences.

The study of egalitarianization, in other words, acts as a mirror of a morally pluralistic society. To be as flexible as possible in this context, we will try not only to describe access to education, but also to look at other issues; in this chapter we will therefore distinguish between three forms of egalitarianization: equal access to higher education, equal opportunity within higher education, and equal opportunity at the start of one's professional career.

Access opportunities

Any study interested in equal access to higher education should pay attention to how much every individual makes use of it, analysed both by socioprofessional category and subject (including resulting career choice).

The different levels of higher education

Equality of opportunity in Belgian higher education has not been a great success. In spite of the progress of middle class and female students, lower income groups are still poorly represented. According to De Lannoo (1979 and 1983), the number of male students from lower income groups increased from the second half of the 1950s until 1968–9, yet from then onwards there has been an uninterrupted decrease in the relative size of the group. On the level of subject choice, too, significant differences between social origin and the choice of study subject continue to exist: in medicine, law and applied sciences there is strong representation of the higher and poor representation of the lower socioprofessional levels. The opposite pattern, on the other hand, applies to religion, social sciences, psychology and educational sciences. Given such numbers, we can clearly speak of an incomplete and stagnating process of egalitarianization within university education.

Several authors have pointed out that the deceleration in the growth of the number of university students and the ebbing away of the egalitarianization process, go hand in hand with the accelerating growth of the number of students in higher *non*-university education, where trends towards equal opportunity persist.

According to the egalitarian view, however, equality does not stop with access to higher education. It appears that working-class students not only choose university studies leading on to lower professional status but also – and particularly so in the physical and biomedical sciences – obtain fewer degrees of distinction during his/her undergraduate years, and choose less ambitious postgraduate studies. As far as the suspension of academic study careers is concerned, very clear forms of social inequality exist. Complementary or advanced studies abroad (i.e. at doctorate or postgraduate level) show similar effects, although less obviously: the scholarship system – the policy instrument par excellence in relation to the financial aspects of studying, and therefore intrinsically geared towards egalitarianization – does not help finance complementary studies (Loosveldt, 1987). Other research has been carried out regarding more qualitative facts as well. There is a significant link between the level of education of the student's father and their own intrinsic motivation for the subject under study; this also affects their interest in its specific content. It helps them to avoid feeling a complete stranger in the relatively new situation, but to enjoy feeling 'at home' instead.

Opportunities at the start of a professional career

A final aspect of the ongoing responsibility of higher education to promote equal opportunities is the guidance of its students at the beginning of their careers and during their career development. Here a similar experiential hypothesis has been put forward: working-class children show different (less ambitious and less self-confident) job application behaviour, and they develop their careers in other (more passive) ways.

The birth of an ideology

The quote 'For unto every one that hath shall be given, and he shall have abundance: but from him that hath not shall be taken away even that which he hath' (Matthew 25: 29) inspired Professor Dr Herman Deleeck (1981) to the naming of the Matthew effect. Under the influence of sociocultural and sociopolitical factors, a large part of the benefits of government social policies will proportionally tend to go more to higher than to lower social categories. The well-off will get a bigger piece of the resources cake. However, this is not a new phenomenon.

The situation was already censured two hundred years ago both by confessional and non-confessional groups. With the slogan of the French revolution – *Liberté, égalité, fraternité* (liberty, equality, brotherhood) – inspiring several revolutionary movements, it is evident that the egalitarianization of education also subscribes to this credo.

It could be argued that social provision is nearly as old as the (concept of the) university itself. In Flanders, the state organization of social provision received new life after World War II. The experience of the war renewed the solidarity between different social groups, and movement towards social equality was able to breathe afresh. Voluntary collaboration by students and the personal involvement of cooperators in providing services were powerful contributory forces. As part of the prevailing social idealism, an increase in university education was envisaged through the provision of financial and material resources.

A second wave of expansion occurred in the 1960s and the early 1970s, the result of sustained economic growth at the end of the 1950s. Personal involvement was minimized in favour of the institutional intervention of administrative and professional 'experts'. The state's role in the entire process was increasingly emphasized. The professionalization of the social sector was partly cause and partly consequence of this expansion, which took place as soon as it was socially and financially feasible.

However, as the social and budgetary situation grew worse, a decline in funding took place. 'The right to education is a demand which, like many others, was only slowly conceded to, and more precisely, only at the moment when these demands could be fitted into the economic and political situation' (Verbrugghe *et al.*, 1977: 1).

Values and views within the sector

Values and priorities throughout the history of the social sector have changed. There has been a shift from the 'Martha to the Mary perspective' (Lammertyn, 1995: 19). Reference is made here to another parable from the

Gospel according to Luke, where Jesus and his disciples visit the house of the two sisters.

Teams with a Martha perspective will orientate themselves to the efficiency with which they can complete the technical and result-directed activities. They prefer standardization of tasks and an extensive division of labour. Teams with a Mary perspective orientate themselves to individually directed care and personal concern. They prefer a task content that allows for the personal differences between clients. They look for empathy and involvement. In other words: both perspectives show different values and different organizational cultures.

Social services also have the choice between *universalism* and *selectivity*. Universalism sees services and benefits for the entire population as a social right, whereas selectivity relates to services provided on the basis of individual needs, usually defined after a study of the means of subsistence. Selective services and benefits take into account the financial situation of an individual or a household.

Another disputed issue in connection with the character of social care is the choice between 'in cash' or 'in kind' benefits, i.e. between (financial) provisions, subsidies, financial aid, etc. on the one hand, or goods and services on the other.

Supporters of 'in kind' benefits state that this form is more efficient and more effective than providing amounts of money that can be spent freely. Supporters of allocating benefits in the form of money counter this point of view by stressing the consumer's greater sovereignty and freedom of choice. Moreover they argue that income transfers are a more efficient means to reduce problems such as poverty than 'in-kind' benefits. Too many resources go to the system and its staff.

Another problem is that of coordination and participation. Social workers often claim to be concerned with the whole person. However, clients' problems usually have many causes, as mental, physical and environmental factors influence the functioning of clients and their opportunities in life. At the same time we see that each social worker and the organizations they represent are specializing more and more. Coordination is the answer to this contradiction.

As opposed to coordination strategies, which look at how benefits can be related to each other in different ways (to reflect different social policies), participation strategy aims to distribute between the providers of benefits and the client the power of decision making. Central to this view is the idea that clients will be guaranteed claimable and efficient services only when they hold a position of authority in them.

Other changes are also evident in the increasingly public and professional role of welfare workers: caring is a fully fledged profession, for which full remuneration is demanded, with normal labour relations. Moreover, the qualifications of the staff have increased. However, there is a class difference between the 'experts', who mostly come from the middle classes, and the clients, who are mostly from lower socioeconomic classes. Because of this, professionals do not always understand their clients' behaviour and value patterns. This may lead to the professionals – also because of time pressure – only paying attention to aspects of the problem that are relevant to their own role and expertise. Labelling clients as hopeless, multi-problematic, chronic, inaccessible or (on the contrary) as 'good' clients is thus another expression of a specific professional technology and of the way in which specific organizations are structured.

Funding systems

Higher education in Flanders (as opposed to elementary education) is not free. Although a substantial amount of the costs of higher education are paid for by taxpayers, the student is required to pay an enrolment fee that could cynically be described as an attempt to limit the number of applications. Naturally, such a 'restraint fee' is contrary to the idea of equality. Moreover, in addition to this enrolment fee, other costs of studying and living can be substantial.

Scholarships are intended to achieve the real egalitarianization of higher education in Flanders. A considerable amount of government intervention is spent on them, and the number of candidates is similarly large. But in addition to the quantitative importance of the scholarship system, its qualitative meaning should also be pointed out, for scholarships are of a completely different nature than other education provision. The most important difference lies in the fact that scholarships are selectively paid to (the family of) the applicant. Moreover, it consists of direct financial interventions.

The alternatives to scholarships, specifically study pay and study loans, have been analysed in detail. The evaluation of these alternatives indicates that scholarships are, despite everything, the best solution for Flanders. The appealing alternative 'study pay' refers to the work the student delivers and the compensation offered to him/her (and not to his/her parents) by society. This option is chosen by those who want to put emphasis on the fact that an 18-year-old is an adult, on the student's independence from home, and on the professional earnestness the student develops in studying for his/her future job. Students, however, are often seen by society as less adult and less independent from the family than their 'working' age-peers, and have a barely latent image as party-animals; this probably explains the unconscious resistance that makes such a concept, which would strongly support the movement towards equality within education, difficult to discuss in Belgium.

The alternative 'study loan' derives from the idea of the transitional stage of 'needy student' later changing to 'well-paid functionary'. This is unsatisfactory because graduates can no longer be assured of a well-paid job, combined with the fact that it is precisely graduates of the lower social class who have a lower chance of employment; study loans are contrary to the principle of equality.

State provision (given to all students, rich and poor) complements selective provision (only for students coming from lower socioeconomic backgrounds) and remains an essential supplement to scholarships. State subsidies are used for numerous collective benefits, such as housing, restaurants, social, psychological and medical services, and for supplementary scholarships.

The institutionally dependent nature of collective social provision in Flanders has an important side-effect. The appeal of an institution can be influenced by the quality of such services. At that point, recruitment and egalitarianization go hand in hand, like a remarkable pair of non-identical twins. If such recruitment benefits motivate the institution to invest in equality, one is able to trade-off ends and means. If the development of equal opportunities is used for blatant recruitment, however, one must ask questions about the institution's motives. In this context it becomes important to strive for regionally based social provision, such as that seen in Belgium's unsurpassed eastern and southern neighbours, Germany and France.

More than just money

Each country somehow tries to promote equality of opportunity, usually through a mixture of direct and indirect, selective and universal measures. If policy-makers want to think about the quality of this mixture for specific student groups, they should at least look at all the available policy measures for those groups. In doing so, they must not only think about money.

It is common knowledge that inequality is the result of sociocultural barriers that appear very early in the student's educational career. The system of scholarships, which has no hold over these factors, can consequently only play a minor role. Educational inequality, generated by social stratification, clearly cannot be fought by educational measures only.

Education throughout the centuries has been a system controlled by the ruling groups in society. The values, interpretations and underlying principles of education cannot be separated from those dominant social values. In this respect, the movement towards equality means that space must be given to those who do not belong to the dominant group. Formerly this used to be mostly girls and working-class children, whereas now there are other groups as well, such as immigrants, and the disabled. We have to work on their behalf, I believe. But I am afraid I am just one member of the unjustly dying race of those who find the making of a more equal educational system to be as yet unfinished, and for whom it must thus remain an obsession.

References

Cantillon, B. (1982) Studietoelagen en de democratizering van het hoger onderwijs, *De Nieuwe Maand*, 25(9): 669–77.

De Lannoo, I. (1979) Slagen en mislukken in de universitaire loopbaan, *Politica*, 29(2): 111–29.

De Lannoo, I. (1983) *Democratiseringstendenzen in de samenstelling van de studentenbevolking Kultuurleven*, 50(7): 609–15.

Deleeck, H. (1981) De democratisering van het hoger onderwijs: feiten en middelen, *De Gids op Maatschappelijk Gebied*, 72(6–7): 507–33.

Deleeck, H. and Storms, B. (1989) Blijvende ongelijkheden in het onderwijs: 10 jaar later, *De Gids op Maatschappelijk Gebied*, 80(12): 1119–38.
Lammertyn, F. (1995) De zorg voor welzijn. Actuele antwoorden op oude vragen, in H. Baert (ed.) *Welzijn en gezondheid in 2002*. Kiezen en/of delen, Leuven: LUCAS.
Loosveldt, G. (1987) Onderzoek naar de democratisering van het behalen van een tweede diploma, *De Gids op Maatschappelijk Gebied*, 78(4): 307–24.
Verbrugghe, B. *et al.* (1977) De democratisering van het onderwijs, het ontnuchterend ontwaken uit een al te mooie wensdroom, *De Gids op Maatschappelijk Gebied*, 68(6–7): 1–24.
Wellens, J. (1982) De democratisering van het onderwijs. Beschouwingen vanuit een rechtvaardigheidsperspectief, *Onze Alma Mater*, 36(2): 125–48.

9

The Urban/Metropolitan University: Land-grant University of the Twenty-first Century

Joel E. Anderson

Universities, whether public or private, represent major financial investments. We should not be surprised that governmental officials and community leaders look at our intellectual resources with envy and feel entitled to access to them for help on a substantial number of societal problems. A premise of this chapter is that we should feel obliged to share campus intellectual resources as much as we can in order to elevate the lives of people in our communities. I shall address the issue by recalling the record of one group of universities that succeeded to a great degree in taking knowledge out to rural people and helping them to use it to make their lives better. I shall also take note of another group of universities that are endeavouring, more or less successfully, to do the same thing in very different settings.

The land-grant universities in the United States

Peter Magrath (quoted in Campbell, 1995: xii), President of the National Association of State Universities and Land-Grant Colleges, has spoken of the land-grant universities as 'one of the truly great educational wonders of the world'. These institutions, which date from the signing by President Abraham Lincoln of the Morrill Act of 1862, were to be established by the states, funded indirectly by grants of land from the federal government. Reflecting the ever-growing spirit of democracy, they were intended to make higher education, particularly in agriculture and the mechanical arts, available at low cost to the children of common people. Higher education was to be practical and improve and enrich the lives of ordinary people. The original plan envisioned one land-grant institution in each state in the federal Union. This in effect created a de facto national system of institutions of higher education.

The practical mission of the land-grant institutions to make knowledge useful was emphasized with the adoption of the Hatch Act in 1887. This federal legislation provided funding for the establishment of 'agricultural experiment stations' at land-grant universities to conduct research that would improve agricultural production. The practical mission of making knowledge useful was emphasized more dramatically with another innovation through federal legis- lation: the Smith-Lever Act of 1914 resulted in the establishment at the land- grant universities of the 'cooperative extension service'. 'Cooperative' denoted that costs of the system were shared by the federal, state and local governments.

The extension service – in an earlier day often referred to as the 'agricultural extension service' – was established to disseminate knowledge, possessed on campus or discovered at the experiment station, to the farm families living throughout the state who could use the knowledge to increase agricultural pro- duction and otherwise improve rural life. As a result of the Smith-Lever Act, in most states the land-grant campus organized an extension service that included 'county agents' in each county of the state as well as a staff of experts – 'spe- cialists' – at the state level who provided support for the county agents.

Although I had little notion of any connection to a university, I can recall from my own childhood on a farm the work of county agents in my neighbour- hood. They brought to farmers free knowledge and advice about the science and technology of farming. They would assist in testing the composition of the soil to determine what nutrients were missing and which fertilizers were needed to enhance crop growth. They advised on animal and plant diseases and insect problems and would instruct in the inoculation of livestock and the application of insecticides. They provided extremely helpful information on soil and water conservation and a host of other subjects important to the farmer.

The county agents had the benefit not only of their own college education but also the growing body of knowledge developed by scientists back on the land-grant campus, particularly at the agricultural experiment station. The experiment stations conducted research on issues and problems specific to their respective states. An experiment station in one state might develop a hybrid corn that grew well in the specific conditions of that state, while an experiment station in a different state with different climate and soil would develop a hybrid that flourished there.

County agents were not there just to help the men. There were county agents, called 'home demonstration agents' in my youth, who provided know- ledge and advice to the farmer's wife on making clothes, cooking food, plan- ning healthy diets, preserving food through the winter and summer months, practising good hygiene, and beautifying the home.

These extension agents elevated rural life in the United States. They helped make farms more productive, farm families more prosperous, and farm life more healthy and wholesome and livable. (See Rasmussen, 1989, for a history of the extension service.)

In 1989, the seventy-fifth anniversary of the cooperative extension service, the stationery of the extension service in my state carried the line, 'Linking people to research'. I found that statement riveting and attractive. Linking people to research? That is an immense challenge, but I could reflect on my experiences growing up in rural Arkansas, and I knew that it was true. It was a legitimate claim.

I think this is the missing piece in higher education, at least in my own country: too often we do not succeed in linking people to research – or in less simple language, we fail at technology transfer or the diffusion of knowledge. As a result, we have much useful knowledge discovered and refined by fine minds on campus, but that knowledge stays on campus, sometimes in professional journals, communicated either ineffectively or not at all to people beyond campus who might use it. In short, we do not link people to research.

The changing land-grant universities

The land-grant universities in the United States are not what they used to be; and they are more than they used to be.

In each of the 50 states in the USA, the land-grant campus established as a result of the Morrill Act of 1862 is today regarded as the leading university – often referred to as the 'flagship' campus – or at least one of the top two or three universities in the state. The land-grant campuses have had the advantage of longevity, more time to grow and gather strength. Yet their status has to some extent been diminished with the passing of time as each has come to share its state territory with other highly regarded state universities, and the land-grant university's dedication to the outreach mission has also to some extent diminished. There appear to be two primary reasons for these changes.

First, rural America has changed. The agrarian population has fallen to only 3 per cent of the national population. In the 1990s, while the colleges of agriculture and the agricultural experiment stations remain strongly connected to agricultural interests, agriculture is a less dominant interest in the economies of most states and in the lives of land-grant universities. The cooperative extension service has been most directly affected by the changes in rural America. The people to be linked to research are fewer in number and not so readily identifiable as in earlier times. Indeed, the cooperative extension service has sometimes appeared to be an organization looking for a mission, perhaps similar to the March of Dimes after the Salk vaccine essentially eliminated polio.

Second, most, if not all, of the original land-grant universities have become, or aspire to become, comprehensive research universities. The rise of the research university to a kind of normative status – what every university faculty wants their campus to become – has been analysed by Ernest L. Boyer (1990), late president of the Carnegie Foundation for the Advancement of Teaching. In general, faculty at research universities give first priority to research. Teaching and outreach activities are devalued. Despite the fact that research universities might also deserve, in Peter Magrath's language, to be identified as an educational wonder of the world, they do not connect as strongly with the people of their states and their problems as the land-grant universities once did through the cooperative extension service.

The land-grants now march to a different drummer. They are not as strongly orientated as they once were to giving the people – the owners of public universities – what the people want. I would submit, however, that as we look to shaping universities for the new millennium, or at least for the new century, that we take a leaf from the notebook of the architects of the original land-grant institutions. We should dedicate our institutions to giving the people we serve what they want and need. It seems an over-simple point. Yet universities arose as instruments for achieving purposes bigger than and outside themselves. They do not exist for faculty and administrators. They exist to serve.

I would point to a book (1995) by an eloquent apostle of land-grant universities, John R. Campbell, former president of Oklahoma State University. Although Campbell speaks with passion for the land-grant universities, it is revealing that the title of his work is *Reclaiming a Lost Heritage*. He notes the decreased enthusiasm of public policy makers for higher education in the United States, and he believes that to gain increased support, universities need to learn from the earlier record of the land-grants:

> If land-grant institutions are to enjoy a high level of public support, it is imperative that they stay close to their basic constituencies – those who need and use their services. The relationship between land-grant institutions and their constituents might be compared with a stream-fed lake. The lake's level is related to the rate of water inflow; if high, lake level will be high. Similarly, if the inflow of public support is high, colleges and universities are enabled to grow, to be more productive, to render expanded services to the public. When institutions fail to respond to public concerns, needs, and problems, they cannot reasonably expect to continue receiving the same level of public support.
>
> (Campbell, 1995: 32)

In my judgment, Campbell is very much on target, although the land-grant institutions may not be quick to heed his message.

The rise of the urban/metropolitan universities

During the last 50 years or so, public urban/metropolitan universities in the United States have emerged in sizeable numbers. As a group these institutions have come to prominence since World War II. Most of them were established or enlarged to meet the increased demand of citizens for higher education, with the returning veterans of war and then the post-war 'baby boom' generation strongly fuelling growth in college enrolments.

In more specific terms, state officials found that the land-grant campuses, often located away from population centres, were unable to meet all of the rising higher education demands of citizens. The metropolitan areas included significant numbers of place-bound people who could not move away to attend college. Due to family and other responsibilities, these students in urban/metropolitan areas would often hold jobs while attending college. As a consequence, state-supported universities have appeared and grown in one after another metropolitan region across the nation. (Some people refer to them as urban universities; others refer to them as metropolitan universities. While I view the latter term – metropolitan – as more inclusive and more appealing, I use the terms here interchangeably.)

A striking characteristic of these urban/metropolitan institutions is that their leaders have embraced public service as a major component of their missions, reminiscent of the land-grant universities. Typically the focus of the urban/metropolitan universities is on their immediate regions, i.e. their metropolitan areas. The language of outreach, extension, professional service, and applied research are common in their vocabularies.

The focus on the immediate metropolitan area came about, in part, to differentiate them from the land-grant campuses with their statewide focus on agriculture. The focus on the metropolitan area also came about, in part, because cities constitute dynamic, demanding environments. My own institution is one of the urban/metropolitan universities, and I can testify that to a surprising extent every discipline on the campus is the object of demands from some group in the community, and all of the faculties have accommodated those demands in varying degrees. In short, if a campus is responsible for serving myriad needs of a metropolitan area, it has its hands full.

There is now a Coalition of Urban and Metropolitan Universities in the United States with 53 members, including two international affiliates, made up of universities from metropolitan areas with populations of at least 250,000. Their presidents have all embraced a declaration[1] that includes this language:

> We, the leaders of metropolitan universities and colleges . . .
>
> - reaffirm that the creation, interpretation, dissemination, and application of knowledge are the fundamental functions of our institutions;
> - accept a broad responsibility to bring these functions to bear on our metropolitan regions;
> - commit our institutions to be responsive to the needs of our communities by seeking new ways of using resources to provide leadership in addressing metropolitan problems through teaching, research, and service.

I believe that these are the institutions that have the key to success in the next century, as the land-grants had it in an earlier day. They are committed to making knowledge useful to their constituents in the metropolitan regions they serve.

Who are the urban/metropolitan universities?

It is useful to see the urban/metropolitan universities against the backdrop of the land-grant universities. Every state today has at least one land-grant institution, and some 19 states, mostly in the southern part of the United States, have two or more campuses designated as land-grant institutions. In most instances these states established second campuses for African American students during the time when education was segregated by race, with separate public educational institutions for whites and African Americans in the South. This policy came to an end with the civil rights movement of the mid-twentieth century.

Most of the land-grant universities are classified as research universities in Carnegie categories, and they offer a comprehensive set of baccalaureate, master's and doctoral degree programmes. While literally dozens of institutions could be named here, the University of Maryland, Ohio State University and the University of Illinois can be cited as examples of the land-grant group. In addition to being viewed as flagship campuses in a majority of their respective states, the land-grant universities generally are older, more fully developed, better funded, and enrol larger numbers of students.

A review of the group of urban/metropolitan universities shows that most states now boast at least one. Many of these universities fall into Carnegie master's categories, a few fall into the doctoral categories, and still fewer into the research categories. A closer examination would show that their master's and doctoral programmes tend to be orientated more toward professional fields than to the arts and sciences. These institutions tend to be several decades younger than the land-grants, and their immediate origins more diverse. A number of the urban/metropolitan universities first existed as private institutions, two-year colleges, university extension centres, or some other educational entity before their state governors and legislatures made them public universities.

Whereas the typical land-grant university student lives in student housing on campus and enrols for full-time studies, the typical metropolitan university student commutes to campus and enrols for part-time studies while holding a part-time or full-time job. Literally dozens of representative institutions could be named. Georgia State University in Atlanta, the University of Alabama at Birmingham, Wayne State University in Detroit, and Wright State University in Dayton can be cited as examples of this emerging group of institutions. Located in the nation's metropolitan areas, these institutions are where the action is, where the accomplishments of humankind are most apparent and where the problems faced by people at the dawn of the new millennium are most intense.

Examples of outreach activities

Metropolitan universities have opened up their intellectual resources to their communities in numerous ways. Anyone interested in seeing the rich variety of those activities and reading about them in detail need only spend time in the quarterly issues of the eight-year-old journal, *Metropolitan Universities*, published by the Coalition of Urban and Metropolitan Universities.[2] From that and other sources one will find that metropolitan universities are frequently involved in consulting and policy studies for government agencies on a wide variety of subjects. Many are involved with their communities in economic development activities, particularly small business assistance and workforce training. These universities are also frequently involved with the local schools, from kindergarten through high school, in a variety of partnerships from training teachers to assisting at-risk students. And metropolitan institutions have played a role in responding to the ongoing, seemingly insatiable demand for training in the use of computers.

Many of the foregoing examples are not necessarily urban. They could very well occur in a rural town, between a university there and the community. However, the frequency and strength of demands from the community are much greater in cities than in towns, in part because of differences in scale. In the city the fine arts community is bigger. The government offices and agencies are bigger and more is expected of them. The schools are larger and are beset with many more at-risk children. The economic stakes are greater in the city. Crime is more likely to be a serious problem. City leaders in these and other important issue areas of community life often have a sense that there are people – experts – at the university who could help them. My institution recently carried out a strategic planning process that extensively involved people from the community. (On each task force the ratio of community representatives to campus representatives was 2:1.) One of the strongest recommendations directed to the university at the end of the planning process was to work with the community to solve problems in the community (UALR 2000 Oversight Committee, 1994: 5–7).

Some kinds of interactions with the community are, however, necessarily urban and cannot take place outside a city. For example, located in the heart of the city, the University of Missouri at Kansas City has had the opportunity in 1995 to join in efforts to revitalize the urban core.[3] By definition, such assistance can only be given in a city where urban decay is a problem.

Some university relationships with the community depend on a critical mass of numbers of clients or customers, numbers not available in small towns. Wichita State University is located in a population centre of sufficient size to sustain an arts institute that increases access to the fine arts for all segments of the city's diverse population by offering inexpensive non-credit courses in music, dance, theatre and the visual arts.[4] Similarly, there would not be enough clients in most small towns to keep open a tax clinic to help the working poor appeal Internal Revenue Service rulings. But in Atlanta the numbers are sufficient, and Georgia State University law faculty and students have operated such a clinic for five years.[5]

Not only are there large and demanding community problems nearby to universities located in metropolitan areas, but proximity also gives other opportunities. Last summer my institution, at the request of the Governor of Arkansas and of the director of the state's Department of Education, conducted a study of the roles of the department and its organization, operations and internal communications (UALR 1996). In the second stage of the study, 44 faculty and staff members from the University of Arkansas at Little Rock along with 14 volunteers from the private sector interviewed all 224 employees in the department in one week. It would not have been feasible to have asked the same 58 people to do the same thing if the Department of Education had been located 100 miles away. This opportunity came because the university was located in the governmental capital of the state, where large governmental agencies are located. This example also illustrates a remarkable strength: the sheer numbers of highly competent people employed at universities. What other organization could have so easily marshalled 58 people for such a project?

Obstacles to outreach by metropolitan universities

Despite the opportunities and the formidable resources of urban and metropolitan universities, and despite the very impressive records they can boast in reaching out to their communities, they have faced significant obstacles in making good on their pledges to provide access to their great stores of expertise. As we contemplate the university of the twenty-first century, we need to recognize these obstacles. We will find that the land-grant experience is relevant.

Although the pioneers of the land-grant universities might want to dispute this, the metropolitan universities today, in comparison with the land-grants, confront a much more diverse and complex group of constituencies external to the campus. It is a great challenge to be responsive to the legitimate demands of all of them. Further, in the heyday of the land-grants where there were few if any competing institutions, it was easier for members of a state legislature, no matter what area of the state they represented, to feel that the land-grant university belonged to all of them and was addressing problems in their home districts. One might logically infer that metropolitan universities should identify selected niches, selected community issues or relationships, on which they could focus their resources and efforts and build their supporting constituencies. Whether this inference can be translated into a tenable strategy in the demanding urban environment remains to be seen.

As a result of the diversity of interests and needs served in a metropolitan area, metropolitan universities must navigate through dangerous political waters. It is not an exaggeration to say that in metropolitan areas many problems, and particularly their possible solutions, are controversial. No matter how honourable the intentions and essentially neutral the university's methods, some powerful interests may be offended by the consequences of the university's involvement. Life in an ivory tower has its advantages!

Metropolitan universities have had only limited success in achieving the infrastructure necessary to effective outreach. There is in almost all disciplines represented by faculty much potentially useful knowledge on the shelf; but there are no extension agents to bring that knowledge to the persons and situations where it would be useful. The land-grant institution had a college of agriculture and home economics on campus where instruction of college students occurred, an agricultural experiment station where research relevant to the agriculture of the state was conducted, and an extension service set up to disseminate knowledge and make it useful to rural people across the state. In contrast, with few exceptions, at metropolitan universities the faculty and other campus professionals are the on-campus instructors, the researchers, and when it occurs, the extension personnel, too. Although one can make a virtue of this necessity and say it enriches teaching, the reality is that the infrastructure for effective outreach remains inadequate.

The infrastructure issue backs up to faculty in three other ways. First, faculty hired at metropolitan universities have typically graduated from doctoral institutions where research was the prized activity, and outreach activity that made knowledge useful to people beyond the campus was not modelled at all by their faculty mentors. Even if responsive to campus leaders who encourage faculty to become involved in outreach activities, metropolitan university faculty often will be unprepared for such roles.

Second, I think we often overlook teaching schedules in our analyses of the slow growth of public service and outreach activities of faculty. The point is not just that faculty members must devote substantial time to teaching but that teaching schedules require that they meet classes at regular times each week. For the sake of students, these schedules are 'rigid'. If they are to be done well, outreach activities that require considerable time away from campus, or that arise on short notice and need a week or two of intensive effort, may simply not be compatible with the classroom obligations of faculty members. Moreover, in recent years in the United States there has been increased emphasis on teaching by college faculty. They are being asked to do it more and better. To the extent that time devoted to teaching increases, one can expect time devoted to the outreach mission of the institution to decrease.

Third, as has been analysed by Ernest Boyer (1990) and others, the prevailing notions of faculty roles and rewards at American universities emphasize research over teaching and public service. Faculty values tend to be more aligned with those of their academic disciplines across the nation, which often define research as the most prestigious role; they are less aligned with the missions of the institutions that pay them, which may desire more focus on teaching or outreach.

Although metropolitan universities typically have a number of faculty who, despite all the constraints, are enthusiastic about making their professional expertise available to their communities in meaningful ways, the three observations just made about faculty represent serious infrastructure issues in the development of metropolitan universities. There are three fundamental options for relief. One option is that faculty numbers be increased and average teaching assignments reduced so that each faculty member would have more flexibility to provide professional expertise to the community. A second option is to achieve funding for professional personnel, other than classroom faculty, who would be twenty-first century versions of the land-grant university's county extension agents. Their full-time role would be 'linking people to research'. A number of institutions have responded to their dilemma over faculty time with modest success by establishing community-orientated centres and institutes with budgets that permit them to buy a portion of a faculty member's time to free the faculty member to assist in applied research or other outreach activities. A third option is to elevate the value and rewards for outreach activities, which could result in a reallocation by faculty of their time from research to outreach activities.

There is another important time constraint that limits the metropolitan university's sharing of its expertise with external groups and organizations: the competing demands on the time of presidents and vice-presidents. Such institutional officials need to do more than express strong support for public service activities by their institutions. From time to time they need personally to lead such efforts.

My observation has been that universities do not mesh easily with other dissimilar organizations. It may take the authority and involvement of the president or chief academic officer to remove barriers within the university and to keep a cooperative effort with an external group moving forward.

Also, the authority of the president or chief academic officer is sometimes necessary in order to pull together the disparate elements of the university that need to be involved in a project. For example, at my institution the chancellor (president) personally led the aforementioned study of the state Department of Education. The provost (chief academic officer) led a year-long study of the troubled public school system of the City of Little Rock, a study involving a core interdisciplinary group of nine faculty members that tapped expertise of a variety of other faculty and staff members on campus as needed (Anderson *et al.*, 1997). These two institutional projects made significant demands on the time of the chancellor and provost, but it is difficult to imagine that either project would have been done as well without the advantages that came with the authority of the project leaders. This may be a constraint in urban outreach that we do not learn by studying the land-grant experience.

There is a final lesson that we should learn from the land-grant experience, yet one rarely finds it mentioned in the literature about metropolitan universities. The county governments helped to fund the infrastructure of the cooperative extension service. While a greater amount of money was contributed by the federal and state governments, the fact that the county government helped with funding gave extension personnel incentive to stay in touch and be responsive to the concerns of local officials. It also meant that county officials indeed had a claim on the service of the county extension agents and were not reluctant to ask for it.

Metropolitan universities have been reluctant to ask for financial support from the local governments in their metropolitan areas. In my judgement metropolitan universities should begin long-term efforts to secure such support. Not only would it give the universities greater financial strength, which in turn would enable them to make their intellectual resources more readily available to the community, but also it would cause the university and the local governments to know each other better and to expect more of each other. As we strive to shape and prepare our institutions for the new century, the proposition that partial funding by local governments should be sought by the metropolitan universities, needs to be taken seriously.

Conclusion

Our universities, no less than other institutions, need to adapt to changing times and circumstances. Their usefulness and, therefore, their survival depend on it. I believe our universities will be successful in adapting if we exhibit a fundamental commitment to meeting the needs of the people. If we are committed to serving their needs and not ours, it will keep us alert and push us to change as the years pass. In an earlier day the land-grant universities showed such a commitment to a remarkable degree and organized their resources in such fashion as to make it possible for them to meet the needs of the people they were meant to serve.

To an impressive degree, the metropolitan universities are committed to serving the people of their metropolitan areas with more than just instructional programmes. They are also committed to making the remarkable resources of a university campus available to solve problems or otherwise elevate the life of the community. They have not had an easy time of it. Obstacles have been numerous and significant. Yet there is a growing number of metropolitan universities, each a laboratory in which experience is being gained in carrying out their ambitious missions. They are making a habit of watching each other and sharing their experiences.

All colleges and universities could find it instructive to watch the urban/metropolitan universities in the United States in order to learn how to reach out and link people to research in the twenty-first century.

Acknowledgements

Appreciation for research assistance is expressed to Jim Lynch, Senior Research Specialist, and Robin L. Wilson, Research Assistant, in the UALR Institute of Government.

Notes

1. This declaration appears with an invitation to join the Coalition of Urban and Metropolitan Universities in each issue of the journal *Metropolitan Universities*. The publisher of the journal may be addressed as follows: Marilyn Matson, Publisher, *Metropolitan Universities*, Towson University, 7800 York Road, Towson, Maryland 21252-7097.
2. The journal *Metropolitan Universities* frequently has devoted a full number to a single topic with particular attention to the role of the metropolitan universities. For example, full numbers, with volume and number cited here, have been devoted to the public schools 2(1) and 5(2); regional development 2(3 and 4); urban studies and

urban centres 5(4); public health 6(2); university-community partnerships 6(3). Also, the issue of faculty roles and rewards at metropolitan universities received significant attention in 5(1), 7(4) and 8(1).
3. See the descriptions of exemplary programmes provided to participants at the conference, 'The New Realities: Challenge and Response', Third Conference of Urban and Metropolitan Universities, University of Arkansas at Little Rock, Little Rock, Arkansas, 19–21 March 1995. Entitled 'Neighborhood Revitalization', the description of the University of Missouri at Kansas City programme was provided by Lucinda Ellison Lu.
4. Ibid. Entitled 'College of Fine Arts Institute', the description of the programme at Wichita State University was provided by Wendy Hanes and Kathy Holm.
5. Ibid. Entitled 'Georgia State University Tax Clinic', the description of the Georgia State University programme was provided by Michael Baxter.

References

Anderson, J., Briscoe, D., Chamberlin, G., Davis, P., Gitchel, W., Lynch, J., Sewall, A., Terry, A. and Wood, D. (1997) *Plain Talk: The Future of Little Rock's Public Schools*. Little Rock, AR: University of Arkansas at Little Rock.

Boyer, E. L. (1990) *Scholarship Reconsidered: Priorities of the Professoriate*. Princeton, NJ: The Carnegie Foundation for the Advancement of Teaching.

Campbell, J. R. (1995) *Reclaiming a Lost Heritage*. Ames, IA: Iowa State University Press.

Rasmussen, W. D. (1989) *Taking the University to the People: Seventy-Five Years of Cooperative Extension*. Ames, IA: Iowa State University Press.

UALR 2000 Oversight Committee (1994) *Expectations for a Metropolitan University: Interim Report of the Oversight Committee, UALR 2000*. Little Rock, AR: University of Arkansas at Little Rock.

University of Arkansas at Little Rock (1996) *A Study of the Arkansas Department of Education*. Little Rock, AR: UALR.

Part 3

Governance

Management, leadership, administration, collegiality, bureaucracy, participation, autonomy, accountability are key words to be found in the six chapters of Part 3. Authors have concentrated on different levels of governance and decision making – departmental, institutional and system – and it is clear from their contributions that power is shifting between levels, that the balance between internal and external steerage (and the links between them) is changing, and that new tools (e.g. quality assurance, information technology) are being deployed to support decision making. In a situation of considerable turbulence, the relative absence of success criteria except at departmental levels is a noteworthy feature of discussions of governance.

Leadership at the departmental level is the subject of Chapter 10. Drawing on a study of seven departments in Swedish universities, Bennich-Björkman considers the factors that make for successful departments. Leadership, a sense of mission, an intellectual community, a focused research agenda are all associated with success. In contrast, individualism, management rather than leadership, an absence of community, are characteristic of less successful departments.

In this study, success is defined in terms of reputation, with a particular emphasis on international reputation. But it is more than the sum total of the reputations of individual academics. Are academic freedoms compromised by strong leadership where individual interests are subjugated to collective purposes? For Bennich-Björkman, such compromise is a necessary prerequisite for departmental success.

In Chapter 11, de Boer addresses governance and management at the institutional level in Dutch universities. He describes the 'participatory revolution' of the 1970s and a 'managerial revolution' of the 1990s. Both, he believes, have led to greater politicization and bureaucratization of decision making and a decline in professorial authority.

Current modes of governance in Dutch universities are set by new legislation that came into law in 1997. Thus, academic freedoms and their limitation are essentially 'set' for the universities by external authorities. The rise of the evaluative state and an increased marketization are among the external factors that have shaped internal university governance and decision making. If these can be described as 'managerialism', the term requires critical scrutiny in relation to the realities within institutions. As de Boer contends, although managerialism may not necessarily shift power towards managers, it may give academics new opportunities and discretion, new ways of 'playing political games', 'cosmetic' change with adherence to old values.

National policy making in a federal state and its implications for individual universities is the subject of Chapter 12. Perellon discusses recent changes in Swiss higher education in terms of four 'transformations': spatial transformations (involving merger of institutions); funding (contingent on structural change); accountability (new evaluation procedures); governance (more executive-level decision making). The capacity of individual universities to contest and obstruct the implementation of 'top–down' change is clear from Perellon's examples of what has actually happened in relation to these policies.

Chapter 12 serves to remind us of the gap that exists between the policy and practice of governance in many countries and how the authority of different levels of governance are interlinked. In particular, changing relationships between the universities and the state have implications for the locus of authority within universities, with an executive level of institutional authority taking over powers from professorial and basic unit levels.

In a chapter which examines the changes that have occurred in university systems in central and eastern Europe, Darvas places particular attention on the emergence of strong institutional actors, managerial and professional/academic, in steering processes of change. He also points to the diversity of developments in the region and rejects the notion of a single line of (western-shaped) development. A multiplicity of interests and actors, a restricted role for government, and the emergence of intermediary or buffer organizations are described.

Darvas reminds us of the success with which universities in central and eastern Europe preserved their autonomy under restrictive political regimes. He asks whether this power of academia will be used for conservative or radical purposes in the future.

The processes of governance, rather than its structures and interests, are the focus of Nedwek's chapter and its concerns with the implications of information technology. He describes a familiar context of quality, accountability and institutional effectiveness dominating policy agendas and a surrounding climate of confusion and scepticism, both inside and outside the universities.

Nedwek argues that the application of information technology is able to enhance the productivity of all parts of the university. In so doing, tasks and roles are redefined. Collaboration with organizations beyond the university becomes the norm. Traditional university values of academic disciplines and peer review may give way to increased entrepreneurship and independence. Greater choice, independence and responsibility for learners is but part of the changing distribution of institutional power in these circumstances.

The final chapter in this Part examines the Scottish Higher Education Funding Council's (SHEFC) perspective on the role of the governing body of a higher education institution in securing the appropriate balance between institutional autonomy and accountability for the use of public funds. Sizer and Cannon consider the framework of accountability within which institutions operate and draw contrasts with the recommendations of the Steering Committee for Efficiency Studies (The Jarratt Report) in the UK in 1985 and the Higher Education Management Review (The Hoare Report) in Australia in 1995. The authors present SHEFC's view on the role of the governing body in determining the strategic direction of the institution and the effective monitoring and implementation of this by the executive management of the institution.

10

Why Universities Need Leaders: The Importance of Departmental Leadership

Li Bennich-Björkman

Introduction

The struggle for excellence is a major concern for academic institutions, in teaching as well as in research. These primary tasks are performed at the 'bottom' of the academic hierarchy: at the departments, institutes or by whatever name the basic units are addressed in different national settings. Looking at these primary units, it is possible to identify a large variation in the quality of the research and teaching. How can these differences be explained? Is it merely a question of individual qualities, or are there institutional conditions that determine performance to a certain extent? In other words, can we find organizational characteristics which seem conducive to excellence in research and teaching? This chapter contributes to the crucial question on what makes some departments provide excellent research and teaching while others do not. The focus is on relating differences in academic performance on the departmental level to variations in steering, control and leadership. It is argued, on the basis of empirical results from a study on Swedish university departments (Bennich-Björkman, 1998), that there indeed exists a strong relationship between the presence of a visible and marked intellectual and organizational leadership and academic performance.

A crucial issue to explore further, underpinned by the conclusions in this chapter, is thus the subtle balance between the necessary individual freedom for scholars and graduate students on the one hand and the equally essential leadership and community structure on the other. There is definitely a need for universities to pose more openly questions regarding the balancing of individualism and community so that organizations conducive to excellence in research and teaching can be encouraged and created.

Why is the focus on departments crucial?

Academic freedom, interpreted as a right freely to select areas for research without being subjected to political or other external demands, has historically been highly cherished and safeguarded (Hagstrom, 1965). However, modern universities are no longer the exclusive elite institutions of the nineteenth and the first half of the twentieth century, with opportunities for face-to-face contact between students and professors. More than anything, today's universities – in Europe, in the US and in Japan – are large organizations that aim to offer higher education on a mass level, while still conducting advanced research and providing research training (Clark, 1983, 1995). The major changes in the last decades in the social and economic conditions influencing the universities – most of all the transition from an industrial to a post-industrial society – have introduced new challenges for the higher education sector. Undergraduate teaching has expanded tremendously, and graduate education has followed suit. Consequently, the essential questions of balancing community, leadership and traditional academic freedom have successively made their way onto the agenda.

Today, leadership in other areas of society is a much discussed phenomenon. In private organizations, in corporations, public authorities and in bureaucracies (Wilson, 1989), an intensified focus on leadership is a significant characteristic, driving a fast-growing budget for leadership training, management courses and (not least) sophisticated recruitment procedures. In academic settings, however, the debate seems rather unfocused and limited, if not non-existent. Is leadership in academia different, therefore, from leadership in other formal organizations? The core activities of academia differ from bureaucracies in that what is undertaken is not a rule-performing activity, subject to direction (Eriksson, 1997). The academic environment, again, is not the same as its corporate equivalent. University research is basically a non-profit-making activity. Individual academic freedom is highly cherished as an operational, historic and generic feature; autonomy is a touchstone of academic life.

However, not even in higher education have the tendencies towards greater emphasis on leadership passed totally unnoticed. An awakening interest in the quality and content of academic leadership has, above all, made assessment of and demands on the higher levels of the system commonplace, underscoring the need for strategic decision making and more initiative (Trow, 1984). The preoccupation with issues of academic leadership, however, often grinds to a halt when we approach the basic units of the international academic system, namely the departments (Eriksson, 1997). That is all the more strange, since it is in the departments that research and teaching – which constitute the *raison d'être* for universities – takes place.

Furthermore, it is no secret that even individual departments possessing equal resources perform their tasks with varying success. While some perform excellently, producing research of high quality and constantly attracting hordes of talented new students, others muddle through with great difficulty, surviving but not being able to turn vicious into more virtuous circles. Although such a pattern can be recognized in almost every university, historically there has been a great (and in one sense justified) reluctance to interfere in the affairs of departments, or even to use differences between them as a point of departure for more genuine and open self-criticism. The reason for this is most obviously to be found in the traditionally enjoyed autonomy on the part of professors and academic teachers. Collegial decision making, in combination with a far-reaching respect for academic freedom and professional autonomy, has contributed to a 'hands-off' attitude. Most significantly, governments historically have kept a distance; their conduct has been partly based on the idea of universities as an independent 'power' in an intricate system of checks and balances.

The last decades have, however, witnessed something of a revolution in the relationship between governments and universities throughout Europe, particularly in Britain (Clark, 1995; Tvede and Kyvik, 1996), but definitely changing the traditional conditions in other national higher education systems as well, Sweden included. One reason, among many, for this move towards more regulative and 'active' government control and surveillance is to be found in a growing lack of trust in the universities' own capacities to safeguard quality and excellence in the era of the mass university (Trow, 1994; Bennich-Björkman, 1998). Not least, this present state of affairs – which needless to say in a long-term perspective may prove to be quite harmful to the inner life of universities – is driving a closer interest in how excellence is cultivated at the basic level. In order for universities to recover initiative and develop evaluative practices, the mechanisms and processes that sustain excellent teaching and research at the basic level should be given more focused attention.

The focus of this chapter is solely on the question of how organization and leadership affect performance at the departmental level. Empirical data from a recently completed study on institutional differences between excellent and stagnant departments in Sweden form the basis for a discussion on how leadership at the basic level can make a crucial difference.

The study was conducted in a Swedish context, investigating the intellectual and social life of seven university departments in three social science disciplines: ethnogeography, psychology and economics. Four of the departments – one in ethnogeography, one in psychology and two in economics – were identified as innovative research (and teaching) establishments, while the remaining three – one in each of the three disciplines – were considered as stagnant. The selection of the departments was made through a reputational method. A large number of active scholars in the three disciplines were asked to select departments or persons they considered to be innovative or creative. The organization and 'climate' of the seven departments picked out was then investigated through semi-structured interviews with graduate students, lecturers and professors. Approximately 150 persons were interviewed during the field work.

For the sake of simplicity, the innovative departments will henceforth be addressed as the A departments, while the stagnant ones will be referred to as B departments.

Regarding department size and gender balance, the seven departments are not very different from each other. They are all medium-sized organizations, with a staff ranging from 15 to 20, and a stock of active graduate students of between 20 and 401. Among the faculty there is a pronounced male dominance in all the departments, while women comprise the majority of the graduate students.

Economic resources for research and research training vary, but not as much or as systematically as might be expected from the difference in 'output'. While the A departments have rather generous faculty grants and support from external sources and research councils, that is also true of at least one of the B departments, which is quite well-off. Instead, the factor discriminating most between the groups of A and B departments is mobility among the faculty. The A departments generally have a more mobile faculty (except for department A1). Academic mobility in the Swedish context is usually low, so these statistical 'hard' factors do not take us very far in explaining differences in performance. Instead, let us turn to the more 'soft' variables of organizational climate, leadership styles and norms.

Is organization and leadership a crucial factor?

As organizations, universities are 'bottom-heavy' (Clark, 1983: 1). But does leadership at the department level differ that much? It is not an unreasonable objection, since the departments in the study are part of one still unified, state-controlled body. Beyond the departmental level lies the faculty boards. Beyond that stands top university management; ultimately, universities are subject to political authority too. However, the profound differences found between the seven departments forming the core of the inquiry – and that includes departments which were sometimes parts of the same university – give us reason to suspect that the internal organization differences could be largely responsible. One of the internal factors which appears as a key variable is leadership. 'Leadership' will here be defined as incorporating a qualitative dimension, as opposed to 'management', which refers more to formally appointed positions (Eriksson, 1997).

A leadership presence is a crucial characteristic of the innovative departments, while its absence signifies the stagnant ones. Furthermore, the innovative and the stagnant groups differ with regard both to the presence of administrative leadership and the way that it is exercised. While the A departments possess a strong organizational leadership, it is typical of the stagnant departments that they have appointed 'managers', but lack leaders. Also the innovative research environments in the study combine this organizational leadership with marked intellectual authority. However, 'authority' in this context should be clearly distinguished from authoritarian rule. Authority, as defined here, is clear and visible – even explicit – intellectual leadership exercised by one, a few or many of the senior members in a research environment. However, it should not be understood as a repressive leadership in the sense

that it demands obedience to certain views or opinions, as is commonly understood by authoritarian rule. On the other hand, it is not a tolerant leadership
either, if that is understood to be a willingness to accept most perspectives and
views. Intellectual authority as exercised in the A departments could be defined
as the holding of clearly expressed, underpinned and competent views by the
senior members, while not demanding obedience.

Another concern that falls within the realm of a general discussion of leadership is on what grounds status and recognition is acquired in the A and B departments respectively. In other words, what is the appropriate overall authority
structure? The different ways that the departmental hierarchy is constructed
and sustained reveal profound differences in recognition patterns between the
innovative and the stagnant departments. It is sometimes claimed that creativity presupposes horizontal relations; in other words, that what is required is
actually a lack of hierarchy. In contrast, the pattern emerging here indicates
that hierarchy is part of the successful, as well as of the unsuccessful, research
environment. The distinction instead is on what grounds the hierarchical patterns are built. While the innovative departments present hierarchical patterns
built on *competence*, a professional authority (Blau, 1994), the stagnant ones
uphold *positional* (or in Blau's terminology, bureaucratic) hierarchies. Status
and recognition could thus be distributed according to – at least – two different
logics. The junior members of the innovative departments experience a hierarchy primarily based on respect for the specialized knowledge and competence possessed by the seniors. In contrast, the junior members and the
graduate students in the stagnant departments observe a hierarchy grown out
of formal position in the system. Putting it differently, the distinction could be
described as one between intellectual and positional recognition.

Constructing a mission

In the study, four departments were identified as innovative and three as stagnant. There are significant similarities between the leaders of the four successful departments. At all four departments, the leaders have been able to define
and pursue a common purpose for the department. Burton Clark's seminal
concept of the 'organizational saga' as a unifying force in excellent colleges
(Clark, 1992/1970), as well as the partly deliberate creation of corporate cultures (Deal and Kennedy, 1982), comes to mind. The leaders are described by
the members as providing them with a sense of belonging to a community and
of being part of the collective that is the department. This community also has
a purpose in which all the members unite. In other studies, such a sense of purpose has sometimes been labelled a 'mission' (Deal and Kennedy, 1982).

The actual content of the 'mission' varies between the departments. In some,
there is a common striving for the department (not just individuals) to acquire
an international reputation. That implies both publishing in the most prestigious journals and also being frequently cited, thus making a mark in the international scholarly community. This may seem self-evident, but in a small

country like Sweden an international orientation is not always easy, since the national scene is an alternative to international publication. For one of the A departments, the 'mission' is mostly referred to as an explicit ambition to contribute new perspectives and a new direction to the discipline. In other words, the members of this department regard the contribution to disciplinary renewal as their common aim.

The sentiments of a common purpose are most clearly encouraged and developed in two of the four departments, where one of the members states that 'the consensus about what the department wants to be – an excellent research institute – is very crucial'. A question to be asked is, in a potentially individualistic environment like the university, how is it possible to create and sustain such feelings of collective sharing? Before attempting to provide a tentative answer, the situation at the B departments will briefly be considered.

In contrast to the A departments, the B departments have 'managers' – in the sense of formally appointed supervisors – but hardly leaders. There is likewise a lack of any commonly shared ambitions or aims; very few of the members in the B departments are able to identify any kind of unifying corporate 'glue'. Instead, a significant feature of these departments is that many of the members are strongly individualistic: 'Everybody does their own thing' sums up their point of view.

The creation of intellectual community

We now move on to another characteristic that unites the A departments: it is not through magic that they are able to create widespread feelings of belonging among their members. It is achieved mainly because there is a striving, through different means, to create a sense of intellectual community. A department, an academic research and teaching environment, is much more a result of its leadership than just a collection of academic scholars working on their individual pieces and careers. It is, and must be created to be, an arena for intellectual and scholarly collaboration evolving around mutually shared research interests and topics. Consequently, the A departments are departments where there exists a limited research agenda; their research is focused on a limited number of topics in which they more or less could be said to specialize. Obviously, from the perspective of the individual scholar or graduate student this restricts the freedom to select research problems completely freely. While still possessing some room for individual choice, *disciplined individualism* is imposed and expected. Even though there are no formal restrictions on the selection of research topics, there is anyway a clear tendency to direct (for example) graduate students to topics and problems where the department already possesses a certain competence. Putting it differently, the research profiles of the senior members constitute a structural limitation on graduates' choices of topics.

Furthermore, the A departments are academic establishments where the senior members share basic theoretical and/or methodological perspectives. Since there exists a shared basic framework, collaboration is greatly facilitated.

Universities (as well as departments and individuals) obviously intensely defend their autonomy and academic freedom; this has tended to make academic leadership a highly sensitive issue. In some academic environments the idea of it has been subjected to far-reaching scepticism and scorn. That is the case in the B departments, where the notion of direction (in the sense of gathering scholars around certain common themes or clearly identifying a research profile for the department) is strongly rejected. Neither a leadership by the full professors nor a more collective leadership from the graduate students is recognized as legitimate in the eyes of the faculty of the B departments. While the full professors play – in particular in comparison to their counterparts in the A departments – a minor role in research matters, the graduate students' selection of research topics is quite unrestricted. They receive few or no signals indicating areas or topics of specific interest to the department or where the senior members would be expected to have an accumulated competence. On the contrary, they are encouraged to seek out as little guidance as possible in this crucial phase of graduate education, in order to safeguard their independence of mind and integrity. Freedom, independence and autonomy are the values that are safeguarded, while leadership, steering and control are strongly repudiated. This *radical individualism* is a prominent characteristic of the B departments' organization. A further, and serious, consequence of this lack of intellectual leadership in the B departments is their failure to establish well-functioning intellectual forums; in other words, to establish seminars. In order to mould a group identity, arenas for meetings and discussion have to be provided; through such mechanisms an intellectual and social glue is created that benefits the environment. For such a glue to become efficient and strong enough, there is most probably a need for a minimum level of mutual research interests. The lack of any joint intellectual direction or leadership in the B departments creates a logic where the disparity between research interests becomes too wide, so that such a minimum level, or threshold, is not reached.

In the A departments, an intellectual leadership – both individually and on a more collective basis – is developed and visible. There exists a belief – for some, a strong conviction – among the professors in these departments that specialization – a limited research agenda – is conducive to high quality, and in the longer run, to creativity.

The organizational leadership

In all the innovative departments it is possible to identify organizational entrepreneurs. In some cases, they are the same as the major intellectual leaders, but not always. Characteristic of these organizational entrepreneurs is their genuine concern and interest in the way that the departments as organizations work. 'When you create an organization, you must think about the purposes you should aim for together. Our goal is very explicit. Our purpose is to conduct research on an international level and not to preoccupy ourselves with national publication', explains the director of department A4. It is also significant that these leaders are themselves mentally prepared and ready to take on the role as leader. When asked, in contrast to the formally elected managers of the B departments, they positively confirm their position as leaders. A common denominator among the directors of the innovative departments is their ability to conceive of their units as agencies of a common purpose rather than as a looser framework for individual plans and ambitions. The organizational leaders in the A departments regard it as challenging and highly worthwhile to experiment with different organizational solutions, and these directors also radiate a fascination with the prospect of creating and forming institutions.

Another significant feature of what can be called an organizational leadership in the innovative departments is the ability of the directors and additional leading persons to express genuine and permanent concern for others. This feature is often described by the members of the departments in terms emphasizing that the leaders are involved in a disinterested manner in the department as a whole. One of the leaders is described as being respected for his way of being 'extremely unselfish and altruistic'. Over and over, members return to descriptions of the leaders as caring about the department and those working there, and not only about their own research or career. 'It is quite possible to imagine another kind of leader though, one who merely does his own thing', adds one graduate student.

What about the situation in the B departments? While intellectual authority, as seen above, is avoided, so is organizational leadership. The position as head of administration is hardly used strategically but is regarded as a 'dogsbody' post, which circulates among the senior members and is reluctantly taken on. Rather a typical exclamation originates from the head of administration in department B1, who states that 'I do not have any ideas about [intellectual] leadership – I rather avoid it.' Again, we can return to the a priori scepticism towards authority and leadership embedded in the individualistic tradition; even if persons occupying leading positions in the B departments have organizational ideas and visions, they would be hard to bring into existence since there is a predominating expectation of non-leadership.

Conclusions

Universities need leaders, not only managers. Most of all, leaders are needed at the basic units of the academic system, in the departments. Why is that? First and foremost, without leaders who have organizational vision, the strength and potential inherent in the organizational structure – the possibility that individuals can gain from each other and make use of each other's competence and advantages – are most definitely lost, which shows in the cases of the B departments. Instead of developing these basic units into more communal structures, the apparent risk is that they will stay a collection of loosely linked individual plans and ambitions. Developing departments into something beyond is the great challenge, one that makes the difference between success or mediocrity.

The importance of belief and conviction is not less applicable to the world of scholarly activities than that of corporate or bureaucratic behaviour. The leaders and directors of the A departments have established in the minds of their department's members the conviction that the department derives its purpose from their shared directions and collective identity. A shared awareness of common goals has contributed to making these departments collective rather than merely individual establishments.

The significance of 'singularity of purpose' has been commented upon by Clark as one of the benefits of heading in the same direction. But it is the leader's role to make others share what he or she believes in. The leader or leaders must imbue the minds of the members with perceptions of the department as a totality. The traditional values of autonomy and individualism make such efforts hard to achieve.

In creating a climate that fosters creativity and excellence, the presence of intellectual authority – of intellectual leadership, both individually and collectively – is further determining. A climate that leads to high achievement is closely tied to a clear professionalism and competence, while the extended tolerance and freedom of the B departments, in contrast, seemed to lead to diffuse signals and high levels of uncertainty. In the A departments, senior members with incisive views, which they are willing occasionally to defend openly and in public, convey to younger members the conviction that research carried out in the department is significant and important. Intellectual authority creates meaning, gives purpose to research, nurtures commitment and dedication, instead of the B departments' belief in the relativity of things, encouraged by 'tolerance' and freedom.

Furthermore, the intellectual community created by the drive towards 'specialization' and a limited research agenda in the A departments greatly facilitates collaboration between individual members; both between senior members and between seniors and graduate students. Communication and intellectual interaction are triggered through closeness in research interests, sometimes even leading to beneficial relationships of mutual dependence. In such relations, as is the case in all situations of genuine collaboration, thoughts and ideas have to be confronted and further developed in interaction, which in some happy cases can lead to innovative breakthroughs and scholarly progress.

References

Bennich-Björkman, L. (1998) *Organizing Innovative Research. The Inner Life of University Departments*. Oxford: Elsevier Science.
Blau, P. (1994) *The Organization of Academic Work* (second edition). New Brunswick, NJ: Transaction Publishers.
Clark, B. (1983) The contradictions of change in academic systems, *Higher Education*, 12.
Clark, B. (1992/1970) *The Distinctive College*. New Brunswick, NJ: Transaction Publishers.
Clark, B. (1995) *Places of Inquiry. Research and Advanced Education in Modern Universities*. Berkeley, CA: University of California Press.

Deal, T. E. and Kennedy, A. A. (1982) *Corporate Cultures. The Rites and Rituals of Corporate Life*. Reading, MA: Addison-Wesley.

Eriksson, C. B. (1997) *Akademiskt ledarskap*. Uppsala: Acta Universitatis Upsaliensis.

Hagstrom, W. (1965) *The Scientific Community*. New York: Basic Books.

Trow, M. (1984) Leadership and organization: the case of biology at Berkeley, in R. Premfors (ed.) *Higher Education Organization*. Stockholm: Almqvist and Wiksell.

Trow, M. (1994) Academic reviews and the culture of excellence, in T. Nybom (ed.) *Studies of Higher Education and Research*, vol. 2. Stockholm: The Council for Studies of Higher Education.

Tvede, O. and Kyvik, S. (1996) *Doktorgrader of Forskaropplaering: Internasjonale Erfaringer of Perspektiver. En Sammanlikning av 9 OECD-land*. Olso: Norsk Institutt for Studier av Forskning og Utdanning.

Wilson, J. Q. (1989) *Bureaucracy: What Government Agencies Do and Why They Do It*. New York: Basic Books.

11

Changes in Institutional Governance Structures: The Dutch Case

Harry F. de Boer

Introduction

Unlike many other institutions, universities have shown an ability to adapt to changing conditions. By sticking to the basic values and ideals of scholarship, universities have managed to 'survive' (van Vught, 1995: 194). It is widely believed that this adaptability has resulted from the self-governance of scholars (Nisbet, 1971). 'Self-governance' refers to personal authority (grounded in functionally based expertise) and collegial authority (collective control by a body of peers through norms congenial to the expression of expert judgement – Clark, 1983).

During the last three decades, however, this system of self-governance has come under pressure in many countries. Two 'revolutions' have occurred in western Europe: the first during the late 1960s and early 1970s, and the second in the late 1980s and early 1990s. I will argue that the dominant position full-time professors once had in the traditional collegial structure (or at least in the formal structure) has declined as a consequence of the two revolutions.

The first revolution – labelled here as the 'participation' revolution – set out to change the university authority structure by implying that full-time professors had to share power with other academics, non-academics and students. The second revolution – here referred to as the 'managerial' revolution – seems to want to increase the formal powers of administrators at the expense of academics. It looks like full-time professors may lose another battle. Does a situation in which professors lose (some of) their dominance over the formal authority structure imply that the intrinsic values of scholarship will be undermined? If that is the case, universities may be in jeopardy.

I shall deal with this question by discussing the two major changes in the governance structures of Dutch universities. The first major change in The Netherlands took place around 1970. The second one happened around 1997. First, however, I shall start by discussing the two major changes in a more general way. Then I shall present the Dutch case by describing the participatory style of governance (which existed from 1970 till 1997) and the managerial style of governance (which came in from 1997). In the final section I will make some comments about institutional governance, in particular relating to managerialism.

Participatory governance

The first 'revolution' in The Netherlands, as in many other countries, affecting the traditional authority structure of the academic community, concerns the process of 'democratization'. In most higher education systems in Europe, traditional, consensual relationships within universities were undergoing far-reaching changes. Junior academics, non-academics and students were joining full-time professors on the governing bodies of the university. Representatives of various groups of the academic community were allotted a substantial number of seats in university senates, faculty meetings and other committees within the institutions. Advocates of this participation model of governance employed several different arguments. Some of the motives for participation are better communication and exchange of information, a better use of the available knowledge, experience and expertise, more commitment and less obstruction to the pursuit of goals (Drenth, 1990).

One of the consequences of this shift towards a participatory model of governance was that the academic community became much more a political organization. The various groups of the university community, with their different values and preferences, were given the opportunity to promote their interests. Decision making by consensus based upon shared values was more or less replaced by decision making by negotiation or coalition building.

Another consequence has been that the 'new democracy' has imposed regulation and bureaucratization on (Dutch) university life. Because the concept of bureaucratization is closely related to governance, I will elaborate upon bureaucratization a little further. According to Daalder (1982: 205), universities became the breeding ground *par excellence* of regulations (see also Shils, 1983: 28). Rules, forms and 'channels' had become more prominent; informal understandings and conventions had become less prominent in the administration of universities. Under the 'new democracy' there was now the need to regulate the exercise of powers between bodies that should govern 'together' ('horizontal governance'). Additionally, the new modes of governance have contributed to mountains of paper, described by Daalder (1982: 206) as 'the documentary revolution', leading to a substantial increase in the number of professional administrators.

The introduction of a new governance structure in 1970 was not the only cause of a trend towards bureaucratization. There are other contributing factors as well. There is, for instance, a widespread belief that the increase in higher education has also contributed to the growth of administrative tasks within universities. Such a growth has an impact on governance: collegial governance based upon shared norms becomes more difficult as the size of organizations increases (Tolbert and Stern, 1991).

However, it should be noted that the concept of 'bureaucratization' is rather complicated. Gornitzka *et al.* (1998) make a distinction between academic and administrative bureaucratization within universities. The first refers to the amount of time academics spend on administrative matters; the second concerns the number of administrative positions in relation to other positions. Therefore, not only absolute numbers but also relative numbers (ratio of academics to administrators) should be taken into account in indicating a tendency toward bureaucratization.

Another indication of the growth of bureaucracy in universities nowadays stems from a study on governance structures of 131 institutions in western Europe. This study shows, among other things, that on average about 80 per cent of all the rules and procedures within universities are laid down in regulations. In other words, the degree of formalization – generally seen as a feature of bureaucracies – is rather high (de Boer and Goedegebuure, 1996). Such formalization of rules and procedures contrasts to the less formal procedures feasible in a governance process based upon shared norms.

Bureaucratization may also increase, just because it seems to be reinforcing. According to Shils (1983: 28), 'it is in the nature of bureaucracies to extend themselves. More tasks, quite reasonable tasks are discovered; it then becomes necessary to increase the administrative staff for that purpose. So, at least, it seems to administrators.'

The growth, both in the amount of administrative work and the the number of administrators with their own values and preferences, has caused a pull towards 'rationalization'. Mintzberg (1983) argues, for instance, that administrators will try to 'rationalize' and 'standardize' policy processes, which may be regarded as another feature of bureaucracies. Another development that has had an impact on university governance concerns the growing importance of (strategic) managers within universities. Changes in higher education and society at large affect the internal life of universities and have led to a growing attention to and importance of (strategic) management (see, for instance, Dill and Peterson Helm, 1988; Neave and van Vught, 1991). One of the questions coming to the fore concerns the validity of traditional conceptions of 'shared authority' in the rapidly changing world of higher education. This brings me to the second revolution in authority structures within universities.

Managerialism

The second attack on the authority structures of the academic community started in the middle of the 1980s. From this time on, governance structures of universities are being debated or revised in many countries (see, among others, de Boer, 1996). Participatory structures were being criticized for their inefficiency (they were slow and cumbersome) as well as in part their ineffectiveness (they were inward-orientated and neglected outside demands). Especially in hard times, universities have difficulty in reaching (strategic) decisions. Typically the problems of the participatory mode of governance are caused by time-consuming decision-making processes, a high level of deliberate avoidance of criticism by any academic unit of another, or the fact that many academic deans anticipate rejoining the faculty, meaning they are reluctant to burn bridges behind them (see, among others, Cole, 1994). Another problem might be that a vast majority of academics focus appropriately on their teaching and research and know little about or show little interest in the economics of the university (Cole, 1994).

Efforts to improve management efficiency seem to be designed to increase the power of administrators (especially vice-chancellors, deans and chief executives) at the expense of academics and students. Many academics fear that the traditional right of professionals to control their work may be stripped away. This new 'revolution' in governance structures appears to move in the direction of 'managerialism'.[1]

According to Pollitt (1990) and Trow (1994: 11), 'managerialism' indicates some kind of ideology, a set of beliefs. It is a new set of assumptions and techniques. It is centred around the idea that good management is essential for any organization – private and public – and, consequently, that managers should be given the 'right to manage'. They should have the freedom to make decisions about the use of organizational resources to achieve desired outcomes. The three Es – economy, efficiency and effectiveness – should be the leading values in the governance and management of public organizations. The key elements for managerialism in general are (Pollitt, 1990; Clarke and Newman, 1997):

- an emphasis on the public, conceived in terms of individual customer choice, with rights to choice and quality;
- the creation of markets and quasi-markets, and the commitment to competition;
- a greater scope for individual and private sector provision: individuals are to become more self-reliant and provide for themselves;
- the separation of the purchaser role from the provider role;
- the growth of contractual or semi-contractual arrangements;
- more emphasis on performance targets and accountability;
- flexibility of pay and conditions.

Not all these elements of the managerial ideology can be found throughout higher education systems to the same extent. In British higher education, for instance, Trow (1994) distinguishes two forms: the *soft* and the *hard* concept of managerialism.

The soft concept sees managerial effectiveness as an important element in the provision of higher education of quality at its lowest cost; it is focused around the idea of improving the 'efficiency' of the existing institutions. The hard conception elevates institutional and system management to a dominant position in higher education; its advocates argue that higher education must be reshaped and reformed by the introduction of management systems which then become a continuing force ensuring the steady improvement in the provision of higher education.

(Trow, 1994: 11)

The soft-liners criticize universities for their complacency, their administrative inefficiency, their indifference to establishing links with industry or to broadening access to the population as a whole. Nevertheless, they hold the opinion that universities should be governed by their own norms and traditions, with a more effective and rationalized management still serving functions defined by the academic community itself. The hard-liners on the other hand do not have this trust in the wisdom of the academic community. They advocate business models of management. They try to transform universities into organizations similar to ordinary commercial firms so that they can be assessed and managed in roughly similar ways. Middlehurst (1995: 85) gives a more neutral description of 'managerialism' as

> making decisions and designing systems of control and cooperation that direct the work of others so that compliance with policy and directives is assured. Leadership is ascribed to the individual (or small group) at the apex of a hierarchy, who is assumed to set the tone of the organization and to establish its official objectives.

A common feature of managerialism in higher education is the government's withdrawal of trust in the academic community to manage the university efficiently and effectively. Though this kind of 'corporate rationality' (Neave and van Vught, 1991: 242–4) is nowadays rather old fashioned in the corporate world, it sets the tone in higher education. The result of tighter management, meaning a partial repudiation of collegiality, may be that universities move much closer to an industrial pattern of organization, with senior management teams and strategic plans, line managers and cost centres. Just as universities have moved closer to a corporate model of management, so private corporations have become more collegial; large rigid hierarchies of line managers have tended to be replaced by more loosely coupled networks of team managers (Gibbons *et al.*, 1994). Managerial structures in higher education reflect top–down, line management, with executive power at all levels in the hands of 'individual leaders'. Such a shift is apparently the result of distrust in the capability of academics to administer their own institutions.

Husén (1996: 16) argues that increased centralized government of universities, with detailed control exercised through an administrative hierarchy, leads to conflicts between administrators and academics:

> on one side, we have the insistence on collegial autonomy exercised by scholars whose competence has been thoroughly assessed in peer reviews and, on the other, we have hierarchical decision-making machinery that takes decisions in assemblies constituted by representation of interest groups and executed through a hierarchical administration.

The tendency towards greater directive control, through a line-management structure in order to obtain greater administrative efficiency, tips the balance from academics to administrators. However, one of the main problems is that in a university academics possess the 'line' expertise necessary to evaluate the feasibility of strategic proposals (Dill and Peterson Helm, 1988). Thus, the new mode of governance may increase the inherent tension between bureaucratic authority, derived from organizational position, and professional authority, based on specialized, technical expertise. The managerial revolution not only establishes a much tighter organizational framework, but also creates a managerial entrepreneurialism that competes with as well as complements the academic norms. There seems to be a competition between managerial and academic values for possession of the university's soul (Gibbons *et al.*, 1994). The outcome of the competition is hard to predict. Will there be a winner? Or will there just be losers, in the sense that such a competition will distract attention from the real issues, possibly paralysing the university?

What has caused this 'managerial revolution'? There is ample theoretical and empirical support for the proposition that as the environmental context of an organization alters, there is a pressure for change within the organization, including the structure of authority (Dill and Peterson Helm, 1988). As argued elsewhere (de Boer, 1996), the rules of the game in higher education have changed quite substantially, and these changes in the rules of the game have had an impact on the governance structures of universities.

Probably the most influential change concerns the role of government, or to be more precise, its changed role and the consequences of this shift. A clear trend to be discerned in many European higher education systems since the mid-1980s is that the tasks of central authorities have been reorientated towards *ex post* evaluation and monitoring instead of *ex ante* comprehensive planning. Meek and Goedegebuure (1991) conclude that

> firm beliefs in the virtues of regulation, planning mechanisms, and government co-ordination appear to be replaced by a philosophy in which the government's role is confined more to setting the boundary conditions within which the higher education system is to operate, leaving more room to manoeuvre at the institutional level.

Neave (1988: 11) refers to this process as the 'rise of the evaluative state':

> The Evaluative State is then a rationalization and wholesale redistribution of functions between centre and periphery such that the centre maintains overall strategic control through fewer, but more precise, policy levers, contained in overall mission statements, the setting of system goals and the operationalization of criteria relating to output quality.

This shift in governmental steering paradigms – from the interventionary state to the facilitatory or evaluative state (Neave and van Vught, 1991) – has had profound consequences for higher education. One of the consequences of the withdrawal of the nation-state that is highly relevant to a discussion of institutional governance structures is the 'marketization' of higher education

(Williams, 1995). 'Marketization' in the broadest sense means (among other things) that students have become customers, researchers have become merchants, with more institutional autonomy, new funding mechanisms, multiple sources of income for universities, etc. Marketization has not taken place in every country to the same extent, but in most countries an orientation towards 'the market' began more than two or three decades ago. Consequently, internal resource allocation and financial management have become much more complex (Williams, 1995). According to Williams (1995), academic criteria were once able to determine resource allocation decisions when resources were plentiful, but this is no longer the case. There is a real difference in the planning for growth and the planning for decline. The changing patterns of finance have a clear impact on the increasing managerialism of universities (see also Rasmussen, 1995). Such a conclusion is in line with the observation of Barlow *et al.* (1996) in their study of public managers, namely that economic pressures are one of the most important explanations of the rise of managerialism.

Universities are now operating in an environment of scarcity and competition, which rests uneasily with a participatory mode of governance. The values and the structural mechanisms of the period of growth are now being applied in a new period of a strategic policy making in which academic decision makers must confront the most substantive and divisive issues (Dill and Peterson Helm, 1988). Operating in a (quasi-) market demands quick responses and sometimes hard decisions. Rosenzweig (1994) holds the opinion that hard and divisive problems cannot be dealt with in the absence of strong, risk-taking executive leadership. As competition, conflict and demands for survival increase, decision making tends to become more centralized and less participatory (Zammuto, 1986). In centralized structures leaders can marshal resources rather quickly. The pressures toward managerialism are market driven, economically derived and socially influenced. The salience of managerial norms has increased as environments have become more competitive, complex and turbulent (Goodstein *et al.*, 1996). Competing for students, controlling university costs and research competition have become critical strategic environmental contingencies that have strengthened the desire to increase the power of management.

In sum, changed circumstances – the changed role of the government and, consequently, the marketization of higher education – have put the participatory modes of governance under pressure. These participatory modes of governance were established in periods of prosperity,[2] a situation quite different from higher education in the 1990s. Strategic decision making combines with managerialism quite well (when compared with participatory governance). Moreover, competition emphasizes efficiency, which is clearly linked to the philosophy of managerialism. Shifts in the competitive environment of universities, mainly caused by a change of the role of government, have increased the relative importance of managerial norms that emphasize rationality, efficiency, management of uncertainty and the desire for greater flexibility.

To elucidate the differences between the two concepts of governance, in the next two sections the 'old' governance structure (an example of participatory governance) and the 'new' governance structure of Dutch universities (an example of managerial governance) are described.

The participatory governance structure of Dutch universities (1970–97)

Following campaigns during the 1960s to democratize the universities, the governance structure of Dutch universities was prescribed in national law for higher education (Act of Higher Education and Scientific Research; Dutch abbreviation 'WHW'), with its origins in the 1970 University Governance Reorganization Act. The main formal governing bodies of Dutch universities are described in the WHW.

At the *central* level there are several actors: the university council, the executive board, the rector magnificus and the board of deans. The *university council* is a representative body and consists of 25 members drawn from the university community: at least one-third are academics, a maximum one-third are non-academic staff, and a maximum one-third are students. The number of council members may be extended by a maximum of five external lay members. All members, the lay persons excluded, are elected by and among the university community. Members serve for at least a two-year period, except for students who serve for a one-year period. The meetings of the university council are public. The chair of council is elected from its own members.

The university council has the final say on the budget, institutional plans, annual reports, general academic procedures, and rules and regulations. The authority of the council is stipulated in national law. Some responsibilities are delegated to sub-committees.

The *executive board* consists of three members: the rector magnificus who is a member ex officio, and two appointed members. All three persons are appointed by the minister of Education, Culture and Science. Though here the mechanism for appointment is not election but selection, the university community (especially the board of deans – see below – and the university council) have the right to place nominations before the minister. The meetings of the executive board are not public, though the board reports to government.

According to the WHW, all powers are assigned to the executive board at the university level except powers specifically assigned to the university council. The main functions of the executive board concern policy design, financial advice, building and grounds, personnel matters and policy implementation. The executive board and the university council govern the university.

The *board of deans* is composed of the deans of the faculties and chaired by the rector magnificus. The board of deans has mainly advisory powers relating to teaching and research. Apart from its role in nominating the rector magnificus, its chief function is the granting of doctoral degrees.

The second level of governance within a Dutch university is at the *faculty level*. At this level the following main actors can be distinguished: the faculty board, the faculty council, the dean, and two standing committees: the 'research committee' and the 'education committee'. The role of the faculty board and the faculty council and the relationship between them is similar to that at the central level for the council and the executive board, though of course decisions at this level concern faculty matters.

The *faculty board* is the executive body at faculty level and consists of a maximum of five persons. The dean holds the chair. The majority of board members are academics. The faculty board has the authority to administer the faculty except for those responsibilities which are the province of the faculty council. The faculty board is accountable to both the faculty council and the university-wide executive board, which it has the right to advise.

The *faculty council* consists of a maximum of 15 persons, of whom at least half are academics. Remaining members are non-academic staff and students. As at the central level, the faculty council can extend its membership by the appointment of five lay persons. One of its main duties is approval of the faculty budget. The faculty council may delegate some of its responsibilities to the faculty board. The *dean* chairs both the faculty board and council and is elected by the faculty council from the full-time professors of the faculty. In most cases the dean is in office for two or three years.

The members of the *education committee* are appointed by the faculty council. Half of the members are students. This committee has advisory powers for faculty teaching programmes and it evaluates examination procedures annually. The *research committee* is also appointed by the faculty council and it has a majority of academic members. This committee has advisory powers for the design and implementation of faculty research programmes.

At the *base unit level* – the third level of governance – the 'disciplinary research group' (DRG; *vakgroep*) is an important governing body. These DRGs are small clusters of professors and their assistants working in the same disciplinary area. However, the members of the DRGs are not only academics, but may also include non-academic staff and students. Procedural rules of the DRG are determined by the faculty council and faculty board. Their main functions are the design of study and research programmes. The proposals of the DRGs have to be approved by the faculty council. The DRGs are accountable to the faculty board.

For line management or administrative structures (i.e. supporting activities like finance, personnel, public relations, etc.), the executive board is responsible. At both the central and faculty levels, administrative units exist. Generally speaking, at the central level the administrative units are part of the realm of the *secretary* of the university. At the faculty level, commonly there is a chief executive officer responsible for the administrative units (though the executive board may decide to give the management authorities to the dean). Management authorities cannot be delegated or attributed, only mandated. This means that in the end the executive board is accountable, not the secretary or the other executive officers.

A new governance structure for Dutch universities

Beginning in the late 1970s and throughout the 1980s, a number of criticisms were directed at the way Dutch universities were governed and managed. Government reports as well as individual commentators noted that the system was based on an unstable balance of power between the university council and the executive board, and this created a good deal of suspicion and hostility between the two bodies (Polak Committee, 1979). Other claimed inefficiencies included ineffective articulation of decision making between governing bodies at all levels within the university, slow and cumbersome decision-making procedures, confusion over delegation of responsibilities and authority to the various governing bodies, and an unhealthy tension between management responsibility and academic authority (Daalder, 1982; Drenth, 1990; Netherlands Scientific Council for Government Policy, 1995). But it was not until 1995 that successful initiatives were displayed to change the governance and management structure of Dutch universities. The so-called Steering Group on Quality and Study Capability identified six main problems concerning the participatory governance structure of Dutch universities:[3]

- the governance structure is inadequate for the organization of teaching;
- responsibilities for teaching are not clear. Because of the collective mode of decision making, no individual seems to feel responsible. Also, the structure appears to be highly fragmented;
- the formal separation of powers (between governance and management), especially at the faculty level, is unsatisfactory;
- as a result of the second and third points it is difficult to ascertain who is accountable for the quality of teaching;
- the strong orientation towards research at the expense of teaching has a negative impact on the latter;
- coherence and communication among the various levels is inadequate, which is in part the result of the ambiguous separation of powers between the key academic decision-making units.

The report of the Steering Group and other criticisms of the way Dutch universities have been governed and managed led to the Bill concerning the governance structure of universities. In the summer of 1995 the minister of Education, Culture and Science introduced the Bill – Modernizing Universities Governance Structure (Dutch abbreviation 'MUB') – which formally became law in March 1997.

In the explanatory memorandum attached to the Bill, the minister of Education, Culture and Science stated that a modernization of the governance structure of universities is a prerequisite for improving the quality of the primary processes (i.e. teaching and research). Another reason for fundamental change in institutional governance structures concerned the desire to strengthen the decision-making power of the university as a whole, while decreasing the overall burden of governance and management. The minister argued that the reforms would promote both efficiency and effectiveness.

According to the minister, the new governing structure coincided with the overall government steering strategy to enhance institutional autonomy. It was argued that the new university governance structure offered a good opportunity for the universities to fulfil their tasks in a turbulent environment. The new governance structure was not regarded as an end in itself, but as a means to (a) fulfil the expectations of the institutions' constituencies at large and (b) improve teaching and research.

The MUB leaves ample room for universities to design their own structure within the legal framework (i.e. in comparison with the former Act). The central element in the MUB is the unambiguous assignment of powers and responsibilities, which results in the integration of governance and management competences. Under the previous governance structure it was not always clear who was accountable for what. The new structure focuses more on 'vertical relationships' – that is, on relationships between the central and the faculty levels – while the previous Act stressed 'horizontal relationships'. The main changes in the governance structure of universities are:

- strengthening executive positions vis-à-vis council, at both the central and faculty levels;
- the university and faculty councils will become representative advisory bodies for students and employees instead of 'heavy equipped governing bodies';
- the integration of governance and management/administration. Up to now, governance and management responsibilities have been separated, e.g. council and executive board. The new structure combines governance and management functions in the one body;
- the disciplinary research groups, which up to now were quite powerful, will disappear (at least formally);
- the dean will become the most powerful person at the faculty level;
- a new governing body, the supervisory board, will be introduced (comparable to a 'board of trustees').

At the central level the new structure attempts an unambiguous assignment of competences by investing a great deal of power and responsibility in the executive board. This board consists of three persons who are appointed by the supervisory board. The university council will no longer have decision-making power; one of its most powerful rights – approval of the budget – will be taken away. It will become a representative advisory body to a large extent. It has the right of comment with respect to institutional rules and regulations and important policy documents, such as the strategic plan. The MUB offers two options for the 'new university council': a divided and an undivided advisory body of representatives. Undivided advisory bodies consist of representatives of both employees (50 per cent) and students (50 per cent); a divided system has a separate body for employees and for students. The choice is up to the university. Six universities have decided to install a divided system; seven have decided otherwise.

At the central level a new governing body has been introduced, namely the supervisory board. This body consists of five persons appointed by and accountable to the minister. The most important plans of the university – strategic plans, budget plans, etc. – will be submitted to the supervisory board for approval. The supervisory board will also be the arbitrator when disputes arise between the executive board and the council.

A major change at the base unit level is that disciplinary research groups lose their legal status. They are no longer a formal governing body in the university structure.

The MUB offers two options regarding the executive function at the faculty level. A university may decide to install a faculty executive board or a dean (single-headed leadership). Most universities have chosen this latter option. Within faculties the dean (or faculty executive board) will be the most powerful person (body). S/he is responsible and accountable for the organization of teaching. The dean is appointed by the executive board. The dean does not only have responsibility for the design of courses and other teaching matters, but s/he also has a mandate from the executive board to manage the faculty (including supporting activities like finance and personnel). In contrast to the previous situation, a single person (in most faculties) rather than a representative body will have authority over the faculty.

The faculty council loses most of its powers and becomes an advisory body in which students and employees participate. This council may have a divided or an undivided structure. Disputes between dean and faculty council will be resolved by the executive board.

Discussion

Universities have been very successful institutions for centuries. By sticking to their basic values and ideals, universities as institutions have proved to be resistant to changing conditions, even though there has been much internal change. Traditionally, full-time professors were the heart of the academic community, successfully preserving basic values and ideals. However, in the last three decades two 'revolutions' have affected the dominant position of full-time professors. First, there was the democratization of the governance structure in the early 1970s; recently there has been a shift towards managerialism. To all appearances, full-time professors have lost some of their – formal – power. Does this imply that they are no longer capable of safeguarding the basic values and norms of the university, and if so, does that imply that universities are in jeopardy?

For a number of reasons it is too soon to draw firm conclusions. In this final section I will touch upon some potential consequences of the introduction of managerialism. First of all, the administrative shake-up of universities, which is rather obvious in the Dutch case, might once more rake up the tensions between administrators and academics. This relationship is at the heart of the debates on institutional governance structures; it is a relationship, to use one of Birnbaum's (1989) understatements, that is not always easy. Both administrators and academics hold different – but equally valid – perceptions of reality, more or less sustained by existing authority structures. The simultaneous existence of both a professional and administrative ethos results in a conflict over demands and preferences included in managerial strategy (Bacharach *et al.*, 1991: 219; see Table 11.1). The issue at stake is really one of power: who is the principal and who is the agent?

There are sound arguments that academics should have a say in decision making, because they possess the 'line' expertise necessary to evaluate the feasibility of strategic proposals. It has been argued that especially in complex environments professional experience and expertise becomes critical (Dill and Peterson Helm, 1988). On the other hand, however, what is meant by 'professional' expertise? If it refers not only to knowledge of teaching and research, but to administrative affairs as well, one might be sceptical about the expertise of academics in administration. It is not obviously true that an academic, respected for his or her scholarship, also is an excellent, professional manager.

Another potential effect of the dispersal of managerialism is that it creates 'hybrid' organizations and might have the effect of creating a 'dispersed managerial consciousness', i.e. the embedding of calculative frameworks throughout universities (Clarke and Newman, 1997). It refers to the processes by which

Table 11.1   Managerial strategies

Parameter	Sought out by managers	Sought out by professionals
task	partial; interdependent with other tasks	complete tasks
training	short; on the job; specialized skill	extensive; external; total skill learned
loyalty	to the organization	to the profession
career	ascent in organizational hierarchy	ascent in the professional 'hierarchy'
structure and organization	functional	discipline
project selection	limit individual choice	full choice based on interest and contribution to profession
rules and regulations	accountability/ administrative authority and sanctions/tight control and direction	collegial influence and advice/rituals and ideology
autonomy	underspecification of ends and over-specification of means	extensive autonomy and participation in determination of ends as well as means
supervision	close supervision	general supervision only; professional standards of evaluation

actors come to find their decisions, actions and possibilities framed by the imperatives of managerial coordination: competitive positioning, budgetary control, performance management and efficiency gains. Actors within the institutions are increasingly aware that managerial agendas and the corporate calculus condition their working relationships, conditions and processes.

It should be stressed, however, that the concept of managerialism is rather broad, new and vague, which makes its outcomes highly uncertain. It offers an incomplete set of instructions and incentives to those supposed to implement them, leaving considerable room for judgement and discretion (Clarke and Newman, 1997). Furthermore, instructions and invectives might not only be incomplete, but contradictory as well. Within managerialism, at least three variants can be distinguished (Clarke and Newman, 1997): an efficiency-orientated approach (stressing productivity and managerial control), a market-orientated variant (stressing competition and contracting), and a user-orientated variant (stressing service quality and responsiveness). These variants might all be present in a single university, and can easily produce tensions and dilemmas. For example, audits (performance measures, standards, inspection) potentially – and often actually – conflict with entrepreneurship and the market (flexibility, responsiveness and dynamism). Contracting, tight specification and close monitoring may be in conflict with norms of partnership and collaboration.

Another unintended outcome of the introduction of managerial leadership might be that enhancing the market responsiveness of department units erodes the power of the executives at the central level and the strategic coherence of the university as a whole. Additionally, high levels of internal competition might arise, running the risk of 'tribalism'.

It is far too soon to conclude that managerialism per se tilts the balance of power towards managers. It can also offer professionals new areas of opportunity and discretion, new ways of playing political games. Or it looks as though they play it the way it was intended to, but in essence they stick to old values (cosmetic operations). It is clear therefore that the introduction of a new concept is not just a simple displacement of one concept by another. New concepts are rarely straightforward; change is seldom linear.

Notes

1. An indication for the change can be found in some adjectives used to describe universities: businesslike university, corporate university, adaptive university, enterprise university or entrepreneurial university (Wasser, 1990: 121).
2. Governments spend more on higher education today than ever before, the difference being that before expenditure was on a small elite system, and today it is on a mass system, with a decline in expenditure per head, but not overall.
3. This Steering Group was composed of the minister of Education, Culture and Science (chair), the chairmen of the intermediary organizations VSNU (universities) and HBO-council (polytechnics), representatives of collective student organizations and two civil servants of the ministry.

142 *Harry F. de Boer*

References

Bacharach, S. B., Bamberger, P. and Conley, S. (1991) Negotiating the 'see-saw' of managerial strategy: a resurrection of the study of professionals in organizational theory, in S. B. Bacharach (ed.) *Research in the Sociology of Organizations*. Greenwich: JAI Press.

Barlow, J., Farnham, D., Horton, S. and Ridley, F. F. (1996) Comparing public managers, in D. Farnham, S. Horton, J. Barlow and A. Hondeghem (eds) *New Public Managers in Europe: Public Servants in Transition*. Basingstoke and London: Macmillan.

Birnbaum, R. (1989) Leadership and followership: the cybernetics of university governance, in J. H. Schuster, L. H. Miller and Ass., *Governing Tomorrow's Campus: Perspectives and Agendas*. New York: Macmillan.

Boer, H. F. de (1996) Changing institutional governance structures, in P. A. M. Maassen and F. A. van Vught (eds) *Inside Academia: New Challenges for the Academic Profession*. Utrecht: De Tijdstroom.

Boer, H. F. de and Goedegebuure, L. C. J. (1996) *Bestuursstructuren Vergeleken; Een Internationaal Comparatieve Beschrijving van Bestuursstructuren in Zeven Europese Landen*. Enschede: CHEPS.

Clark, B. R. (1983) *The Higher Education System*. Berkeley, CA: University of California Press.

Clarke, J. and Newman, J. (1997) *The Managerial State: Power, Politics and Ideology in the Remaking of Social Welfare*. London: Sage.

Cole, J. R. (1994) Balancing acts: dilemmas of choice facing research universities, in J. R. Cole, E. G. Barber and S. R. Graubard (eds) *The Research University in a Time of Discontent*. Baltimore, MD and London: The Johns Hopkins University Press.

Daalder, H. (1982) The Netherlands: universities between the 'new democracy' and the 'new management', in H. Daalder and E. Shils (eds) *Universities, Politicians and Bureaucrats: Europe and the United States*. Cambridge: Cambridge University Press.

Dill, D. D. and Peterson Helm, K. (1988) Faculty participation in strategic policy making, in J. C. Smart (ed.) *Higher Education: Handbook of Theory and Research*, vol. IV. New York: Agathon Press.

Drenth, P. J. D. (1990) *Universitaire Democratie, Toen en Nu*, Rede Gehouden ter Gelegenheid van de Opening van Het Academisch Jaar aan de Rijksuniversiteit Limburg, Maastricht, 3 September.

Gibbons, M., Limoges, C., Nowotny, H., Schwartzman, S., Scott, P. and Trow, M. (1994) *The New Production of Knowledge; The Dynamics of Science and Research in Contemporary Societies*. London: Sage.

Goedegebuure, L. C. J. and de Boer, H. F. (1996) Governance and decision-making in higher education; comparative aspects, *Tertiary Education and Management*, 2(2): 160–9.

Goodstein, J., Boeker, W. and Stephan, J. (1996) Professional interests and strategic flexibility: a political perspective on organizational contracting, *Strategic Management Journal*, 17: 577–86.

Gornitzka, A., Kyvik, S. and Marheim Larsen, I. (1998) The bureaucratization of universities, *Minerva*, 36(1): 21–47.

Husén, T. (1996) The idea of the university: changing roles, current crisis and future challenges, in Z. Morsy and P. G. Altbach (eds) *Higher Education in an International Perspective: Critical Issues*. New York/London: Garland Publishing.

Meek, V. L. and Goedegebuure, L. C. J. (1991) Change in higher education: the Australian case, *Australian Educational Researcher*, 16(4): 1–26.

Middlehurst, R. (1995) Changing leadership in universities, in T. Schuller (ed.) *The Changing University?* Buckingham: SRHE and Open University Press.

Mintzberg, H. (1983) *Structure in Fives: Designing Effective Organizations*. Englewood Cliffs, NJ: Prentice-Hall.

Neave, G. (1988) On the cultivation of quality, efficiency and enterprise: an overview of recent trends in higher education in Western Europe, 1986–1988, *European Journal of Education*, 23(1 and 2): 7–23.

Neave, G. and van Vught, F. A. (1991) Conclusion, in G. Neave and F. A. van Vught (eds) *Prometheus Bound; The Changing Relationship Between Government and Higher Education in Western Europe*. Oxford: Pergamon Press.

Netherlands Scientific Council for Government Policy (1995) *Higher Education in Stages*. The Hague: NSCGP.

Nisbet, R. (1971) *The Degradation of the Academic Dogma: The University in America, 1945–1970*. London: Heinemann.

Polak Committee (1979) Gewubd en Gewogen: Evaluatierapport van de tijdelijke wet universitaire bestuurshervorming, *Tweede Kamer* 1978–9, 15: 515.

Pollitt, C. (1990) *Managerialism and the Public Services: Cuts or Cultural Change in the 1990s?* Oxford: Blackwell.

Rasmussen, J. G. (1995) Management in Danish universities: new legislation and organizational change, *Higher Education Management*, 7(3): 335–44.

Rosenzweig, R. M. (1994) Governing the modern university, in J. R. Cole, E. G. Barber and S. R. Graubard (eds) *The Research University in a Time of Discontent*. Baltimore, MD and London: The Johns Hopkins University Press.

Shils, E. (1983) *The Academic Ethic*. Chicago: The University of Chicago Press.

Tolbert, P. S. and Stern, R. N. (1991) Organizations of professionals: governance structures in large law firms, *Research in the Sociology of Organizations*, 8: 97–117.

Trow, M. (1994) Managerialism and the academic profession: the case of England, *Higher Education Policy*, 7(2): 11–18.

Vught, F. van (1995) The new context for academic quality, in D. D. Dill and B. Sporn (eds) *Emerging Patterns of Social Demand and University Reform: Through a Glass Darkly*. Oxford: IAU Press/Elsevier Science.

Wasser, H. (1990) Changes in the European university: from traditional to entrepreneurial, *Higher Education Quarterly*, 44(2): 110–22.

Williams, G. L. (1995) The 'marketization' of higher education: reforms and potential reforms in higher education finance, in D. D. Dill and B. Sporn (eds) *Emerging Patterns of Social Demand and University Reform: Through a Glass Darkly*. Oxford: IAU Press/Elsevier Science.

Zammuto, R. F. (1986) Managing decline in American higher education, in J. C. Smart (ed.) *Higher Education: Handbook of Theory and Research*, vol. II. New York: Agathon Press.

12

Changing the Rules of the Game: The Transformation of Decision-making Patterns in Swiss Universities Since the Early 1990s

Juan-Francisco Perellon

Introduction

Swiss higher education is at a crossroads and faces perhaps its most important challenge in recent years. A new political and economic context has opened a 'policy window' that should permit the reconstruction of the entire tertiary education system. As we will see, the 1990s appear to be the crucial moment for the introduction of fundamental reforms. But it would be wrong to suppose that present changes are the product of the 1990s. As has already been shown (Leresche *et al.*, 1996; Perellon, 1998b), the social and intellectual referents underlying the current transformations have been building up since the mid-1960s. Therefore the present changes can only be completely understood through a sociohistorical analysis (Perellon, 1998a).

Furthermore, it is worth noting that the proposals to transform the system have mainly come from the various central bodies charged with the redefinition of university policy. This top–down implementation of change has provoked some opposition at the lower level of individual institutions. As a consequence, the form that the new Swiss higher education policy will take, especially concerning the universities, will largely be the result of the reaction – positive or negative – of academia itself.

Finally, another important element in the current changes in Swiss universities is the role played by the political structure of the country. Federalism imposes an unusual mode of task sharing between the federal government and the cantons. As far as higher education is concerned, universities are under the direct financial and political responsibility of the cantons. But the federal authorities have also partially contributed to their funding since 1968. On the other hand, the federal government is in charge of the federal institutes of technology, which are especially related to the instruction of technical and engineering sciences. This constitutes the dual structure of Swiss higher education. In autumn 1998, the *Fachhochschulen* – higher vocational colleges – will complete Swiss tertiary education and become the 'third way' to higher education in Switzerland.

The central–local division of scientific work has been widely criticized because of the autonomy left to the cantons in the general organization of 'their' universities. In that sense, some political actors have argued for a more rational way of task sharing, one that will take into account the higher education needs and demands of the entire country. Since the early 1970s, the spatial organization of Swiss higher education institutions has been described as irrational and ineffective. Federal government has worked on many suggestions for the creation of a 'Swiss university' that will be able to build the future of higher education; it is now starting to put these proposals into practice.

After a brief presentation of the Swiss higher education system, this chapter focuses on four major transformations that have been suggested for the reorganization of Swiss universities. It also analyses the extent to which these changes have been implemented to date, and explains the main difficulties that have been encountered.

The Swiss higher education system: an overview

A system characterized by elitism

In Switzerland, access to university remains to a large extent the privilege of a small minority. According to OECD figures, only 8 per cent of the adult population holds a university degree, which is one of the lowest rates found among developed countries. Currently, only 13 per cent of those aged 21 (entry age) are enrolled in a university (Office Fédéral de la Statistique, 1995: 65). Nevertheless, it must be underlined that access to higher education in Switzerland is also possible through two other channels – the federal institutes of technology and the new *Fachhochschulen*. In that sense, the wide non-university sector of Swiss higher education registers a higher level of enrolment and, to some extent, provides a more positive picture of access to tertiary level education in Switzerland. Twenty-seven per cent of new entrants were registered in non-university institutions in 1993 (Office Fédéral de la Statistique, 1995: 62); 13 per cent of the population hold a tertiary-level non-academic degree (Conseil Suisse de la Science, 1993).

Types of tertiary level education

Swiss higher education has traditionally been composed of two main channels. The first, the federal institutes of technology (EPF – Ecoles Polytechniques Fédérales), are owned and controlled by the federal government. They focus on natural sciences and are asked to provide knowledge that can be applied to advanced technologies. There are two such institutes, one in Zurich and one in Lausanne.

The second component consists of ten universities. They depend directly on the cantonal authorities and have the task of providing broad academic knowledge. Since 1996 there have been universities in three (German, French and Italian) out of the four linguistic regions of the country.

There are also differences of internal organization between the universities and the federal institutes. The EPFs are to a large extent organized in a similar way to American universities. Federal authorities appoint their president, who is responsible for the internal management and general promotion of the institute. The two EPFs are coordinated by a special board, the Conseil des Ecoles Polytechniques Fédérales (CEPF), whose main task is to organize the division of labour between them. In addition, the board defines general policy and provides a link with the Federal Department of Internal Affairs, which directly controls EPFs. It is important to highlight these organizational features of the federal institutes because they are often used as the starting point of a debate on – or even a useful model for – the transformation of the universities.

In fact, since they belong to cantons, Swiss universities have to a large extent developed autonomously. Each of them is organized according to a particular cantonal legislative framework. There is no equivalent of the CEPF for universities. In contrast, there are many actors involved in the definition of university policy and they are organized according to a rather complex structure (see for instance Weber, 1993; Leresche *et al.*, 1996). With regard to internal organization, universities are also different from the federal institutes, since the rector is not appointed by the political authorities but elected by his/her peers.[1]

Since the 1960s, however, the cantonal autonomy in the management of universities has been challenged on a number of occasions, mainly because of the lack of coordination between the different institutions. Two events were particularly important. First, in 1965 the Swiss Science Council (Conseil Suisse de la Science – CSS) was set up; it was the first body responsible for coordinating university policy. Second, in 1968 a federal law on financial assistance to cantonal universities was passed (Loi fédérale sur l'Aide aux Universités – LAU).

This law stipulated that federal government had to take part in the financing of cantonal universities through two sorts of subsidies. On the one hand, the federal authorities partly finance running costs and investments under SFr 300,000[2] but, on the other hand, they also allow public funds for other investments over SFr 300,000.[3] Cantonal autonomy, however, has not only been eroded through financing. The LAU widened the tasks of the Science Council and thereby allowed federal intervention in the definition of university policy. In addition, the LAU established a new coordinating body – the Swiss University Conference (Conférence Universitaire Suisse – CUS). For this reason, the LAU was more than a simple legislative framework. It allowed the involvement of federal government in universities, which had long been the exclusive province of the cantons.

In that way, the CUS and the CSS have emerged, since the 1970s, as the key actors in university policy. Some 20 years later they were joined by a third body, the Science Agency (Groupement pour la Science et la Recherche – GSR), to form the main forums of discussion on the transformation of Swiss university policy.

Some key actors in Swiss higher education policy

The Swiss University Conference

The Swiss University Conference is a control body the cantons were 'forced' to accept in return for the subsidies provided to their universities by the LAU. Its main task is to coordinate the activities of the universities.

In addition, while respectful of cantonal sovereignty and the autonomy of universities, it makes sure that 'common rules are established in the various institutions; equivalence and reciprocity principles are applied in the conditions for admission, in teaching and in exams rules' (Leresche *et al.*, 1996: 68); it also contributes to establishing the 'financial needs of universities, both in terms of current expenditure and long-term investment' (p. 68).

The CUS is composed of 29 members, representing cantons with and without universities, the National Research Council (Fonds National de la Recherche Scientifique – FNRS) and other actors concerned with higher education policy.

The Swiss Science Council

This is a consultative body of the federal government in the area of scientific research. It was set up in 1965, but its tasks were made clearer in 1969 when the LAU was passed.

> The CSS is nominated by the Federal Council [government] to collect, examine and establish national policy in the areas of science and research. The Federal Council decides on the membership of the CSS taking account of the different parts of the country and of the relevant interest areas.
>
> (FF 1968, II: 1639, art 19)

Science Agency

The Science Agency was established in 1990 by the federal government. Like the CSS it takes part in the definition of university policy and in the coordination of the higher education system. In addition it 'encourages the mobility of researchers, teachers and students; promotes the creation of centres of expertise within Swiss higher education institutions; reinforces international cooperation; and fosters links with the private economy in order to develop innovative technologies' (Leresche *et al.*, 1996: 77).

Since it was created, the Science Agency has become the most 'visible' body in Swiss university policy. It is playing an important role in the coordination and reform of the internal organization of universities.

Pressures for change

As outlined above, attempts to coordinate the fragmented structure of Swiss university policy date back to the mid-1960s. However, relatively little had been achieved until the 1990s. More recently, the pace of change has increased as a result of three crucial events.

Budgetary cuts

While throughout the 1980s subsidies to universities were growing in line with increasing numbers of students, since then budgetary restraint has become the norm.[4] In this respect, Switzerland is following the trends seen in many other European countries. As a result, universities are forced to compensate for lower public financing, both from federal and cantonal authorities, through alternative sources of funding. This is being done through a wide range of university activities, particularly those of research.

New links with Europe

The 1990s have seen a growing concern for the possible isolation of the Swiss scientific community. First, financial problems have sparked parliamentary debates about whether Switzerland should continue to participate in a number of international research programmes. Second, the rejection of membership of the European Economic Area in a referendum (6 December 1992) has raised some uncertainty about Switzerland's participation in European research programmes (EUREKA, COST, COMETT) as well as exchange programmes (ERASMUS).

The result is that those in charge of research policy are increasingly looking for solutions in order to avoid a total isolation of Swiss researchers from international networks, which would be fatal for both academia as well as for industry.

Listening to civil society's demands

A third important trend is the increasing recognition of the opportunity provided by stronger collaboration with external agencies, particularly business.

Pressures on academic staff to abandon their 'ivory towers' are growing. As suggested by the Conférence Universitaire Suisse (1994: 150), it is worth pursuing links between academia and the commercial sector because it is beneficial both to research and to universities. As a result, many universities have set up different bodies especially concerned with increasing links with society as a whole. Examples of these bodies are the WWZ (Wirtschafts-wissenschaftliches Zentrum – Centre for Economy-Science Studies) at Basel University, SOVAR (Soutien et valorisation de la recherche – Centre for Research Incentive) at Neuchâtel University.

Furthermore, universities have developed specialized centres of studies and research which are closely related to the demands and needs of political bodies as well as economic agencies: for example the CREA (Centre de recherche en économie appliquée – Centre for Research in Applied Economics) at Lausanne University, the GPA (Groupe de physique appliquée – Applied Physics Unit) at Geneva University, and the Micro Technical Institute at Neuchâtel University.

New directions in Swiss higher education policy

It is quite difficult to describe completely the transformations that are now taking place within Swiss universities. Every institution is a unique universe with its own rules of organization and particular types of relationship with the external environment. Because of these differences, the changes adopted affect each institution differently.

It is worth noting that the decisions affecting university policy are taken by cantonal authorities, in response to the instigation of the federal government. Generally, legislative change concerns both the internal organization of the universities as well as their relationships with the external environment. Particularly, new funding and accountability systems (as well as new types of management and governance) are being introduced. To some extent, these internal changes are affecting the overall Swiss higher education system.

The remainder of this chapter focuses on the measures adopted, and then gives some specific examples.

Spatial transformations

Since the 1960s there has been concern, particularly within the Science Council, about the high number of university sites. It suggested that similar programmes be merged in a single location (CSS, 1967: 13). Since the 1990s, budgetary constraints have provided an opportunity for the Science Council to raise again the issue of the excessive number of sites. In 1993, a report entitled *Major Orientations for the Development of Swiss Universities: Landscape 2000* was published. Its subtitle, *Quality, Competitiveness, Autonomy and Division of Tasks* gave a clear indication of the change of direction in higher education policy.

The report suggested that a number of universities could be merged. This would improve the competitiveness of Swiss universities in relation to their counterparts abroad, particularly in the field of research. The report argued that Switzerland was too small a country to allow ten universities to undertake leading research and to offer programmes that are often very similar.

An identical line was adopted by the Science Agency. Through its former Director, H. Ursprung, it explicitly favoured rationalization of the Swiss university system. The objective was to combine similar teaching and research programmes in order to constitute some 'centres of excellence'. These centres are expected to be internationally recognized and to cover all the subjects within a given discipline. The process would allow both savings and rationalization of the higher education sector.

According to H. Ursprung, the spatial reorganization of the university system had to be based on three clusters of institutions: the federal institutes of technology, the universities of the French-speaking cantons, and those of the German-speaking cantons (which possibly would include the Italian-speaking university). The division of tasks between the various institutions of a cluster should be decided by a council composed of university rectors, scientists and representatives of the economy (Ursprung in Zendali, 'Qui osera le coup d'état qui sauvera les universités malgré elles?' *Le Nouveau Quotidien*, 27 May 1993).

With regard to French-speaking cantons, Ursprung argued that

> the Universities of Geneva and Lausanne, together with Lausanne's federal institute of technology, could form a cluster. Geneva, where the CERN is based, could take high energy physics, which would be abandoned by Lausanne University. In return, Geneva would give architecture to Lausanne's EPF, which in turn could give up basic chemistry to Lausanne University. It is a process in which everyone gives and everyone receives. It allows savings and by the same token the creation of a critical mass in the three areas.
> (Ursprung, 'Universités, unissez-vous!' *L'Hebdo*, 16 April 1992)

These proposals were met with little enthusiasm by the individual institutions. While they did not oppose any sort of restructuring, they were (and still are) concerned with losing some teaching and research programmes. Instead of a transfer of tasks, what they suggested, through their respective rectorates, was the constitution of a university network. In addition, the rectors agreed that any transformation should not be imposed from above, but should be initiated by individual institutions. As the former Rector of Lausanne University put it, 'we aim for the sharing of resources, the abandonment of programmes which are duplicates of other ones, the harmonization of appointment procedures, and the sharing of particularly costly investments' (P. Ducrey, 'L'université romande est un mythe', *Le Nouveau Quotidien*, 18 December 1992).

The current debate on university policy is thus characterized by a constant tension between the push by the federal government towards amalgamation and the resistance to such moves by individual institutions and cantonal governments. However, despite disagreement about the way change should be

brought in, there is widespread consensus that principles of cantonal autonomy in higher education are increasingly outdated. Given that Swiss universities are now supposed to be competitive on an international level, the need
for reform is widely accepted. As pointed out below, some projects already
exist; however, while they fulfil rational economic requirements, they militate
against plurality within academia.

Funding: new context and new forms

Changes in higher education financing are obviously related to budgetary
restrictions, at both the federal and cantonal levels. However, such changes are
also going to affect the relationship between cantons running a university and
those that do not. Not least, the thorny issue of whether business should contribute to higher education financing has to be addressed.

At the federal level, changes suggested through the LAU are likely to result
in a shift from a financing method based principally on the number of students
to one that takes into account, among other elements, progress towards amalgamation. In addition, performance indicators are also likely to affect federal
subsidies in the future. Among the performance indicators suggested are the
number and size of grants received from the National Research Foundation
(Fonds National Suisse de la Recherche Scientifique – FNRS), the number of
degrees awarded, and the number of publications of faculty staff.

Although none of these proposals has been adopted to date, the simple fact
that such suggestions are being made indicates a substantial shift in the overall
approach to university policy. Federal authorities will no longer subsidize institutions while allowing them the same degree of autonomy. Federal funds will
be increasingly conditional upon progress towards structural change.

It should be stressed that all these proposals are being discussed and none of
them has yet been adopted. However, problems likely to emerge in the implementation phase are already evident. First, a financing method based solely on
research grants would result in a two-tier university system. Second, the
number of degrees awarded could lead to a relaxation of exams and admission
procedures in order to produce larger numbers of graduates; this would
thereby increase federal subsidies because in Switzerland there are no limits on
the intake of students.

Financing is also being reconsidered by the cantonal governments, many of
which have budget deficits. Generally, university budgets have been considerably reduced, which has again raised the issue of the amalgamation of teaching
and research activities.[5] To share resources is a sensible way to minimize the
drawbacks of budget cuts. The form adopted is the fixed budget. As a result,
individual institutions have more room for manoeuvre in defining their spending plans, but they also need to set up the appropriate structures.

A third element of change in the complex financing system of Swiss universities concerns the inter-cantonal level. Currently, cantons that do not run a
university pay a fee of SFr 8,914 per year for each student undertaking higher

education in another canton. In March 1996, the canton of Zurich rejected the existing agreement and claimed the payment of full fees, estimated at SFr 19,000 per year. A new agreement has been negotiated, and the result is a three-tier system of fees. For each student in the humanities or social sciences the fee amounts to SFr 9,600 per annum, SFr 23,000 per annum for natural and technical sciences, and SFr 46,000 per annum for medicine. Since a number of students are unlikely to return to their canton of origin, peripheral cantons (Ticino, Jura and Valais) are eligible for a 5 per cent rebate.

A new accountability requirement

The current transformations of the Swiss higher education system are also concerned with notions of universities' accountability to their funders and to society as a whole. It has been argued that universities are not sufficiently open to the external world. They do not pay enough attention to society's expectations and requirements. Since in the past the level of financing was kept at a constant level, universities are not used to justifying their expenditure. This situation is changing substantially.

Universities themselves have shown some concern for this issue, and have set up internal evaluation procedures. However, the introduction of widespread evaluation procedures in Swiss higher education is relatively new. Its goal is not only to strengthen accountability, but also to guarantee high-quality teaching and research. However, while higher education institutions in Europe and in the US are used to being evaluated, it is only since 1991 that such a policy has been adopted on a national scale in Switzerland (Federal Council, 1991). According to political authorities, the introduction of such procedures is the best way to manage science and to cope with budget reductions.

According to the principles of federalism, some federal policies, such as higher education, are implemented by the cantons. This is why almost all of the cantons are adopting new laws for their universities, which include evaluation policies. These mainly concern teaching, because research is evaluated by the National Research Foundation. The main goal of evaluation is to map the strengths and weaknesses of individual institutions and to find solutions for improving teaching and learning.

Comparatively, Switzerland is definitely a latecomer to higher education evaluation. With the exception of Geneva University and the federal institutes of technology, such procedures are still experimental. Arguably, up to now, Swiss academia, as the majority of other higher education systems in the world, has valued research too much in comparison with teaching as a measurement of the quality of universities. Patterns of career advancement were based mainly on achievement in research. The introduction of teaching-evaluation procedures is supposed to redress the balance between teaching and research so as to create some kind of pedagogical portfolios (as is the case in the US).

It should be noted that these developments are still at a very early stage. Rather than being part of a coherent project, they are a response to new pressures coming from policy makers. Nevertheless, there are good reasons to believe that evaluation procedures will play an increasingly important role in the near future. Current reforms at the cantonal level show a trend towards contractualization whereby budget allocation will be based on pre-defined criteria; this de facto requires the introduction of evaluation procedures to determine the extent to which the different objectives – both qualitative and quantitative – are being achieved. How much evaluation will be required by contractualization is not known. What is sure, however, is that such changes are opening the way for a radical rethinking of how universities are organized and governed.

New forms of governance

Much of the transformation discussed in this section is the result of decisions taken in the 1970s. One of the reasons often mentioned for the delay between policy decisions and effective implementation is the internal structure of universities, which is unable to adapt to changing circumstances.

Despite federalism, Swiss universities are all organized according to the same principles. To a large extent, they are part of the 'continental model' of university organization as stated by Clark (1983). Faculties (and within them institutes, departments and/or sections) constitute the key elements in the decision-making process, which is to a very substantial extent controlled by professors. They are able effectively to contest decisions taken by the rectorates. The latter constitute the executive power in a university and are generally composed of three to four people who take responsibility for different areas (teaching, financing, external relations). The team is formed of university professors who represent the institution in negotiations with the authorities. The rector has little room for manoeuvre in his or her policies. S/he is appointed by his/her peers for a two-year period and can be considered a *primus inter pares* more than a true manager. Furthermore, the short duration of the mandate does not allow any time to carry out substantial reforms.

The second element in the university government is the Senate. It has the task of acting as a check on the power of the rectorate and discussing the general orientation of the institution. The Senate includes professors, representatives of the non-professorial teaching and research staff, students and technical and administrative staff.

In addition, universities are directly ruled by cantonal governments. Particularly on spending decisions, institutions have very little autonomy. Funds granted must be used for specific purposes and cannot be shifted around. Finally, all appointments, confirmations of appointments and even promotions (or demotions) must be approved by the relevant cantonal government (Perellon, 1998a). All this limits the effective autonomy of individual institutions in the management of their own affairs.

This division of responsibilities has been criticized by the federal authorities. In 1993, the Science Council argued that in order to reform university policy, a new organizational structure was needed: 'The sharing of responsibility and specialization require . . . clearer and more efficient planning and governance. Success of reforms depends to a large extent on changes to the internal structures of universities' (CSS, 1993: 43).

In practice, the key issue is that university executives lack the institutional means to adopt reforms. The two-year time limit on the appointment of a rector and the dependence on cantonal governments are the main limitations on their capacity to bring about change. Thus, the direction of reform should be towards strengthening rectorates and increasing universities' autonomy in relation to cantonal authorities. This should be done through the extension of the tenure of rectors to four years, as well as making it possible for them and their team to give up academic responsibilities for the duration of their appointment.

More generally, the reinforcement of the executive level would lead to a concentration of decision-making powers (on the spending of public funds and the general organization of the institution) in the hands of the rectors.

It is worth noting that quite strong opposition has emerged in many universities to this new form of governance. In Lausanne University, for example, a recent investigation showed that a great majority of the professors are opposed to the nomination of the rector by the political authority. The head of the institution should be chosen from within the academic community and not from any other sector of society.

But at the same time, the transformation of the governance model of many of the Swiss universities also includes the setting up of new bodies with greater responsibility for the general management of the institution.[6] These bodies, called Conseils Académiques or Conseils de l'Université are composed of relevant individuals from the political and economic sectors of the cantons: they have a wide range of responsibilities, for example fostering links between universities and society.

Furthermore, some proposals have been made to transform these new bodies into the control boards of the institutions. By doing this, the political authority would lose many of its responsibilities (appointments, spending of funds). These bodies would become the true decision makers for the organization and management of the institution. The rectorate would become the commissioner of the decisions taken by these bodies and would represent the institution to the outside world.[7]

In sum, the direction of reform is towards a more effective model of governance. Since universities will be given a fixed budget and autonomy concerning spending decisions, it is essential that there is a centre within the institution with effective power. Presumably, the reinforcement of rectorates, and more generally of executive power, will be to the detriment of professors and of legislative bodies. This would result in a reduction of the democratic character of decision-making procedures, which is a cause for concern.

These reforms will result in a less fragmented system in terms of internal organization, which should ease the process of resource sharing and concentration of activities. The greater involvement of external actors, through the establishment of Conseils Académiques, will make universities more responsive to the needs of society. A possible result, which is nevertheless opposed by some within the institutions, is an increase of the financing of higher education through commercial funds.

Some examples

What has been done so far? Here are some specific examples.

Spatial transformations

A good example of the establishment of resource sharing and activity concentration is provided by the universities of Bern, Neuchâtel and Fribourg. Under the name of BENEFRI these currently form a network. Student exchanges are facilitated, and individual programmes often offer courses on more than one campus. However, no changes have been made to the internal organization of these universities. Each institution has kept its decision-making powers intact. Nothing has really been done to merge the institutions or to develop a common strategy for management or governance.

In parallel to BENEFRI, a project of close cooperation has emerged between the Universities of Geneva and Lausanne (about 50 miles apart). This project is rather interesting since it constitutes a middle way between merging and networking. Research and teaching activities will be reorganized on both sites, which will harmonize their internal structures as well as decision-making and evaluation procedures. While it is still not known how the power will be shared between them and what kind of governance they will develop, both sides have already rejected the idea of having a common structure of governance (one executive and one legislative).

Funding

The biggest changes so far have been in the area of funding. As regards federal funds, substantial progress on a new bill has already been made (Joint Report, 1998; Perellon, 1998b). In parallel, budget constraints at the cantonal level have imposed a rethinking of university financing. In particular, university budgets will be established on a block grant basis so as to allow more effective planning. Finally, the new inter-cantonal agreement reviewed above has been adopted. While the payment of full tuition fees by the cantons without universities has been rejected, varying the amount paid according to the subject studied is a better reflection of the costs of the various degrees.

New forms of accountability

Switzerland is a latecomer in the development of comprehensive evaluation procedures in higher education. However, it is now catching up. For instance, Fribourg University mandated an external evaluation covering all aspects of its activities. The results, however, have not been published, which highlights the strong reluctance to accept higher levels of accountability.

Geneva University has also adopted an evaluation system in which three teaching and research units are assessed each year (Roulet, 1994). Lausanne University is currently working on a project for the generalization of evaluation across the whole institution.

But these efforts should not hide the fact that evaluation of teaching is still underdeveloped. Only a few institutions have set up comprehensive evaluation procedures, and in most cases these procedures have only recently been introduced. Generally, the evaluation of both the institution and teaching is the sole responsibility of the university. Nevertheless, it should be noted that pressure for the introduction and generalization of such procedures has emerged from the different external bodies concerned with university policy, especially the Swiss Science Council.

New forms of governance and relations with the authorities

One of the most controversial issues in the debate on higher education reforms is the concentration of power in the hands of the executive (rectors) and the establishment of external supervisory boards. But these new models of governance also run the risk that decisions on the general academic policy will be taken without the participation of the entire academic community.

The introduction of a strong executive is needed as a result of increased financial autonomy and independence from the cantonal governments. In practice, however, such autonomy remains very limited. The case of Lausanne University is particularly instructive. There, a cantonal Bill was submitted to the relevant academic and non-academic bodies for consultation purposes. The result was a clear rejection by the academic community. In fact, the Bill included only partial provision for increased autonomy. For instance, the rector and the members of the Conseil Académique would be appointed by the cantonal government, which implies a limitation of the University's independence from government.

Instead of increased autonomy, the Bill would increase the state's control over the University. The only element of autonomy that concerns financial management is de facto trivialized by the lack of autonomy of the decision-making bodies within the institution. The case of Lausanne shows the dilemma currently facing policy makers: on the one hand, a reform of the system of governance is needed; on the other, such change encounters strong resistance from the academic community.

Conclusion

On the basis of the preceding account of current developments in the Swiss higher education system, it seems that a key obstacle to the implementation of reforms is the adoption of a top–down approach.

Decisions are taken by federal and/or cantonal authorities, and universities are consulted relatively late in the policy-making process. For this reason one doubts the actual significance of the current reform movement. Autonomy for universities remains none the less the key issue over the next few years. In particular, there should be ample room for manoeuvre in the management of finance and of human resources. In this context, the power relations within institutions will be considerably modified, as has been shown, by a reinforcement of the executive levels of the universities – formed by the rectors and the different bodies responsible for internal organization – and by the redefinition of relations with public authorities and, more broadly, civil society.

But as they are being introduced, these changes might provoke some opposition from the academic community. For the professors in particular the reinforcement of the rector's power will, to a large extent, mean the weakening of their 'privileges' within the institution. But more generally, new forms of internal organization and power distribution might reduce the level of participation in decision-making processes by the academic community through the existing different legislative frameworks (Senate for the whole institution; Faculty Council for the faculty level).

In parallel to the changes within the institutions, the relationship between cantonal governments and universities is being redefined. Through contractualization, public authorities should become actual partners of universities and not just funders, as is the case now.

Despite their importance or extent, the transformations suggested – or wanted – are being implemented quite slowly within the different institutions. If change must occur in deed, it must first occur in word and minds. And this is not yet the case. Not yet.

Notes

1. In addition, it is important to point out that this dual higher education structure will very soon be completed by a new channel. As mentioned in the introduction, the new higher vocational colleges (or *Fachhochschulen*) are intended both to provide advanced vocational training for university-equivalent degrees and also to open up access to tertiary education to a larger proportion of the young population. Nevertheless, as these colleges will only be effective from autumn 1998, they are not further analysed here.
2. These are called 'basic subsidies' (*subventions de base*).
3. These are called 'investment subsidies' (*subventions d'investissement*). It is important to emphasize that this legislative framework is currently under revision. Proposals have been formulated to modify the patterns of funding and to bring in a more competitive system.

4. It is worth noting that 1986 (for the period 1986–91) was the last year when the Parliament accepted the whole budget for science and research proposed by the CSS. Since then, budgets have been considerably reduced, which has caused many political interventions in the Parliament.
5. For example, Lausanne University will have to reduce its budget by up to 7 per cent by the year 2000 in relation to the 1996 budget. This will represent almost SFr 20 million. The same problem has emerged in Zurich University, where the cuts amount to SFr 150 million by the end of the century.
6. For a general view of the new models of governance proposed by the different university laws, see CUS (1994).
7. It is interesting to note that this model of governance, where nothing is said about the participation of the academic community in the decision-making process, has been especially recommended to the cantons by the Conférence Universitaire Suisse (1994).

References

Clark, B. R. (1983) *The Higher Education System*. Berkeley, CA: University of California Press.
Conférence Universitaire Suisse (1994*) Plan pluriannuel des universités et hautes écoles suisses pour la période 1996–1999*. Berne: CUS.
Conseil Suisse de la Science (1967) *Le développement des universités suisses*. Berne: CSS.
Conseil Suisse de la Science (1993) *Grandes orientations pour le développement des universités suisses : Horizon 2000. Qualité – Compétitivité – Autonomie – Répartition des tâches*. Berne: CSS.
Leresche, J.-Ph., Jaccoud, Ch., Bolay, J.-C. (1996) *Les territoires de hautes écoles. Genèse d'une politique*. Lausanne: IREC/EPFL.
Office Fédéral de la Statistique (1995) *Les indicateurs de l'enseignement en Suisse. L'enseignement en mutation dans nôtre pays*. Berne: OFS.
Perellon, J.-F. (1998a) Uneasy partners: analysing the changing relationship between universities and political authorities in Switzerland. Paper presented at 'The Governance of Universities in a Comparative Perspective' conference, Lausanne, April.
Perellon, J.-F. (1998b) The challenge of change: the politics of higher education reform in Switzerland, *Tertiary Education and Management*, 4(3): 199–207.
Roulet, E. (1994) Un exemple suisse: l'évaluation des unités d'enseignement et de recherche de l'Université de Genève, *Gestion de l'enseignement supérieur*, 6(2): 139–48.
Weber, K. (1993) Higher education policy in Switzerland, in L. Goedegebuure, F. Kaiser, P. A. M. Maassen, L. V. Meek, F. A. van Vught and E. de Weert (eds) *Higher Education Policy: An International Comparative Perspective*. Oxford: Pergamon Press, 265–89.

Legislative sources

Federal Act on Financial Assistance to Cantonal Universities (Loi fédérale sur l'aide aux universités), FF 1968, 1633–60.

Federal Council (1991) Ordonnance relative à la loi sur l'aide aux universités, FF 1991, 1035–61.

Joint Report OFES (1998) *Projet de Révision de la loi fédérale sur l'aide aux universités (LAU). Rapport explicatif à l'appui du projet de loi mis en consultation.* Unpublished.

13

Higher Education Development in Transitional Societies

Peter Darvas

Introduction

Universities seem to be able effectively to define their political and social positions even under the worst economic conditions and most restrictive political regimes. Moreover, institutions and powerful academic agencies appear to be the only ones who can provide a solid and long-term answer to the 'what kind of university?' type questions. An ability in and quasi-monopoly of self-definition do not necessarily imply unlimited autonomy, sovereignty or progress, however, as universities' experience in the region of central and eastern Europe (CEE) as well as in countries of the former Soviet Union certainly confirms.

Since January 1996, my own education and understanding has benefited from participation in efforts to change higher education at various levels: as adviser to the Minister of Education in Hungary I helped draft an amendment to the law on higher education, which marked out the critical issues and strategies facilitating effective government progress at institutional and training levels. Later on, during the implementation phase, government strategy was focused mostly on public finance and the government's decision-making powers, institutional integration and management capabilities, improving the training structure, educational programmes and methods. For the last year and a half, as director of the Higher Education Support Programme at the Open Society Institute, I had the opportunity to work more closely throughout the CEE region at institutional level with innovative members of academia, as well as institutional leaders, to support their efforts in various ways. Whereas this work did not explicitly assist the development of a systematic analytical framework, I still feel I gained some significant experience through practical involvement with governments, sponsors and users, institutional leaders and academic agents of change. As a result, I propose to focus my analysis on the most critical – and perhaps exciting – issue of higher education in the CEE region: *change*; more precisely, I propose to look at how primary agencies in higher education and participants in policy making usually approach change, and how they develop their own strategies of change.

My practical involvement and experience in the change processes has stimulated the following observations. (The observations will, however, for the moment, remain without further empirical verification.)

Changes in higher education in the 1990s questioned the relevance of a single line of development, despite the massive and relatively straightforward political and social expectations of reform in the early stages of the post-Communist transition.

There is no single discernible direction of change that is typical of the entire region; instead, there is a series of independent environmental factors and conditions, resulting in a variety of change patterns.

One significant shared set of characteristics is the changing role of governments, a departure from monolithic decision making, and the proliferation of actors and stakeholders.

Among the variety of interest groups, a newly emerging group comprises those who represent individual institutional perspectives and concerns; furthermore, within institutions, a relatively new distinction is emerging between managerial strategies and concerns on the one hand, and the professorial or academic power of faculty on the other.

Evolution and higher education change

My first observation is that practical experience in higher educational change at both governmental and institutional levels raises questions about the relevance of an evolutionist approach, which is perhaps analytically flawed; more critically, it might actually prove to be detrimental if applied in more practical advisory activities. Since the late 1970s, new and more elaborate and reflective approaches have been discernible in international scholarship. For example, the yearly reviews of (mostly western) European trends in higher education in the *European Journal of Education* have questioned the borders of higher education's metaphorical space, debated the chaotic nature of higher education organizations and tried to identify new actors in the policy-making process. Accordingly, the analysis of change has progressed from discussion of simple functions and coherent structures to the analysis of various, often conflicting, interests, objectives and trade-offs in policy making, all resulting from the multiplicity of actors, stakeholders and other participants in higher education. Yet, as soon as countries of the CEE region took the path of post-Communist transition, analysts and advisers – either sceptical or optimistic – shared the essentially evolutionary perspective that a country's ability to catch up in higher education depended on its political and economic performance.

On the one hand, there seemed to be relative consensus among the main political actors on the most fundamental political goals.

- *To establish or restore the high prestige and sovereignty of higher education and scientific research by liberating them from political subordination.* According to this reform objective, the traditional authority and institutional forms of high-level knowledge need to be restored. This can be assisted by the reconstruction of academic freedom and by increasing the prestige of higher learning, which should be protected from undesirable external political influences. Proponents of this direction (mostly within the circles of academic faculties) argue that the locus of these desired values is centred within the historical universities, which represent the prestige and academic ethos of some hegemonic training and research fields. Furthermore, as part of these traditions, policies should support the disciplinary structure based on chairs and corporate decision making based on collective bodies and councils.

- *To support the democratization and marketization process by providing the newly emerging intellectual and professional skills demanded by the post-Communist transition.* Changes should respond to the global problems of the present, such as the increase in youth unemployment, the need for more stringent financial accountability, the challenges of technology and a new balance between basic and applied science, etc. These kinds of changes began in western Europe in the 1980s, when (once again in the history of higher education systems) the trend of amalgamation gave way to that of diversification. Accordingly, new roles for the state, institutions and the individual were envisioned. The role of the state should be decreased and new forms of evaluation should be established to correct the ineffectiveness and inefficiency in the system. Higher education leadership should be armed with new managerial skills that would help to cope with the increasing complexity.

- *To transform the elitist and closed system of higher education by opening up access and by making it part of lifelong learning.* Accordingly, reform should lead to comprehensive higher education with massive enrolments. Changes should move toward the higher education reforms that occurred in the West between the 1950s and 1970s, but which bypassed Communist regimes. Higher education should become part of the mass education system. Universities should be socially more responsive, and reflect the values of modern societies.

Parallel to the political goals, there was a second order of policy objectives also present in the public debates, including:

- making more effective use of public resources by integrating a highly segmented institutional structure;
- increasing institutional funds through private and fee-based provisions;
- making higher education management more effective and professional by giving institutions more autonomy, leaders more authority, and requiring more accountability;
- making provisions, programmes and services more responsive and transparent by increasing the diversification of training programmes and degrees, and integrating research and education.

On the other hand, it was less obvious at the beginning how the fundamental political goals might compete with one another and how they might be in explicit conflict with the policy objectives. Just to quote a few examples of potential conflict: academic sovereignty and external responsiveness; supporting new demand and demanding more effective management; opening up access and finding alternative resources. These are not necessarily in conflict with one another but could easily create a segmented policy arena, as they indeed have mostly done in central Europe.

The evolutionist view is unacceptable not only because it has a reductively normative perspective of what constitutes progressive change, but also because it assumes the existence of simple causal relationships. By now, it is almost common knowledge that relating the development of a market economy with the development of democratic institutions is questionable. Similar doubts should be raised about the relationship between the market economy and democratic institutional cultures on the one hand and the development of higher education on the other. In reality, the performance of the economy or the advancement of democratic political institutions has not at all resulted in the unequivocal development of higher education.

Furthermore, by being involved in practical activities focused on influencing change, I have had to recognize the importance of accidental factors; the more higher education is subjected to political interference, the less coherent the nature of the change. Coincidences, temporary alliances, the importance of personalities and personal conflicts may make any ambitious analytical explanations irrelevant or trivial.

Factors of change

Instead of monocausal and reductive explanations of higher education change, there are in fact significant variations in agenda and direction, and in space and time as well. These variables include:

- the extent to which long-term academic traditions and higher education systems – embodied in the corpus of knowledge and social expectations – were disrupted by external events, such as the disappearance of countries;
- the extent to which the legitimacy of traditions and structures that had emerged during the previous half century were questioned by radical political reforms, typically by the collapse of the Communist regimes;
- the degree of dependence on the inherited institutional, infrastructure and curricular framework (including the availability of equipment, materials, textbooks, methods, etc.);
- the extent to which governmental budgets and other users' financial capacities limit adequate sponsorship for the maintenance and/or development of higher education;
- the level of importance academics and other intellectuals give to public life and political reforms;

- the access of countries, and thus national higher education systems, to international know-how, support, information systems and to the global academic market place;
- the extent to which market reform in general, and the structural elaboration of labour markets in particular, define new, more diverse training and other needs and constitute a competitive environment for higher education.

The possible outcomes of the interplay between these independent factors include the relative autonomy of members of academia and that of the institutions, relative dependence on government, the extent of structural (both vertical and horizontal) and institutional diversification, the increasing rate of participation in higher education, changes in the composition of the academic community and its willingness to control quality.

I would like to emphasize that a model based on these independent factors and outcomes is intended to offer an alternative to evolutionary models: disruption or de-legitimization may not necessarily impede higher education changes; the political influence of academics and intellectuals does not inexorably contribute to their increasing independence; emerging markets and competition do not ineluctably stimulate similar changes in academia; and restrictive finances do not have to restrict the agenda for change. The actual outcome of the independent factors, the agenda, the trends and the actors depends on the particular national settings and dynamics.

A changing role for governments, and the proliferation of participants

The most significant trend in higher education change is the changing role of governments and the proliferation of actors, stakeholders and participants in policy and decision making, stimulated and accompanied by the increase in the overall size, as well as the complexity, of higher education.

One possible reason why this trend appears to be more noticeable in the CEE region than elsewhere is that under Communism, mass participation in higher education change was restricted and could not accompany any growth and diversification of programmes. It should also be noted that the emergence of independent actors or a policy arena not determined or supervised closely by the government is still far from reality in some countries. Especially in some CIS (Commonwealth of Independent States) countries it is quite remarkable that governments, often in claiming to assist the market, try to centralize decision making in higher education even further.

Nevertheless, following the end of the Communist regimes, previously restricted groups vigorously reasserted their stake and values. These historically delayed trends were accompanied by newly emerging expectations. As a result, change no longer means the emergence of a new dominant social group restricting or replacing earlier dominant values and objectives. Instead, issues and objectives constitute a complex net at both governmental and institutional levels.

Moreover, influential higher education actors at both levels tend to be protective, if not conservative, of their own sovereignty in issues like knowledge adequacy, relevance, quality, selection, regulations and procedures. Therefore, as many agents of change emerge, participants – often the same as those who initiated change – establish formidable opposition to changes of other origin.

Two main phenomena may be distinguished within this trend: the first trend is that government policies are becoming more restricted both in context and content. Until now decision making has been generally monolithic, and strategic decisions were dominated by ideological considerations. Furthermore, it is often asserted that present-day political resistance to higher education change stems from the government's cautious – if not passive – policies, policies caused by internal divisions. However, the relationship between government and higher education institutions is more complex. We cannot simply argue that higher education is subordinate to governmental politics. It is true to say, however, that institutions are still strongly dependent on state support, members of staff have remained civil servants, and governmental agencies still have considerable influence on admissions, training, research and certification.

Yet the relationship between government and higher education has another side, one that should not be ignored, namely the strong involvement of higher education in politics. This has affected the political 'spin' of reforms just as much as governmental interference has. Mihaly Bihari, a Hungarian political scientist, pointed out in a lecture in the late 1970s that there is a curiously easy transferability of power. While in CEE we cannot speak about stabilized interests and a solid professional position, the social structure has remained rigid. Educational capital can be easily transferred to economic capital or to political capital and vice versa. Higher education is not separated from these circles of power, as the coordination and control of institutions is organized through the same bureaucratic channels.

We should recognize that in western Europe the collective identities of disciplines and specialist professions have had a relatively longer period to emerge, compared to the post-Communist period of the CEE countries. At the time that higher education in the West was constantly being challenged by external (social, economic and technological) interests, the CEE countries had to deal with complex institutional division and bureaucratic control, which became quite formal as higher education grew and became increasingly complex. Central control was becoming more of a forum for informal lobbying and bargaining for diverse academic interests. Thus, governmental authority, considered to be a basic source of *external* control in the West, was instead an *internal* source of influence in the East.

Changes in the government–higher education relationship are expected to occur in both context and content. For context, governments are refocusing their efforts away from direct intervention and are now defining proper procedures and institutional structures in which other stakeholders can emerge, express their own objectives, negotiate and act more independently. Also, as markets emerge, governments are using financial incentives and regulations concerning public finances rather than authoritarian imposition and intervention. The content of the governmental role and control is changing as a result of indirect means as well as the emergence of non-governmental sponsors, the introduction of user fees and other forms of non-public finance. Consequently, governments do not have a mandate to take full responsibility for all higher education. Instead, they have the luxury of restricting their attention to priority-setting and public objectives.

As soon as the political changes in the 1980s allowed the emergence of non-governmental organizations, the academic community was in the forefront, taking active part in the buffer organizations and thus institutionalizing its access to politics. Among the buffer organizations, we need to distinguish between those set up by governments as consulting bodies and granting agencies and those set up by members of academia to put pressure on governments and to regulate their own access to the policy-making process by bringing it into a coherent form. Typical examples of the former are the higher education councils, which have the mandate to elaborate strategies and make recommendations on the allocation of state funding. An example of the latter includes the emergence of rectors' conferences, which can become fairly powerful in state–higher education discussions and can also act as an exclusive club restricting the access to politics of some institutions.

Activism at the intermediary levels may bring about two opposite tendencies: protectionism, or reform and innovation. Involvement in politics has legitimated the position of faculty and institutions, often replacing (at least to some extent) professional peer control or social responsiveness. As a result, members of academia and other representatives of higher education institutions focus more on central political and abstract norms and solutions and pay less attention to institutional concerns and operational problems. Frequent political interference in academic matters may also bring about easy political confirmation for some privileged academic circles without instituting adequate control. Therefore the academic community may not be interested in decentralization as it also 'liberates' them from traditional channels of influence. While they gain independence from the industrial governmental lobby (very powerful during the previous regime), they may want to replace it with the pre-war or pre-Communist pattern of centralized higher education governance. Thus, the academic community needs to be liberated not only from governmental interference but also from its own political power to influence that authority.

The emergence of institutional concerns

The interests of higher education institutions in CEE have never been strongly articulated. Buffeted between the strong will of governments and effective defence by the faculties in the name of academic ethos and sovereignty, institutions were merely necessary organizational units, representing alternatives to those two types of powers. This may have either been a direct reflection of the Napoleonic higher education traditions or were clever operational solutions imposed by the Communist governments. The latter is exemplified by the separation of large, traditional multi-faculty universities into small, specialized units. By now, these powerless organizations have lost their legitimacy, effectiveness and feasibility: governments are not able to finance the quantitative growth within these units, which have inflated bureaucracies and a large number of non-teaching staff. These specialized organizations have grave difficulties in following the changing demands of the intellectual labour markets; innovative academics cannot use these institutions as appropriate frameworks for their own initiatives of academic innovation: institutions with the Communist structures and traditions simply do not have enough intellectual resources and innovative energy.

Despite the conservative traditions of higher education – or precisely because of them – no change may be planned or implemented without institutional commitment and implementation. Of all the interested parties, institutional leaders and faculty members have the most at stake in the short term, as the hidden agenda is quality improvement. Therefore the challenge to change will not only originate from the public but will be pressed for internally as well. As employment and working conditions have deteriorated, some institutions and faculties have developed an interest in improving the system as a whole, and increasing the prestige and sponsorship of higher education. As demand and access to higher education increases, the major challenge to higher education will be to meet the diverse needs and abilities of newly entering student groups and emerging regional demands. We may observe several parallel tendencies: new missions, further differentiation, new forms of management and coordination for existing institutions, innovation in curricula, educational structures, methods of teaching and learning, as well as perhaps the appearance of new types of institutions of higher education.

All institutions, existing or new alike, need considerably increased power and freedom to innovate in the substantive issues by the introduction of new training programmes and effective recruitment of faculty as well as students. Universities and colleges face uncertainty, given the fiscal restrictions by governments. The overarching trend is towards pluralism of their missions; there is an accumulation of challenges, including the urge to increase their capacities, or the need to make new provision for post-secondary and postgraduate levels. These challenges are further complicated by political instability at government level and as regards social needs. One conclusion is clear: the reconstruction of both a traditional academic ethos and the prestige of higher learning as a singular mission for universities is all but impossible.

The present indications suggest that existing institutions will remain suspicious and sceptical about the emergence of new institutions. They will use their political leverage to oppose the establishment of new institutions and to protect their title and ethos. This attitude is being observed in most countries of the region. However, existing institutions may need to revise this strategy in the long term. As they become more vulnerable to unstable and complex outside needs, they will have to recognize that they have a strong interest in the emergence of new provision, not only within their own organization but also outside of it. While new institutions may become competitors, they also help to diversify provision at system level and, as a result, old institutions can opt to carry less externally assigned responsibilities. As a result the traditional universities will more easily be able to assume the role of 'research universities' and thus become more independent carriers of high-level knowledge. One way to increase the capability of newly emerging institutions is to balance strict institutional accreditation requirements with 'liberal' governmental authorizations. Thus, although new institutions will need to be accepted by their peers, they can legally function, gradually develop their services, and find alternative financial resources.

The increasing complexity of higher education will result in the clear separation of institutional management from the professorial or academic power of faculty. This separation will contribute to the breaking up of traditional forms of institutional authority and hierarchy, in which academic prestige and authority is directly translated into organizational prestige and authority. Traditional authorities, collective decision-making bodies and councils will not be able to maintain effective and impartial control over the 'business administration' of the institutions. These trends may intensify resistance by the conservative sections within academic communities. Universities will need to develop a corporate-type rationality and administration in order to adjust to external interests. This attention will require some managerial skills, if not technocratic categorizations and standards, to deal with the expanded decision-making options. It is known that higher education institutions were strictly limited by nationwide planning systems that tied their finances, as well as their profile, to training needs to meet the immediate production plans. This subordination contributed to the bad reputation of planning. However, the emerging uncertainties will have to be answered by effective institutional planning, self-evaluation and management of financial, physical and human resources, as institutions gain more independence over their finances and their activities.

The existing institutional framework of finances will not enable higher education institutions even to maintain their physical good standing, much less to grow. Institutions need to increase their independence from governmental sponsorship and to establish new relationships with non-governmental and business partners; they need to find new forms and sources of income. The new income sources will result in new opportunities as well as new urgencies. Typically, the new guarantees of autonomy were established in the collective bodies of higher education institutions that were given freedoms in deciding upon matters of curriculum appointments and other substantive issues. In the meantime, the executive position of people such as rectors and directors remained tied by fiscal problems and by legal means that favoured the collective leadership's decision-making capacities.

Additional sources of income will bring about new sources of control, which can effectively push institutions in new directions. For instance, World Bank loans have effectively focused on the need to have new programmes and new organizational solutions. Similar initiatives will almost certainly increase the share of new 'labour market and technology sensitive' programmes within the system. The increasing practical orientation of universities will result in closer cooperation with businesses. Since higher education is destined to produce less direct income than expenditure, there seems to be little to limit the financial dependence of institutions. New sources of control can reinforce the dependence of higher education institutions on external supervising agents. Therefore new legal provisions should be developed to frame cooperation between the institutions and both regional and local economies and governments. One way to protect the institutions is to provide legal statutes that encourage flexibility in their decision-making process. In Hungary, for instance, government is urging higher education institutions to take non-profit status with trustee-type governing bodies; this represents an institutional separation from the government.

In the meantime, faculty members will need increased autonomy and effective ways of communication and control for substantive issues, including curriculum, academic quality, standards of teaching and learning, decisions about academic personnel, and academic policies. These, however, will need to be separated from the administrative and financial management of the institutions. Increasing complexity will not only affect the organizational framework of universities and colleges, but the disciplinary boundaries as well.

Higher education institutions in the CEE preserved traditional forms of academic hierarchy. In this way, the disciplinary structure of higher learning was accommodated within the institutional structure of higher education. There was little communication between disciplinary boundaries and there were even fewer channels that could have challenged the institutional structure of higher education. Authority within disciplinary programmes has remained tied to the position and personality of chairholders, despite the radical vocationalization and reorientation of the system towards direct industrial and social use. This disciplinary governance has remained hierarchical and elitist, and a rigid disciplinary structure has limited professional innovation and substantive changes in higher learning. Only radical (ergo centrally initiated) revisions of the programmes and provisions were possible. However, the long-term crisis and new challenges facing the academic community require a revision of the disciplinary organization. Within the traditional organization of universities, quasi-independent programmes and schools will need to be established, and the traditional chair structure will, in the long term, have to be replaced by modern departments. The new disciplinary structures could also increase the possibility of cooperation between different higher education institutions, as well as between the research institutions that belong to the Academies of Sciences. However, this kind of cooperation will also involve strong resistance by some institutions that may fear losing their independence and/or privileges.

The traditional faculty, especially the senior professorial staff, will likewise resist these changes in the future, fearing that changes will contribute to their losing control or jurisdiction over higher-level knowledge or other substantive issues of higher education. One way of expressing this resistance is the call for re-establishing the traditional ethos of the universities based on their exclusive knowledge and professional authority. Some of these groups may be able to use their political power to dominate public debate about higher education change, or internal organizational discussion of institutional strategies. However, their resistance is not entirely unreasonable. Institutions of high learning should defend their independence and their balance (in both their substance and curriculum) between external influences and internal constituencies. This they should be able to do through various means of effective professional self-regulation.

Academic quality cannot be improved or even maintained through dominant, extrinsic, political and governmental control. Furthermore, institutional control over scientific and disciplinary activities should be eased through legal and financial support. New forms of professional and programme accreditation, as well as self-evaluation, should be instituted. These should be independent from both governmental and legislative political bodies. Standards of intrinsic qualities, including scientific performance, training requirements, media of exchange within higher education (e.g. credits, courses, degrees) should be increasingly controlled by professional bodies, national and international alike. The policy of developing professional self-regulation, independently from the institutional boundaries of higher education, may be assisted by the separation of institutional accreditation from the accreditation of individual programmes and disciplines. This distinction would also help new institutions to emerge without all of their projected services being operational. If they are implemented, these changes will follow the global trends of a stronger focus on professional self-organization and on increasing the importance of disciplinary boundaries.

Disciplines, faculties and programmes will need to enhance their professional identity. This can provide more protection and a means of self-regulation. These interests will possibly increase their inclination to involve international communication and integration. There are both financial and professional reasons for this, as the disciplinary boundaries of higher learning and science are becoming increasingly international. Furthermore, because the higher education systems of the CEE countries are currently having an identity crisis, internationalization may have a significant role in identity formation. The structures of higher education – disciplinary, vertical and horizontal – will be pressed to follow international trends.

Where will universities go from here? Will they be willing to undertake a radical strategy of institutional reform or will they mobilize to defend their existing positions and privileges, and perhaps try to improve their administrative and financial condition? I believe that either is possible, but neither is probable. The actions and the emerging structure of institutions, governmental control and the social role of universities will reflect a mixture of conservative trends and radical departures towards new developments in provisions and structures.

14

Information Technology and Changing Roles in the Academy

Brian P. Nedwek

In a time of drastic change it is the learners who inherit the future. The learned usually find themselves equipped to live in a world that no longer exists.

Eric Hoffer

Introduction

The rapidity of change in our world is creating discontinuities in the academy. Responding to this accelerating rate of change challenges both learners and an array of individuals and organizations that serve to assist them. An information explosion is requiring new ways of working, learning and serving. Moreover, these activities are beginning to merge in this learning-on-demand environment. Academic leaders and institutional planners are searching for a common language to communicate their perceptions of viable alternative courses of action.

Major environmental changes are underway which, in turn, are transforming education at all levels. Four dominant forces are reshaping higher education: the loss of predictable resources, economic globalization and rising competition, stakeholder discontent and distrust, and (perhaps most important) knowledge age technology. These forces are creating a sea change not just in education, but in all of society. To begin the challenging task of realignment to meet new societal expectations should be a conscious decision. To wait passively and react to a host of changes is a failure of the heart and the mind. It is time to create shared meanings of complex and emotionally charged terms and build a vocabulary that can serve to improve the dialogue among stakeholders within and outside the academy about effective ways to meet the challenges of natural, yet chaotic, change.

Forces reshaping higher education

Historically, academic managers interested in the classic factors of production (e.g. books in libraries, faculty scholarship, credit hours generated) assumed a stable and non-competitive environment (Nedwek, 1996a). They worked in organizations that might have been described as neatly hierarchical and autonomous. Their planning models were naïve 'connect-the-dots' exercises. Education was a public good and the policy agenda was focused on access. Life was good!

Today, leaders are having a difficult time planning as powerful forces converge and heighten their impact on post-secondary education (Peterson and Dill, 1997). As the spheres of learning, work and service merge and recombine like fractiles on the latest screensaver, a new role for higher education is emerging as well. It will be 'to broadly gather information from distributed sources and provide it, on-demand, to individuals and organizations as they require it' (Molnar, 1997: 67). Whether all segments of post-secondary education can or will be responsive to societal needs seems unlikely. But in some areas, the transformation of higher education is already well underway (Dolence and Norris, 1995). Strategic alliances and partnerships with private industry to design and deliver just-in-time training are developing in the American community and technical colleges as well as four-year colleges and universities. For example, California State University-Chico has had a training partnership with Hewlett-Packard to deliver instruction at its corporate sites for several years.

Some futurists foresee the emergence of alternative delivery models. Continuous learning and 'unbundled learning experiences' are driving the design of new methods and models of education (Norris, 1996). Clearly the factory or production model of delivery is unable to respond to the changing workplace of shared governance, high-order skills and rapid change (Oblinger and Rush, 1997). The focus shifts to the learner and new organizational arrangements designed to provide competence-based assessment and certification (Tate, 1995). What are these dominant forces reshaping education and how is the academy to respond?

Loss of predictable resources

As national, state and local policy agenda evolve under changing political leadership in Europe and North America, competition is rising for government funds from multiple sectors of society. Political leadership appears to be moving more to a centrist position as it redefines the role of government in society. One trend is the loss of predictable resources to support higher education, especially in the traditional ways it goes about its business. Moving away from national funding of programmes, legislators are scrambling for funds to support a range of social programmes. In the United States, gaming proceeds, although unpredictable, have emerged as a politically feasible alternative revenue stream.

Table 14.1   Percentage of current revenue fund for higher education institutions

Revenue source	Public institutions			Private institutions		
	1990–1	*1993–4*	*Change*	*1990–1*	*1993–4*	*Change*
Tuition/fees	16.3	18.4	12.9	40.4	42.0	4.0
Federal government	10.3	11.0	6.8	15.4	14.5	−5.8
State government	40.3	35.9	−10.9	2.3	2.1	−8.7
Local government	3.7	4.0	8.1	0.7	0.7	0.0
Private gifts, grants, contracts	3.6	4.0	11.1	8.6	8.6	0.0
Endowment income	0.5	0.6	20.0	5.2	4.6	−11.5
Sales and service	22.7	23.4	3.1	22.9	23.2	1.3
Other sources	2.6	2.7	3.8	4.5	4.3	−4.4

Source: US Department of Education, National Center for Education Statistics (1996)

Left to their own devices, public institutions of higher education have embarked on multiple strategies to offset fewer discretionary dollars from the unpredictable appropriations process. Aggressive fund-raising campaigns and systematic tuition and fee increases are commonplace. Resident undergraduate tuition fees have increased between 39 and 41 per cent between 1991 and 1995 at community colleges, state colleges and universities, and four-year public and private universities. During this same period, the US consumer price index rose by only 11.9 per cent.

The changes to revenue streams in public and private higher education have been dramatic. Table 14.1 reveals how the percentage of current revenue attributed to tuition grew by nearly 13 per cent, while state government's share declined by nearly 11 per cent. When auxiliary enterprises are excluded (e.g. dormitories, hospitals), the state government share of support has declined precipitously. The state's share has dropped to 31 per cent, while tuition and fee revenue has increased to 37 per cent (Callan and Finney, 1997).

Lessened predictability of resources has accelerated the interest in delivering programmes and services that produce the highest return on investment (ROI). Alternative delivery strategies to the traditional place-bound campus format have become highly desirable. Asynchronous delivery strategies, especially Web-based approaches, are emerging as high-yield revenue sources. Whether the ROI of these technologies can withstand the scrutiny of new cost accounting methodology remains uncertain. Three things are certain: death, taxes and rising infrastructure budgetary demands.

Globalization and rising competition

Communications products and services have transformed how business is done today. The continuing expansion of the global economy, coupled with an explosion of educational service providers, heightens the stakes in seeking to create a sustainable advantage for an academic institution in the market place.

Today's leaders are called upon to seek more than operational effectiveness: they must gain strategic positioning, i.e. getting an organization to perform 'different activities from rivals or performing similar activities in different ways' (Porter, 1996: 62).

Creating a sustainable competitive advantage as for-profit delivery agents grow exponentially is forcing post-secondary educational leaders to make the tough decisions to trade-off one set of activities for others (e.g. the choice between expansion of asynchronous learning programmes or improvements in residential living for undergraduates). For-profit higher education is a booming business, with annual growth exceeding 10 per cent. The largest eight companies have grown to a $3.5 billion annual business that is building regional and national franchises (*Chronicle of Higher Education*, 1998). Huge investment decisions to install expensive new technology to compete must be made with uncertainty about break-even points.

Spreading the risk of undertaking new ventures with uncertain long-run revenue streams has created new alliances and partnerships across sectors. Autonomy gives way to altered power relationships if not shared governance. Increased competitiveness among traditional and non-traditional educational providers and the need for major institutions to compete internationally requires new organizational forms. Corporate organizational designs are emerging to provide greater flexibility and adaptability to rapid change (Dill and Sporn, 1995). North American universities are forming partnerships with private corporations to spawn their own for-profit companies to market online education (e.g. UCLA's Home Education Network).

Synergistic partnerships and strategic alliances are forming along multiple paths. Assessment and certification of mastery has led to competence-based programming at a host of innovative institutions, e.g. Western Governor's University, California State University at Monterey Bay. Academic programme delivery partnerships between public and private sectors are growing as classrooms are created in communities, e.g. Arizona Western College and Northern Arizona University's efforts in Yuma. Support and auxiliary service delivery has seen the development of partnerships among private technology giants, public libraries, neighbourhood associations and public state universities, e.g. Cleveland Community Energy Coalition with Cleveland State University. Research parks and investment fund strategies are used to leverage urban revitalization in Philadelphia and elsewhere. Finally, applied research and service strategies abound, e.g. Cal Poly/Ontario Community Centre for Urban Research with California State Polytechnical University and Overtown Neighbourhood Partnerships with Miami-Dade Community College.

Stakeholder discontent and distrust

The academy has fallen from grace. Legislators and the paying public are interested in their 'return on investment' as the cost of education continues to rise far more rapidly than most popular indicators of the cost of goods and services. Quality, accountability and institutional effectiveness dominate the policy agenda. The confusing lack of practical information about the comparative quality of institutions has created a political vacuum, filled quickly by the increased use of 'league tables' in Europe and North America, e.g. McClean's, U.S. News and World Report. Governments have responded with performance-funding strategies, commissions on the cost of higher education, and a range of intrusive measures designed to redefine governance in the academy. A broad array of performance and accountability initiatives have appeared in legislative action in the United States and elsewhere (Kells, 1993; Gaither *et al.*, 1994; Nedwek, 1996b). Regional and specialized accrediting agencies are maintaining the saliency of performance indicators as tools for accountability.

Post-secondary educational administrators are scrambling for marketing tags that either leverage an institution's 'place' in the rankings, or create an alternative way to look competitive. The bells and whistles of information technology may be a seductive way to buy a fashionably forward-looking face for public consumption. Listening to a typical sell from a campus representative to a prospective undergraduate, parents will assume a quality environment as a guide boasts about fibre optic backbones, Web-based tutorials, and global Internet links. The consumer's leap of faith is taken; lots of technology must mean lots of learning.

Knowledge age technology

Knowledge age technology has enlivened the discussion of the mission and identity of the academic village. Senior managers are beginning to understand that knowledge age technology is more than a replacement for the library as the new 'black hole' of post-secondary education with its gadgets; it is introducing new players who are competing for the learner's attention. Gurus of organizational change in this technological era are predicting highly competitive market places where learning happens anytime and anywhere in networked environments.

The education monopoly enjoyed by the academy has begun to crack under the pressure of new players providing competitively priced goods and services. Software companies are creating a series of products targeted to a wide range of learners. Microsoft Corporation has launched its *My Personal Tutor: Preschool to First Grade* suite of programs targeted to building mathematics and reading skills among pre-adolescents. This software is built on a technology that recognizes basic skill needs and provides an interactive tutorial to assist the learner. It rests on the educational concept of 'scaffolding', providing individual exploration along with instructional support to the learner. It is only a matter of time before similar pedagogy and software are available to post-secondary institutions for use in remedial or pre-collegiate programming. Licensing contracts are appearing that allow multiple corporate entities to enter the growing adult learning market. IBM Global Services and Wave Technologies International

Inc. have joined forces to produce the largest technical training operation in the world.

Today, knowledge age technology is viewed as an enabler to transform higher education from a production-centred enterprise to a rich learner-centred environment (Drucker, 1994). Distance learning initiatives fused with new information technology minimize, if not eliminate, place-bound instruction for some degree programmes. The tradition of hierarchical relationships between instructional or service provider and recipient is undergoing substantial change. Computer-supported systems of collaboratories of scientists and students are developing without regard to geography (Finholt and Olson, 1997).

The emergence of collaborative arrangements among learners may be new to the academy, but they have been flourishing in the private sector. In the late 1980s, the term 'community of practice' began to appear. Today these communities are thriving because individuals believe 'they have something to learn and to contribute . . . The work they do is the joint and several property of the group' (Stewart, 1996: 173). Recent studies report increased cooperation among learners when technological tools are part of the learning process (Slavin, 1990). Other unintended and positive consequences of knowledge age technology have been reported. For example, enhanced self-esteem and increased retention rates have been demonstrated (Adams *et al.*, 1990; Hamm and Adams, 1992).

Technology is transforming not just what happens in the classrooms but the full range of support services, from admissions and advising to alumni development and research production. For example, with the advent of relational databases to support administrative systems software, students now have the tools to manage their academic careers. Student services have seen the development of electronic portfolios in career and academic advising. For the faculty and sponsored programme managers, electronic data interchange software is under construction to improve the management of research services.

As with any movement, a new language and artefacts are emerging. Educational leaders, planners, technical consultants and a growing number of faculty speak a new language. Evidence of the institutional transformation process has begun to emerge, with faculty and staff performing new tasks or new ways to do existing ones. Classrooms, for example, are beginning to be connected real-time to current events, and science laboratories are making extensive use of simulations. Gradually heightened performance expectations become regular and predictable. Soon, new roles are articulated; some existing ones are redefined; and others collect budgetary dust. This transformation is marked also by a new vocabulary. Faculty activity is described as mentoring, navigating and coaching. Learning activity includes notions of learner productivity, learner-centred services, and collaborative arrangements among learners.

New artefacts began to appear on the academic landscape by the mid-1990s, including learning malls, electronic villages of reflective practitioners, self-paced learning modules and electronic syllabi and portfolios. Classrooms now contain newsgroups, usernets, bulletin boards, listserves, annotation systems, and shared online environments. A rich set of new roles and responsibilities for senior executives, faculty, staff and students are emerging, with enormous social and political ramifications. We need to focus on specific impact areas and then gain some insights about how innovative institutions are taking on the challenges of the knowledge age.

The emerging knowledge age presents numerous challenges to academic leaders and planners. In this traditionally labour-intensive enterprise, faculty roles and responsibilities in teaching, research/scholarship and service represent the core area of transformation. Academic and operations support staff are experiencing gradual change, as are those internal and external resources available to leadership. These transformations are redefining governance or at least forcing a reconsideration of the academy's basic tenets of control. Let's examine each of these areas to understand better the paths of transition and how change can be leveraged.

The knowledge age and learner–teacher relationships

The traditional American model of higher education was built on the metaphor of an empty vessel to be filled by an all-knowing teacher. Education was a tightly structured enterprise where knowledge was transmitted or transferred from one actor to another. The model produced a place-bound and role-bound architecture. The tools of the trade (classrooms, labs, libraries and offices) were located in one location, a college campus. Expected behaviours of teachers and students reflected a manufacturing process where faculty assumed homogeneity in learner needs and readiness. The process, in turn, gave rise to a host of performance measures, e.g. workloads, seat-time. Efficiency in the use of resources was the dominant administrative value. For the past several decades, planners, administrators and governance officials were focused mainly on the factors of production, especially the teacher.

Instructional delivery became routine and predictable. Reinforced by promotion and tenure standards, traditional faculty roles gained widespread acceptance across the academic landscape. Performance expectations were relatively insensitive to varying institutional missions. The emerging knowledge age is forcing an examination of delivery mechanisms and thus has created a political and professional vacuum for managers and faculty alike. New roles and responsibilities are entering the conversations of rank and tenure committee members, teachers and academy watchers. Today we are witnessing the emergence of new challenges for faculty as they attempt to increase congruity between their role expectations and those of students, administrators and, among others, legislators.

The traditional role of information dispenser/broadcaster is giving way to a more facilitative relationship with the learner. Substantive expertise remains highly valued, especially so at institutions whose mission is the development of basic knowledge. Potentially the most powerful role change is a call to the

Table 14.2   Traditional and emerging faculty roles

Traditional roles	Emerging roles
Course designer	Design team member
Broadcaster (lecturer)	Mentor
Discussion moderator	Model questioner
Evaluator	Guide
Adviser	Facilitator
Discovery researcher	Architect of connections
Subject matter expert	Coach
Scholar	Scholar of the learning process

scholarship of integration, application and teaching as envisioned by Boyer (1990). At some institutions the research agenda has been expanded to include applied scholarship of the learning process.

A new vision is emerging that places the learner first (Barr and Tagg, 1995; O'Banion, 1997). Learning productivity is becoming a key value in curricular design and programme delivery. Networked environments are pressuring the academy to redefine faculty roles (Staman, 1997). Faculty can be model questioners, problem solvers, or a host of other role incumbents (Miller, 1995). Faculty role change from broadcaster to mentor, guide, learning agent and coach is a shift from content expert to process manager. Table 14.2 lists traditional and emerging faculty roles.

The historical model of curricular design and delivery centred on the faculty member as course designer, delivery agent and assessor. The emergent roles of faculty are unbundling these individual tasks and reconfiguring them. For example, multimedia courses are designed by a team of professionals including IT staff, curriculum design specialists and the faculty member. Design and delivery of media-enhanced courses have created a demand for effective faculty development services.

The emergence of the electronic classroom and syllabus is the driving force behind altered faculty–learner linkages and the roles played by supporting staff. Norman (1990) suggests transforming the traditional pedagogy to electronic classrooms through a hypermedia database that is organized into course materials, interactions and products. A theatre metaphor is an instructive guide to the development of electronic classrooms. One of the more successful models is the case of the AT&T Teaching Theatre at the University of Maryland (Norman and Carter, 1994). Some suggest that in designing and supporting Web-based courses we view education as consisting of modes of dialogue and communication between faculty and student, among students, and between student and resources (Boettcher and Cartwright, 1997).

In the emerging pedagogy, instructors are expected to facilitate learning rather than dispense nuggets of truth through lectures. Information can be communicated or shared between facilitator and learner in real-time or asynchronously. Students are expected to take an active role in the learning process. Just as with faculty, learners are expected to have technical literacy across a range of applications. The classroom is no longer merely a room; it is a window to materials, experiences and resources beyond physical space. Staffing electronic classrooms therefore commands a wide range of technological skills to assist in managing the production within this multidimensional learning environment.

An electronic syllabus is the key map across materials, faculty–student and learner–learner interactions and products. A course syllabus is the contract between instructor and learner. Electronic syllabi can set a very different tone for a course by increasing the quality of information available to the learner. Online syllabi can be distributed on a course Web server providing numerous links to a variety of features (MacMinn, no date). A variety of information is made readily available to the learner including:

Course background data
Faculty curriculum vitae
Course difficulty measure, e.g. previous grade distribution

Aggregated performance measures
Grade distribution of current term

Course management data
Assignments to and submissions from learners
Establishing e-mail accounts
Link to administrative software for posting grades electronically
Student roster
Access to individual performance assessment scores

Substantive learning materials
Presentations
Abstract of materials, online documents

Connections
E-mail gateway to the instructor
Listserve
Newsgroups
Website links

Assessment information
Portfolios for storing skill demonstrations

Online syllabi have the power of establishing connectedness across the full range of services provided by faculty and staff. The syllabus is undergoing a transformation from a basic course structure outline to a dynamic resource for the distribution and retrieval of learner-centred information. An added function of online syllabi is the enhancement of the students' ability to manage their own learning environment. For motivated learners who have a degree of technical sophistication and are goal-directed, electronic syllabi can promote independence.

We are only beginning to understand how learners use multiple strategies to acquire knowledge. O'Malley and Chamot (1990) organize these strategies into three types: metacognitive (managing one's path to knowledge acquisition), cognitive (learning process activities), and social/affective (collaborative learning activity and personal development). These strategies can be connected to how students learn in either face-to-face or technology-enhanced settings (Smith, 1997). Table 14.3 presents a matrix of faculty behaviours organized by learner knowledge acquisition strategies and faculty roles.

Table 14.3 contains a rich variety of faculty expected behaviours. Academic leaders, information technology specialists and planners can create their own institutional matrix that reflects the culture of the school. In the process of building a tailored matrix, developers will quickly see the elements of faculty job descriptions emerge. This matrix-building process creates the base for performance assessment. Developers may want a step-by-step approach to building their own departmental, divisional or institutional matrix as a first step in establishing a new faculty development programme.

Table 14.3 captures some of the opportunities available to faculty in meeting the needs of the twenty-first-century learner. The key assumption underlying this array is that the educational process must be learner-centred, with a faculty continuously redesigning tasks to meet the needs of the learner. The learning milieu becomes a 'dynamic, customized pursuit of new solutions rather than the acquisition of a preconceived package of facts' (Smith, 1997: 37). Thus, faculty, whether plying their craft in traditional or virtual learning situations, are expected to be scholars of the learning process.

Learner-centred educational practices help further to customize faculty roles by paying greater attention to the diversity of learning styles. Educators of adults need to understand that their collaborator and facilitator roles are far more important than that of information dispenser. Active and cooperative learning strategies are natural to learner-centred educational practices, but would not be widely deployed in schools that held different values (e.g. reputation in athletics, funded research, prize-winning faculty). Moreover, active and cooperative learning may be especially difficult to achieve in huge undergraduate introductory classes.

Creating and sustaining a learner-centred environment does not come without a price. Post-secondary institutions are only beginning to understand the budgetary and cultural commitment needed to continue the transformation to a learner-centred organization. Only a few schools have taken a holistic approach to faculty development, curricular reform, instructional technology planning and assessment. The University of Central Florida is an excellent example of a carefully planned and systematic approach to pedagogical redesign. They have established a Faculty Center for Teaching and Learning to assist faculty in redesign of courses (see http://www.reach.ucf.edu/~fctl/). The University has also started a team approach to developing asynchronous learning formats (see http.//www.reach.ucf.edu/~coursdev). Complementary additional training in media use, new library technology and information management strategies have been put in place as well.

A knowledge acquisition and faculty roles matrix has direct implications for resource allocation. The transformation of educational models from our

Table 14.3 Faculty roles and strategies for knowledge acquisition

| Faculty roles | Strategies for knowledge acquisition | | |
	Metacognitive	*Cognitive*	*Social/affective*
Traditional	Establishes course goals and objectives	Selects course materials (texts, multimedia)	Advises students on programme/degree requirements
	Sets course timing components (deadlines, sequencing)	Constructs tests and written assignments	Interacts with students through posted office hours
	Provides event-based feedback (assignment reviews, grading)	Broadcasts facts and opinions; creates and disseminates new knowledge	Builds limited team-based learning communities
Emergent	Encourages personal goal-setting in concert with course goals	Establishes links to external resources	Models professional behaviour
	Encourages process-based feedback	Monitors environment for new resources (software, listserves, Web sites)	Sponsors student access to networks of learners and practitioners
	Intentionally merges community service and consultation with student learning	Creates and disseminates new knowledge	Systematic training in small-group dynamics
	Works in teams to design tutorials tailored to student needs	Redesigns learning processes based on systemic assessments	Provides emotional and moral encouragement

current pedagogy argues for re-engineering that promises saved time and financial resources. Some argue that these 'savings' can be ploughed back into enhanced course design and educational planning (Dolence and Norris, 1995; Massy, 1997). It is clear that collaboration and cooperation, coupled with a strong institutional commitment to adequate funding, are essential to the integration of information about teaching, learning and research (van Dusen, 1997).

This centralized and coordinated approach is an effective organizational arrangement to gain immediate results within the faculty. The continuing explosion of new tools and techniques creates discontinuities between dreams and deeds in the classroom. Inspired by the American Council on Education's Teaching, Learning, and Technology Roundtable (TLTR) model, the University of Delaware created a series of new services to assist faculty under the umbrella name of PRESENT (Practical Resources for Educators Seeking Effective New Technologies). See, for example, its 'Tool Kit for Teaching with

Technology' in http://www.udel.edu/learn/technology/ (see de Vry and Hyde, 1997).

The knowledge age and administrative support staff

Information technology tools are transforming how staff deliver support service to the academic and operational functions of the institution. Academic and operations support staff have significant responsibility in assisting the institution to adapt to new roles and the changing environment. There are several redefined roles suggested for academic and support service staff.

- process re-engineer
- missionary/anthropologist
- partner with faculty and learners

Process re-engineering is becoming commonplace in student services divisions. Staff members have key roles to play in bringing in new ideas and ways of doing things to meeting the needs of the twenty-first-century learner. Collaboration and partnership among faculty and other support staff can foster positive interdependence and interaction. In the knowledge age of mediated pedagogy to foster collaborative learning, faculty and staff are engaged in process re-engineering to achieve learning objectives. The basic elements of a collaborative learning environment include interdependence, interaction, individual accountability and responsibility of the learner, interpersonal skills and effective group processing (Johnson *et al.*, 1991; Card and Horton, 1997).

Staff roles in a variety of support areas are under substantial transformation. Information resource professionals are migrating from specialists to generalists who can speak the languages of multiple stakeholders. They are insightful enough to be moving away from a silo mentality toward the integration of core functions. They are the new boundary spanners (Hawkins and Battin, 1997). As *missionaries*, staff can bring new approaches and paradigms to the faculty by creating a clearing-house function with academic departments. As *anthropologists*, staff in the information age can come to realize their role as meaning-makers, especially in the growing conversation about what constitutes efficient pedagogy and effective results. Librarians, for example, are developing an entirely new set of roles as they come to understand the electronic library (Rapple, 1997).

As facilitators of the learning process, staff will need to develop new communication and interpersonal skills as they work in *partnership* with faculty. Re-engineering libraries, career services, registration systems and the like will require staff to find new ways of providing service without compromising quality (Heterick, 1993). They will need to reject conventional wisdom on how stakeholders are best served and focus on preferred outcomes and benchmarks of core functions (Penrod and Dolence, 1992).

Process re-engineering is underway in institutions charting a new transformation path. Parallel to what is underway with faculty role reconfigurations,

Lane Community College has sought to make mid-level managers understand the new roles of coaches, advisers and consultants in the decision-making process (Moskus, 1997). Rensselaer Polytechnic Institute introduced a studio course format in late 1994 to pilot the integration of technology with learning groups. Classroom facilities were redesigned as a consequence of process re-engineering. The physics studio experiment demonstrated how faculty and learner roles become less rigid and more fluid, allowing a transfer of some responsibility for learning from the teacher to the learner (Wilson, 1994, 1997). Portland State University's process re-engineering produced an interdisciplinary curriculum that uses student enquiry and peer mentors.

Let's take a look at three applications in support services – one dealing with students, another with Web-based information services, and a third with faculty – to demonstrate these role transformations. The first case examines the use of electronic portfolios in career and academic advising services. The second application shows the use of the Web for capturing and disseminating student learning information. The last illustration looks at technology applied to research services supporting faculty.

Student services in the knowledge age are undergoing re-engineering and producing encouraging results, for example:

- services controlled by the student;
- portable, lifelong, electronic portfolios maintained by the student and graduate;
- one-card navigation across a full range of services;
- seamless 'front door' to education allowing students to navigate administrative databases, e.g. student records, billing-receivables, financial aid.

Electronic portfolios

This new technology represents the continued evolution of student services and reflects the emerging interest in performance-based assessment practices. Portfolios are collection tools to store evidence of a student's work, progress and demonstrated achievements within specific subject areas or across a curriculum. Computer-based portfolios are designed to save information in electronic format. Unlike traditional hardcopy format, the new technology allows storage of text, sound, graphics and video on CD-ROMs. The new devices can store approximately 650 Mb of information (roughly equivalent to 300,000 pages of typed text).

An excellent example of electronic portfolios is Winona State University's Electronic Resumé. Using Authorware and Skillview, an application template is used by students to create a multimedia resumé that is easily transportable. The product is an interactive resumé/portfolio that contains textual information on student goals, objectives and philosophy, as well as written evidence of past accomplishments, physical evidence of verbal communication skills and authentic assessments of other skills (Winona State University, 1997).

Electronic portfolios represent a new technology that provides multi-sensory information for use by career centre personnel, admissions officers, advisers and other academic services support personnel. For a good overview of the commercially available portfolio programs, see Lankes (1995) and the work underway at California State University-Monterey Bay using Netscape Gold, PageMill, Adobe Photoshop, ColorIt, and other software (see http://www. monterey.edu/students/). For an application at the secondary level that is easily adapted to post-secondary settings, see the Grady Profile at http:// www.aurbach.com.

Web-based information services

Use of the Web is expanding as a tool for capturing and disseminating information about students and their learning outcomes. The University of Colorado at Boulder Student Affairs Research Services uses the Web to collect student satisfaction data and post outcome information (see http://www. colorado.edu/outcomes/index.html). Eastern New Mexico University uses the Web to keep faculty informed about assessment strategies and related educational resources (http://www.enmu.edu/users/testaa/welcome.html). Similar use of the Web in outcomes assessment and information dissemination functions is used by institutional researchers at Montana State University (http://www.montana.edu/~aircj/assess/).

Web-based services are available to support core functional areas as well. There exists an electronic application service available to harried parents of prospective freshmen (http://www.collegenet.com). Peterson's has initiated a free, online admissions site using POLARIS (Peterson's Online Application, Registration, and Information Service). A set of proprietary online forms are accepted by nearly 900 colleges and universities (see http://www.applytocollege.com).

In addition to a growing variety of Web sites within institutions, national organizations are active in building clearing-houses on outcomes assessment strategies and instrumentation. See for example the work of the American College Personnel Association or the growing listserves on student learning and assessment (e.g. listserv@lsv.uky.edu and listserv@uafsysb.uark.edu). An excellent summary of links across sectors is available through the Society for College and University Planning (http://www.scup.org/links.htm).

Electronic data interchange (EDI)

Most grant and contract administrative activity is perceived as a troublesome distraction to faculty researchers and sponsored programme officers. Administrative software to manage the flow of transactions at research universities was constructed largely to track post-award activity. Interest in pre-award tracking using system software from commercial vendors was limited. While automated electronic transactions are well established in commercial applications, they have been late in appearing in higher education. Electronic proposal submission is a key component of pre-award transactions. Grant submission and administration software development is well underway and should be fully operational within two years.

The initial platform for developing electronic transactions is under construction. Rules-governed sets of data fields have been built, and consensus has developed on nationally sanctioned data standards. Application narratives are being developed and field experiments are underway (Graham, 1996).

An alternative methodology is under construction by the National Science Foundation (NSF). Its project, the NSF FastLane, uses the Web as a vehicle to build a research proposal online. The FastLane project contains several features:

1. user searches of the NSF database;
2. direct application for graduate research fellowships;
3. transmission of nominations for recognition, e.g. Medal of Science;
4. proposal review commentary;
5. timely status updates of proposal submissions;
6. smart forms to collate individual and institutional information in the NSF mainframe database;
7. a report template to convey final project report to the NSF by the Principal Investigator; and
8. monitoring status of continuing fund application. For further information and demonstration see the NSF website at http://www.fastlane.nsf.gov/a0/instructions/insappin.htm

The FastLane initiative in all likelihood may not be the model for all EDI applications. There are anticipated limitations in proposal submission routeing and tracking systems, also uncertainty on the tightness of security. Moreover, fear of a potential misuse of information escalates as databases are matched and tied together (Rezmierski, 1996; Rhinehart, 1996). The High Energy Astrophysics Science Archive Research Center uses a remote proposal system (RPS) to carry submitted proposals in response to NASA announcements. Researchers can submit proposals through either an e-mail server or the Web (see http://heasarc.gsfc.nasa.gov/RPS/rps_pr.html for further information).

Private sector initiatives are emerging to compete in this multi-billion federal dollar arena. Software development companies are continuing to work on electronic interfaces with federal government agencies. An interesting project worth monitoring is under construction to allow electronic proposal submission to the National Institutes of Health. A suite of management tools (e.g. proposal development, tracking and management) are available to assist sponsored programme office personnel. InfoEd International, Inc. estimates a pilot version will be operational in early 1998. For additional information consult http://www.infoed.org. Competition among private vendors should produce enhanced software and management tools for use by a wide range of funded-research offices.

The knowledge age and internal resources

Access to resources is changing as the knowledge age emerges. Resources are drawn from within the organization or secured from outside, i.e. its external environment. Table 14.4 displays the conventional perception of internal resources in contrast with knowledge age bases.

Table 14.4   The knowledge age and internal resources

Conventional approach	Knowledge age
Provider-centred	Learner-centred
Information silos	Accessible, integrated databases
Independent, single-purpose space	Interdependent, multi-purpose space
Reputation-driven competitiveness	Time-based competitiveness
Access to goods	Access to networks

Information technology accelerates the interest and capacity to deliver programmes and services from a learner-centred perspective rather than a human resources view. Traditional approaches to database management reinforced information silos under the control of numerous organizational layers. New databases and supporting administrative software have broadened user access. In the physical environment, control over space is giving way to the perception of the interdependence of space. The significance of place for facilities planners is increasing as they seek to modify existing classrooms to increase informal interaction among faculty and students.

Another internal resource has been an institution's reputation as the currency of competitiveness. In the emerging age, time and its efficient use will be more valued than ascribed institutional reputation. Providers of educational services that deliver high-quality programmes any time and any place will be more competitive in the market place than place-bound approaches. The growing adult market segment, either first degree seekers or those upgrading skills and credentials, is far more sensitive to time-based competitiveness than other market segments. Technology also improves the value of networks as an internal resource. The steady movement toward collaborative learning environments for students, multi-party alliances for research development, and multi-organizational approaches to service delivery make access to information networks more valuable than ever.

The knowledge age and external resources

Resources external to a college or university are also changing. Table 14.5 suggests that loyalty to place is becoming less relevant to students as distance learning modes of delivery expand. Government sources of support for the academy are changing as well. Gone are the days of 'no strings' general appropriations from either state or national coffers. Numerous states have moved to quality

Table 14.5   The knowledge age and external resources

Traditional approach	Knowledge age
Loyalty to place	Alumni disengagement from place
General 'no strings' appropriations	Performance funding tied to key measures
Unrestricted giving	Donor conditions
Formal articulation agreements	Collaborative partnerships and time-limited alliances

outcomes factors in higher education budgeting (Layzell and Caruthers, 1995; Banta *et al.*, 1996). South Carolina has taken performance funding the furthest, with legislation that commits 100 per cent of appropriations to performance. Donors today are concerned that their gifts are targeted to meet their needs and expectations of the academy. Finally, the cost of information technology and its application in instruction and research is demanding new kinds of alliances and partnerships across public and private sectors. For example, Northwestern University has received a four-year grant from the Ameritech Foundation to create a regional network-based collaborative environment to support education and research. The Collaboratory Project will provide consulting, training, technical support, applications, tools and services to create a Chicago-regional networked environment (see http://www.nwu.edu/collaboratory/intro/coldesc.html).

The knowledge age, governance and accountability

The market place of higher education is steadily changing as well. Pricing of and access to goods and services in the academy was largely under the control and governance of the producers. The information age suggests that a demand for excellence and enhanced telecommunications will alter the power base of institutions and their ability to control pricing and access. Farrington (1997) foresees a bleak future for marginal institutions. He predicts that colleges with limited prestige and a local market are most threatened and suggests that 'their markets can be invaded by competitors with better faculty and more prestigious brand names. Some weaker institutions will surely lose in the competition' (cited in Oblinger and Rush, 1997: 68).

In the early 1990s interest in learner-centred pedagogy began to emerge. Project-Based Learning (PBL) was a learner-focused pilot that sought to create an environment where the 'student is the problem-solver, planner, manager, students are motivated and take responsibility for learning' (Oakey, 1995: 15, cited in O'Banion, 1997). Just as technology is driving new role definitions for faculty and staff, the PBL project foretells transformation of traditional student roles from passive recipients to active managers of the learning process.

Perhaps the most significant area of change is associated with the assessment and certification of skills and knowledge. This reconceptualization and focus

Table 14.6   The knowledge age and assessment

Traditional approach	Knowledge age
Provider designed	Collaborative
Programmes loosely coupled to learning outcomes	Performance-based learning with immediate feedback
Outcome-based	Process-based
Assumed mastery	Demonstrated mastery
Faculty-controlled	Faculty/learner collaboration

on the learner alters how we establish and support internal accountability methods. Table 14.6 shows striking differences between pre-knowledge age and contemporary issues in the assessment of higher education.

Knowledge age technology affects accountability in higher education in several ways. The transition to knowledge age learning and assessment is marked by faculty and learner collaboration both in the development of outcomes and the methodology to document achievement of competence. Traditional programme models are giving way to performance-based learning with immediate feedback. A host of computer-assisted self-paced modules are available for use by degree-seeking students. Competence-based curricula are emerging in several technology-based delivery initiatives. The Western Governors University, California State University at Monterey Bay and the Arizona Learning Systems efforts make extensive use of administrative software for instruction and academic service delivery.

Knowledge age technology and competence-based programming are forcing a renewed interest in learning processes and the assessment of what works best for which type of learning style. Institutions seeking a sustainable advantage in the new market place are taking seriously the demand for demonstrated mastery at appropriate stages in the learning process. Equally significant, there is some suggestion that assessment will be decoupled from certification. Faculty and programme managers will no longer enjoy a monopoly on the academic process and measurement of its quality. Faculty may likely serve as moderators between the criteria of assessment and evidence brought by the learner (Brown, 1997). The market will be likely to produce a fee-for-service model of third-party certification of competence; as it were, a *Good Housekeeping* Seal of Approval.

The transformation process moves from providing learning opportunities to demonstrating learning success. As outcomes-based programming becomes more commonplace, we should see a continued development of performance funding against predetermined skills and competencies. How the process of articulating skills and weighting them with either discretionary resources (e.g. a funding-for-results allocation model) or direct allocation, remains to be battled out in legislatures and coordinating boards in the states. In this political game of accountability, some institutions and programmes are better prepared to survive than others. Community colleges have long enjoyed success in applying outcome-based assessment strategies, especially in vocational areas. Similarly, professional programmes in allied health professions, nursing and law (among others) have a refined capacity to engage in skill-based assessment.

Summary and conclusion

That the environment surrounding higher education is undergoing rapid transformation is clear. Less understood is how the academy will choose to change as well. One thing is certain. The traditional elements underpinning the design of programmes, services, physical plant and the like are changing in value. Time and place are two crucial resources whose values are moving in opposite direction. Effective time is more dear, while attachment to place is less relevant. The real test of a learning institution or organization is the 'quality of access it provides to academic communities' (Brown and Duguid, 1996: 14). Communities of practice or communities of reflective practitioners (Norris, 1996) are both the product of and force behind the infiltration of information technology in the academy.

The components of higher education are becoming unbundled by knowledge age technology. The processes of education are decoupling the resources from the learner. Faculty are emerging as mentors, navigators and guides to learners, as the professorate seeks ways to redefine rank and tenure rules and standards of promotion. Information age technology is reshaping and redefining issues of faculty autonomy and accountability (Finnegan, 1997). As their roles become further clarified in the knowledge age, it is reasonable to conclude that traditional vehicles of integration within the academy (e.g. academic disciplines and peer review) will give way to increased entrepreneurship and independence. Senior management may begin to see tenure-track faculty slots as untapped sources of scarce funds to support further information technology. Thus, outsourcing core faculty functions to part-time, temporary staff and outsourcing auxiliary enterprises to private sector providers are attractive strategies to develop new revenue streams or replenish existing ones.

Courseware and self-paced modules are facilitating the realization of independence in learners. Documentation of skills to be demonstrated is housed in assessment centres or within portable software programs. Whether students entering the twenty-first century are prepared for such independence remains uncertain. Just as the knowledge age is calling for emergent faculty roles, so too must learners enter the transformation process. Students must become 'strategic learners' and possess a variety of new knowledge acquisition skills (Weinstein, 1996).

Even pricing of goods and services in the academic basket is getting unpacked. Some distance learning providers have begun to create a 'fee for service' model of pricing using subscription service fee structures. For example, Magellan University allows students to subscribe to online lessons, self-testing services and (among others) university library services (see http://magellan.edu/studentservices/summaryandfees/). All these changes see the continuing evolution of greater choice, independence and responsibility as within the control of the learner.

Planning for tomorrow's tomorrow in this effervescent world is not for the faint of heart nor the bankrupt soul. Some will lead and others follow, while a few remain unburdened by a vision of the future. Some CEOs have accepted the knowledge age challenge and are willing to have their time on the tiller judged by how far they have moved the institution into these uncharted waters. Each of us has some inkling about this transformation. How we chose to ignite our passion for creativity and awaken our imagination will shape our future and that of our institutions.

References

Adams, D., Carlson, H. and Hamm, M. (1990) *Cooperative Learning in Educational Media: Collaborating with Technology and Each Other.* Englewood Cliffs, NJ: Educational Technology Publications.

Banta, T., Rudolph, L., Van Dyke, J. and Fisher, H. (1996) Performance funding comes of age in Tennessee, *Journal of Higher Education,* 67(1): 23–45.

Barr, R. B. and Tagg, J. (1995) From teaching to learning: a new paradigm for undergraduate education, *Change,* 27(6): 12–25.

Boettcher, J. and Cartwright, G. P. (1997) Designing and supporting courses on the Web, *Change,* 29(5): 10–63.

Boyer, E. (1990) *Scholarship Reconsidered: Priorities of the Professoriate.* Princeton, NJ: The Carnegie Foundation for the Advancement of Teaching.

Brown, J. S. and Duguid, P. (1996) Universities in the digital age, *Change,* July/August: 11–19.

Brown, S. (1997) Choosing and using assessment for learning. Paper presented at the 'What Kind of a University?' conference, London, England, 18–20 June.

Callan, P. M. and Finney, J. E. (eds) (1997) *Public and Private Financing of Higher Education: Shaping Public Policy for the Future.* American Council on Education. Series on Higher Education. Phoenix, AZ: Oryx Press.

Card, K. A. and Horton, L. (1997) Using computer-mediated learning to foster collaborative learning. Paper presented at the Teaching, Learning, and Technology Tutorial, AAHE National Conference, Washington, DC, 16 March.

Chronicle of Higher Education (1998) For-profit higher education sees booming enrollments and revenues. 23 January, A36.

de Vry, J. R. and Hyde, P. (1997) Supporting faculty exploration of teaching with technology, *CAUSE/EFFECT,* Fall, 20(3): 45–8.

Dill, D. D. and Sporn, B. (1995) University 2001: what will the university of the twenty-first century look like? in D. Dill and B. Sporn (eds) *Emerging Patterns of Social Demand and University Reform: Through a Glass Darkly.* New York: Pergamon Press.

Dolence, M. G. and Norris, D. M. (1995) *Transforming Higher Education: A Vision for Learning in the 21st Century.* Ann Arbor, MI: Society for College and University Planning.

Drucker, P. (1994) The age of social transformation, *Atlantic Monthly,* 274(3): 53–60.

Farrington, G. C. (1997) Higher education in the information age, in D. G. Oblinger and S. C. Rush (eds) *The Learning Revolution: The Challenges of Information Technology in the Academy.* Bolton, MA: Anker Publishing.

Finholt, T. A. and Olson, G. M. (1997) From laboratories to collaboratories: a new organizational form for scientific collaboration, *Psychological Science*, 8(1): 28–36.

Finnegan, D. E. (1997) Transforming faculty roles, in M. W. Peterson, D. D. Dill, L. A. Mets and Associates (eds) *Planning and Management for a Changing Environment: A Handbook on Redesigning Postsecondary Institutions*. San Francisco, CA: Jossey-Bass.

Gaither, G., Nedwek, B. and Neal, J. (1994) *Measuring Up: The Promises and Pitfalls of Performance Indicators in Higher Education*. ASHE-ERIC Higher Education Report No. 5. Washington, DC: The George Washington University, Graduate School of Education and Human Development.

Graham, C. E. (1996) Electronic proposal submission basic concepts, *NCURA Newsletter*, February/March.

Hamm, M. and Adams, D. (1992) *The Collaborative Dimensions of Learning*. Norwood, NJ: Eblex Publishing Corporation.

Hawkins, B. and Battin, P. (1997) The changing role of the information resources professional: a dialogue, *CAUSE/EFFECT*, Spring, 20(1): 22–30.

Heterick, Jr., R. C. (1993) *Reengineering Teaching and Learning in Higher Education: Sheltered Groves, Camelot, Windmills, and Malls*. Professional Paper Series, #10. Boulder, CO: CAUSE.

Johnson, D., Johnson, R. and Smith, K. (1991) *Cooperative Learning: Increasing College Faculty Instructional Productivity*. ASHE-ERIC Higher Education Report No. 4. Washington, DC: The George Washington University, Graduate School of Education and Human Development.

Kells, H. R. (ed.) (1993) *The Development of Performance Indicators for Higher Education: A Compendium for Eleven Countries*. Second edition. Paris: Organization for Economic Cooperation and Development, ED 331 355.

Lankes, A. M. (1995) Electronic portfolios: a new idea in assessment, *ERIC Digest*, December, EDO-IR-95-9.

Layzell, D. T. and Caruthers, J. K. (1995) Performance funding at the state level: trends and prospects. Paper presented at the Annual Meeting of the Association for the Study of Higher Education, Orlando, Florida, 2 November.

MacMinn, R. (no date) AEA Presentation: Toward an Electronic Classroom. See http://kiwiclub.bus.utexas.edu/aea_presentation/aea_presentation.html

Massy, W. F. (1997) Life on the wired campus: how information technology will shape institutional futures, in D. G. Oblinger and S. C. Rush (eds) *The Learning Revolution: The Challenge of Information Technology in the Academy*. Boston, MA: Anker Publishing.

Miller, M. A. (1995) Technoliteracy and the new professor, *New Literacy History*, 26(3): 601–12.

Molnar, A. R. (1997) Computers in education: a brief history, *THE Journal*, 24(11): 63–8.

Moskus, J. (1997) Lane changes: transformation at Lane Community College, in T. O'Banion, *A Learning College for the 21st Century*. Phoenix, AZ: Oryx Press.

Nedwek, B. (ed.) (1996a) *Doing Academic Planning: Effective Tools for Decision-Making*. Ann Arbor, MI: Society for College and University Planning.

Nedwek, B. (1996b) Linking quality assurance and accountability: using process and performance indicators, in B. Nedwek (ed.) *Doing Academic Planning: Effective Tools for Decision-Making*. Ann Arbor, MI: Society for College and University Planning. 137–44.

Norman, K. L. (1990) The electronic teaching theatre: interactive hypermedia and mental models of the classroom, *Current Psychology: Research and Reviews*, 9: 141–61.

Norman, K. L. and Carter, L. E. (1994) An evaluation of the electronic classroom: the AT&T teaching theater at the University of Maryland. See http://www.itz. uni-koeln.de/themen/cmc/text/norman.94txt

Norris, D. (1996) Perpetual learning as a revolutionary creation, *On the Horizon*, November/December, 1–4.

O'Banion, T. (1997) *A Learning College for the 21st Century*. Phoenix, AZ: Oryx Press.

Oblinger, D. G. and Rush, S. C. (eds) (1997) *The Learning Revolution: The Challenge of Information Technology in the Academy*. Boston, MA: Anker Publishing.

O'Malley, J. M. and Chamot, A. U. (1990) *Learning Strategies in Second Language Acquisition*. Cambridge: Cambridge University Press.

Penrod, J. I. and Dolence, M. G. (1992) *Reengineering: A Process for Transforming Higher Education*. Professional paper Series, #9. Boulder, CO: CAUSE.

Peterson, M. W. and Dill, D. (1997) Understanding the competitive environment of the postsecondary knowledge industry, in M. W. Peterson, D. Dill, L. Mets and Associates (eds) *Planning and Management for a Changing Environment*. San Francisco, CA: Jossey-Bass, 3–29.

Porter, M. E. (1996) What is strategy? *Harvard Business Review*, November–December, 61–78.

Rapple, B. A. (1997) The electronic library: new roles for librarians, *CAUSE/EFFECT*, Spring, 20(1): 45–51.

Rezmierski, V. (1996) Electronic data interchange: we are stampeding, *CAUSE/EFFECT*, Spring, 19(1): 40–50.

Rhinehart, P. T. (1996) The use of electronic data interchange under the family educational rights and privacy act, *CAUSE/EFFECT*, Spring, 19(1): 34–9.

Slavin, R. (1990) *Cooperative Learning: Theory, Research, and Practice*. Needham, MA: Alyn and Bacon.

Smith, K. L. (1997) Preparing faculty for instructional technology: from education to development to creative independence, *CAUSE/EFFECT*, 20(3): 36–48.

Staman, E. M. (1997) Launching internet on community college campuses, *Community College Journal*, August/September, 67(7): 12–17.

Stewart, T. A. (1996) The invisible key to success, *Fortune*, 5 August: 173–5.

Tate, R. G. (1995) At the crossroad: higher ed and technology development, *Technos*, Winter, 4(4): 26–30.

US Department of Education, National Center for Education Statistics (1996) *Digest of Education Statistics 1996*. Washington, DC: USDE.

van Dusen, G. C. (1997) *The Virtual Campus: Technology and Reform in Higher Education*. ASHE-ERIC Higher Education Report, Volume 25, No. 5. Washington, DC: The George Washington University, Graduate School of Education and Human Development.

Weinstein, C. E. (1996) Learning how to learn: an essential skill for the 21st century, *Educational Record*, Fall, 49–52.

Wilson, J. (1994) The CUPLE physics studio, *The Physics Teacher*, December, 32(9): 518–23.

Wilson, J. (1997) Reengineering the undergraduate curriculum, in D. G. Oblinger and S. C. Rush (eds) *The Learning Revolution: The Challenge of Information Technology in the Academy*. Boston, MA: Anker Publishing.

Winona State University (1997) *Colleen Toohey's Interactive Resume/Portfolio*. Winona, MN: Winona State University.

15

Autonomy, Governance and Accountability

John Sizer and Steve Cannon

Introduction

In its evidence to the National Committee of Inquiry into Higher Education (The Dearing Committee) the Scottish Higher Education Funding Council (1996) develops a new vision for Scottish higher education. It is a vision of a diverse and flexible mass higher education system capable of meeting the economic and social needs of the country, which recognizes that the fundamental purposes of higher education are to promote the general powers of the mind and to advance learning and research. It is a vision that is partly dependent on a new framework for governance.

In this chapter, concepts of autonomy, accountability and governance are examined from the perspective of the Scottish Higher Education Funding Council (SHEFC, or 'the Council'). It considers the framework of accountability within which higher education institutions operate and draws contrasts with recommendations in the *Report of the Steering Committee for Efficiency Studies* (The Jarratt Report, 1985) in the United Kingdom and the *Higher Education Management Review* (The Hoare Report, 1995) in Australia. It goes on to examine this perspective and these contrasts drawing on both recent research and evidence from the National Audit Office (NAO) reports into *Governance and Management of Overseas Courses at Swansea Institute of Higher Education* (1997a) and the *University of Portsmouth* (1997b). The chapter concludes by drawing on the SHEFC's evidence to The Dearing Committee to suggest a model of governance that maintains the critical balance between autonomy and accountability, and ensures the appropriate balance between the responsibilities of the governing body and its chairman and those of the chief executive and the rest of the senior executive management.

Autonomy and accountability

Sizer and Mackie (1995) have argued that universities enjoy considerable freedoms within a broadly based framework of accountability. While they acknowledged that a reliance on the state for funding means that notions of 'freedom from' that state are little more than illusions, they contend that within a framework of accountability that defines their relationship with the state, institutions continue to enjoy considerable 'freedom to' manage their own affairs. They concluded that if governing bodies were willing and able to accept their responsibility as the first line of public accountability, then the state should be able to respect the autonomy of the institution. If not, then the chief executive and senior management must become directly accountable to the funding councils, which might result in a greater involvement of the funding councils in the affairs of institutions and therefore a further erosion of institutional autonomy.

The Second Report of the Committee on Standards in Public Life (The Nolan Committee, 1996) agreed that 'the exact counter-balance to autonomy is accountability' and drew a clear distinction between the autonomy of a higher education institution and the freedom of an individual academic:

> We do not believe there is an absolute principle that prevents the government, the funding council, or some other public body from attaching conditions to money given to a university . . . the freedom of action of institutions will be circumscribed by the extent of their dependence on public funds, and the public has a legitimate interest in their governance arrangements.
>
> (Nolan Committee, 1996: 36)

The Nolan Committee suggested that universities and the funding councils have struck a practical bargain between the benefits of autonomy and the need for accountability. Quoting evidence from the Higher Education Funding Council for England, the report suggests that this means that 'universities could be required to act reasonably, not to misuse public funds, not to withhold information . . . and not to ignore probity, value for money, or good governance' (Nolan Committee, 1996: 37).

The Committee identified two main models of governance: a broadly collegial model typical of the older universities, and what might be termed a 'managerial model' more typical of the new universities and the further education colleges. It concluded, presumably safe in its assumption that the practical compromise had been reached, that as far as structures of governance were concerned, 'it would be neither wise nor practical to be prescriptive'. The National Audit Office reports on Swansea Institute of Higher Education and the University of Portsmouth raise the question of whether a new bargain now needs to be struck.

Framework of accountability

The framework of accountability within which institutions operate places clear and specific duties, responsibilities and obligations on them, the funding councils and the state (see Figure 15.1).

In essence the basic principle is that funds flow downwards from Parliament through government departments and funding councils to institutions, while accountability flows upwards from the institution to Parliament. The chief executive of a funding council is personally responsible and accountable to Parliament for ensuring that the uses to which the Council puts funds received from the Secretary of State are consistent with the purposes for which the funds were given and comply with the conditions attached to them. He or she is also responsible for securing value for money in the use of these funds.

In order to meet these responsibilities, the chief executive of a funding council is required to be satisfied (a) that institutions have appropriate arrangements for financial management and accounting; and (b) that the uses to which the Council's payments to institutions are put are consistent with the purposes for which they were given. The overall framework is supported by various arrangements to ensure that responsibilities are clearly defined and procedures put in place so that accountability is fully and properly discharged.

The Financial Memorandum between a funding council and an institution is the key mechanism through which the latter is accountable to the former. In Scotland there are 21 identical memoranda between SHEFC and each institution. In effect the memorandum is an agreement between the Council and an institution which sets out the terms and conditions under which the Council

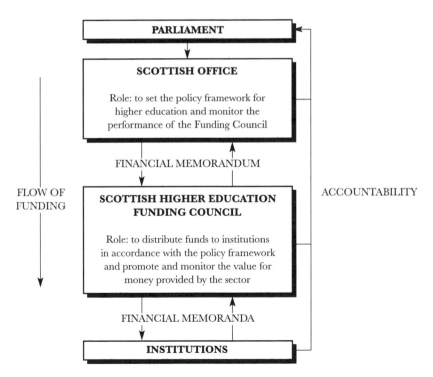

Figure 15.1   Scottish Higher Education Funding Council framework of accountability

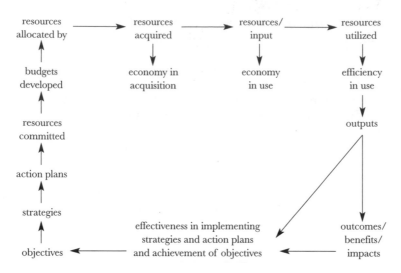

Figure 15.2   Framework of accountability

will make payments to institutions out of the funds made available by the Secretary of State.

The memorandum is underpinned by a definition of accountability which has been elaborated by Sizer (1992) in terms of economy in the acquisition and use of resources, efficiency in the use of resources, and effectiveness both in the implementation of strategies and action plans and in achievement of institutional objectives (see Figure 15.2).

It is in this context that the Council requests institutions to submit corporate plans and financial forecasts and undertakes evaluations of the quality of teaching and learning and research.

SHEFC is a funding and not a planning body. It is absolutely not Scottish Higher Education plc, a holding or parent company with individual institutions as subsidiary companies controlled by the parent company. Institutions in receipt of Council funds are autonomous, and many generate significant funds from other sources. In meetings with chairs of governing bodies of institutions, and in evidence to the Nolan Committee, the Council has emphasized the key role of the governing body in determining the strategic direction and approving the strategic plans of the institution. The governing body has the responsibility of ensuring that the institution maintains its academic vitality and financial viability in the longer term. It is for institutions' governing bodies to form their strategic plans, and to ensure that institutions maintain their academic vitality and financial viability. The Council's responsibility is to secure the most efficient higher education system possible within the funding provided by government, but it is individual governing bodies and senior management teams who will drive the strategic management process.

The role of the governing body

In a rapidly changing environment it is increasingly important that all institutions have a well-developed strategy based on sound strategic analysis. This necessitates institutions having the appropriate internal structures and mechanisms not only to formulate and implement such a strategy, but also to monitor its implementation and as necessary to modify it in the light of changes in the external environment. Unlike company boards, the governing bodies of higher education institutions have on the whole not been designed for strategic management but, rather, as representative bodies of a wide constituency of interests.

In a report of a recent research study on university governance Bargh, Scott and Smith (1996) have argued that governance in universities reflects the outcome of a contest between two alternative models of decision making. First, there is the professional model, in which policy and strategic decisions lie firmly in the hands of the academic oligarchy and its subordinate leader (the vice-chancellor). Second, in the managerial model, the governing body, as the accountable body, and the senior management group impose centrally-driven imperatives relating primarily to economic objectives, such as efficiency and value for money, onto differentiated academic units.

Their research suggests that governing bodies, particularly in the former University Grants Committee-funded universities, are 'caught somewhere between modernity and post modernity'. They derive from an age when their roles and responsibilities were more symbolic than real, when the 'dignified' as opposed to the 'efficient' elements of governance were emphasized. In recent years the emphasis has shifted from the professional model to the managerial, as universities have been challenged by new ideologies and value systems based on the market, consumerism, entrepreneurialism and the overriding need to improve efficiency and effectiveness.

The shift from dignified to efficient roles gives to governing bodies a clear monitoring or surveillance role. In so doing it changes the relationship, or balance of power, within institutions and represents a challenge to notions of professional or collegial autonomy. *The Report of the Steering Committee for Efficiency Studies in Universities* (CVCP, 1985) both recognized and encouraged this shift. The Jarratt Committee urged all universities to examine their structures and develop plans to meet certain key requirements. Governing bodies were encouraged to assert their responsibilities in governing their institutions (notably in respect of strategic plans) and to underpin academic decisions and structures that bring planning, resource allocation and accountability together in one corporate process linking academic, financial and physical aspects. The report identified and sought recognition of the vice-chancellor not only as the academic leader, but also as the chief executive of the institution. It sought to exploit the creative tension between the governing body and senate by recommending the establishment of joint committees to oversee policy, planning and resource allocation, and other key strategic activities.

The report intended to deliver a 'well designed corporate planning process' that sought to make explicit 'the key internal balances between integration and devolution, leadership and participation, Council and Senate as well as ensuring that the academic, financial, social and physical aspects of decisions are interrelated' (para. 3.39, p. 21). The report also sought to establish a new framework of governance appropriate for institutions that were 'first and foremost corporate enterprises', but in doing so it failed adequately to address, define and make recommendations concerning the role of the governing body (and its chairman in particular), and both's relationship with the chief executive and his senior management team. It did not examine the need for a constructive 'creative tension' between the chairman of the governing body and the vice-chancellor or principal; after all the latter was both chief executive accountable to the governing body *and* the governing body's designated or accounting officer ultimately accountable to the Public Accounts Committee in Parliament.

The report of the Australian Higher Education Management Review Committee (CA, 1995), under chairmanship of David Hoare (The Hoare Report), addressed many of the issues identified in the Jarratt Report and went further in its recommendations:

> The governing body of higher education institutions should have ultimate responsibility for strategic direction and development of the university and external and internal accountability, including monitoring and review of institutional strategic performance.
>
> (CA 1995: Recommendation 1, p. 6)

> The role of the vice-chancellor should be to exercise stewardship of the institution on behalf of the governing body, and he or she should be formally accountable to the governing body for performance according to an agreed set of objectives, arrangements and criteria.
>
> (Recommendation 2, p. 6)

The report makes a series of recommendations concerning the structure of governing bodies and the roles and responsibilities of their members; it fails, however, to examine adequately the key role played by the chairman of the governing body. The report acknowledges that the effectiveness of the governing body depends to a large degree on the effectiveness of its chairman but makes little comment and no recommendations concerning the key roles and responsibilities of this office.

While the behaviour of individuals within organizations is undoubtedly influenced by the structure of those organizations, the structure is by no means the only influence. The evidence from the NAO studies at Swansea Institute of Higher Education and the University of Portsmouth supports the research findings of Bargh *et al.* (1996) that effective governance is likely to depend more on interpersonal and largely informal relationships rather than on constitutional or structural arrangements.

Bargh *et al.* suggest that although the majority of governors acknowledge their strategic role in taking responsibility for determining the institution's strategic mission, 'in the complex world of university governance only "knowledgeable actors" can operate effectively' (1996: 22). The evidence they present supports the view that not all governors are invited to play an 'acting role'; those that are often find themselves in minor roles or bit parts. They further suggest that within governing bodies a relatively small 'core group' of governors control the governance process to the extent that some groups of governors are effectively marginalized from important areas of influence. Moreover, the process appears to be self-perpetuating despite the guidance in both the *Report of the Committee on the Financial Aspects of Corporate Governance* (1992) (The Cadbury Report) and the *Guide for Members of Governing Bodies* (Committee of University Chairmen, 1995). While many universities have established a Nominations Committee, Bargh *et al.* found that in practice the process of seeking new members draws heavily on existing members' informal networks via personal recommendations, patronage and opportunism.

Bargh *et al.* also found that the ability of independent governors to initiate strategic proposals depended, to a large extent, on their background knowledge of higher educational issues and their degree of self-confidence to express and volunteer ideas in the company of seasoned executive professionals. This disadvantage is compounded by the fact that lay governors are frequently almost entirely dependent on the executive for information. The executive decides what information it thinks the governing body needs, rather than the governing body specifying what it requires to fulfil its responsibilities. Unless the chairman of a governing body has a clear view of the responsibilities of the governing body and empowers that body accordingly, the executive effectively controls the form and content of how issues are presented to governors, thus limiting and restricting any challenge. Under such circumstances governors are likely to become passive and reactive, shunning the proactive behaviour necessary for the effective performance of their strategic function. The NAO report (1997a) on Swansea Institute of Higher Education found that 'the limited flow of appropriate information to the full governing body' (Appendix 1, para 4.0) was a major factor leading to the breakdown in governance and management at the institution. The study went on to suggest that 'the chairman and the vice chairman were too close to, and were easily influenced by, the institution's senior management and were not sufficiently challenging of it' (Appendix 1, para 125).

The existence of advisory groups (which are often informal and with no constitutional base) to advise the chief executive further serves to marginalize the governing body. Bargh *et al.* concluded that this practice is widespread and generally accepted: 'In both old and new universities the evidence suggests that it is the executive, the senior management team, which takes the "efficient" or most proactive role in the governance process' (1996: 134).

There are similar dangers when members of the governing body itself seek to act without the corporate decision-making process. At Swansea Institute of Higher Education the operation of an executive committee 'left the full governing body in ignorance of many important matters' (Appendix 1, para 125). In its report (1997b) on the University of Portsmouth the NAO concluded there had been a number of cases where governors had exceeded their authority by acting independently of the full board of governors. The report went on to conclude that 'the failure on a number of occasions of governors to act through the established corporate decision-making process was a significant weakness' (para. 3.28).

SHEFC evidence to the Committee of Inquiry into Higher Education

In its evidence to the Committee of Inquiry into Higher Education, SHEFC (1996) emphasized the importance of governance and the role of the governing body. It argued that as institutions face greater and greater demands,

> Governing bodies of higher education institutions will have increased responsibilities for providing strategic direction, ensuring accountability of the Executive, ensuring the effectiveness of key committees and providing specialist advice, particularly in non-academic aspects of institutional management.
>
> (SHEFC, 1996: para. 38)

It expanded on this in its discussion of strategic transformation and change:

> the Council is particularly conscious of the fact that higher education institutions are autonomous bodies. As such, it should be the role of the governing bodies to form their strategic visions and plans within a broader strategy for higher education as a whole to ensure that institutions maintain their academic vitality and financial viability and meet societal needs. This means that governing bodies will have a much more decisive role to play than to which some have traditionally been accustomed. It is therefore important for new relationships of trust and partnership to be established between governing bodies and their executives.
>
> (para. 46)

Thus the principal, or chief executive, has responsibility to the governing body for undertaking strategic analysis, developing strategic plans, for approval by the governing body, to deliver the governing body's strategic vision; he or she also has operational responsibility for delivery of approved strategic and operational plans. He or she cannot be expected to be the sole custodian of the autonomy, continuity and integrity of the institution. The strategic survival of the institution is, in the Council's view, unequivocally the responsibility of the governing body, which ultimately has the responsibility for ensuring that the management of the institution is identifying its priorities effectively.

Under this model the executive is accountable to the governing body. The governing body's discussions and debates are informed by members of the executive but it is the governing body that takes strategic decisions. It is responsible for determining the strategic vision and for the delivery of the strategy plans to achieve that vision. The chief executive manages his or her executive colleagues and accounts to the governing body for the effectiveness with which he or she is discharging the governing body's business, in particular the implementation of operational plans to implement the governing body's strategic plans. This model requires the creation of relationships of confidence, trust and sharing information between principals and chairmen and members of governing bodies; as we have seen, this has not always been universal in the past.

The chairman of the governing body must exert and impose the authority granted to him through the framework of accountability. He or she should ensure that the governing body understands its strategic role and addresses strategic issues. It is the chairman who should have a key role in recruiting the outstanding lay members with not only the 'appropriate mix of skills and knowledge' but also the commitment that ensures regular attendance; who identifies the appropriate key members to chair key committees and work closely with him and the executive; and who ensures that the chief executive undertakes his responsibilities to the governing body and does not simply regard the governing body as a 'rubber-stamping formality'. There are some very good chairmen who fully understand their roles. There are others who appear to have emerged from within the governing body and who may not be able to provide the leadership the governing body requires; perhaps they may be too closely guided by the chief executive. If a governing body has such a chairman it is less likely that outstanding lay members of the type recommended in the Jarratt and Hoare Reports will be recruited. On the other hand there are examples of rapid restructuring of some governing bodies' membership once an outstanding chairman has taken up post.

This analysis leads us to suggest two models of governance. In the first a unitary board approves strategy and oversees its implementation. One would normally expect such a body to have between 12 and 15 members, although in the case of larger, more complex institutions there could be a case for as many as 20 members. The chairman should be a non-executive, and non-executives should be in the majority. The senior executive in the institution (i.e. vice-chancellor) is a member of the body but, equally important, he or she is not the only executive member. All the members of the governing body should carry equal status.

An alternative model involves the establishment of a strategy sub-committee, under a larger governing body, with the authority to act on behalf of that body to formulate and monitor the strategy. Such a committee should be chaired by the lay chairman of the governing body and should involve the vice-chancellor together with respected and senior members of the governing body and the executive staff of the institution. In one sense this model takes us full circle and back to the Jarratt Report recommendation that joint committees of the governing body and senate be established to oversee policy, planning and resource allocation and other key strategic activities. However, there are three important differences. First, it is *not* a joint committee of the governing body and the senate but of the senior lay members of the governing body and the senior executive management team. Second, it is presided over *not* by the chief executive but by the chairman of the governing body and is accountable solely to the governing body. Third, it is more narrowly focused on strategic issues; the Jarratt Report covered operational matters, which are primarily the responsibility of the chief executive and his or her senior management team.

Summary and conclusions

The purpose of this chapter is to stimulate thoughts and ideas and provoke debate. It has sought to place and explain the role of the governing body within the framework of accountability, emphasizing the importance of that role as custodian of the integrity of that information. It has suggested that the Jarratt and Hoare Committees focused on and emphasized the importance of structures while understating the importance of interpersonal relationships within the structure. Drawing on the research of Bargh, Scott and Smith and evidence from the NAO investigations into issues of management and governance at Swansea Institute of Higher Education and the University of Portsmouth, it has been argued that while appropriate structures may be in place, the nature of the relationships between the executive and the governing body, and in particular between the principal and the chairman, are just as important – if not more important – to good governance.

References

Bargh, C., Scott, P. and Smith, D. (1996) *Governing Universities*. Buckingham: SRHE and Open University Press.
Committee on Standards in Public Life (The Nolan Committee) (1996) *Local Spending Bodies*, Second Report, Cm 3270. London: The Stationery Office.
Committee of University Chairmen (1995) *Guide for Members of Governing Bodies of Universities and Colleges in England and Wales*. Bristol: Higher Education Funding Council for England.
Committee of Vice-Chancellors and Principals [CVCP] (1985) *Report of the Steering Committee for Efficiency Studies in Universities* (The Jarratt Report). London: Committee of Vice-Chancellors and Principals.
Commonwealth of Australia [CA] (1995) *Higher Education Management Review*, Report of Higher Education Management Review Committee (The Hoare Report). Canberra: Commonwealth of Australia.
National Audit Office (1997a) Report of Comptroller and Auditor General, *Governance and Management of Overseas Courses at Swansea Institute of Higher Education*, HC222 Session 1996–97, January. London: The Stationery Office.
National Audit Office (1997b) Report of Comptroller and Auditor General, *University of Portsmouth*, HC4 Session 1997–98, May. London: The Stationery Office.
Report of the Committee on the Financial Aspects of Corporate Governance (The Cadbury Report) (1992). London: Gee.
Scottish Higher Education Funding Council [SHEFC] (1996) *National Committee of Inquiry into Higher Education: Submission of Evidence from the SHEFC*. Edinburgh: SHEFC.
Sizer, J. (1992) Accountability, in B. R. Clark and G. R. Neave (eds) *The Encyclopaedia of Higher Education*, vol. 2, *Analytical Perspectives*. Oxford: Pergamon, 1305–13.
Sizer, J. and Mackie, D. (1995) Greater accountability: the price of autonomy, *Higher Education Management*, 7(3): 323–32.

Part 4

Which Futures?

Really, universally, relations stop nowhere, and the exquisite problem of the artist is eternally but to draw, by a geometry of his own, the circle within which they shall happily appear to do so.

(Henry James, Preface to *Roderick Hudson*, 1875)

As the millennium approaches, futures proliferate – predictions, projections, prescriptions, and promises about where today's institutions are going and why. In all areas of life – not least in education – fortune-tellers are at work. As an art-form akin to fiction, prognostication requires an inspired but steady hand. Like Henry James's novelist, the forecaster draws a circle around just a few of the countless relations that shape institutions and influence lives. Selecting one or two strategic facts or potent trends, authors project them forward to create a futurescape where their consequences can be seen. As Bruce Johnstone notes in his chapter, the value of the exercise is to draw attention to these forces and to allow us to think how the future or futures they project 'might be purposely affected'.

Which futures are the university most likely to face? This is a timely question, not just because the turn of a century invites such reflections, but because these are times when major political, economic and technological transitions are challenging higher education institutions everywhere. In the United States, for example, the end of the Cold War has been accompanied by a changing climate for federally funded research in many academic disciplines and fields. Partnerships with industry for research and development have become more common, and universities are also being asked to address consequential social and economic problems in their regions and locales. Around the world, the needs of the changing workplace are increasing demand for higher education while, at the same time, public agencies are shifting the costs to parents and students themselves. The extraordinary growth that higher education enjoyed in the post-World War II era has ended in many countries, and institutions struggle in a climate of constraint to do more with less.

For many educators, today's trends in electronic technology appear to be the single most compelling – and portentous – key to the future of the university. Karl Pister suggests in his essay that the impact of this contemporary information revolution may prove comparable to that of the printing press and the printed book. Indeed, one might cite an even earlier chapter in the history of the book: the production of portable bibles in accessible format in Paris in the late twelfth and early thirteenth centuries. According to Jay Tolson, this 'information revolution' played a direct role in the development of Christian rationalism, 'propelling Europeans toward new ways of understanding the foundations of their faith' (1996: 57). But there were also unintended consequences: 'However much the critical approach to the central text of the Christian tradition might have bolstered the position of the church in the short run, it fostered new habits of mind that in the long run weakened the church's authority' (p. 57).

How will future historians assess the impact of electronic digital technology on today's intellectual communities and their institutional forms? Will the new technology extend or replace print culture, and with what consequences for 'public scholarly and intellectual life'? (Hesse, 1997: 118). Will the contemporary information revolution strengthen the authority universities now enjoy in the creation and distribution of knowledge, or will it blur boundaries between universities and other knowledge producers – for example, commercial publishers, software companies or entertainment firms? Will digital technologies increase student access to improved teaching and learning, or will they – as historian David Noble fears – commodify instruction and lead towards 'the rather old era of mass-production, standardization and purely commercial interests' (1998: 1).

The contributors to this section agree that the future of the university will be intimately entwined with choices academics make about digital technology. Tony Bates sees cause for optimism. 'The wise use of technology', he suggests, 'can simultaneously widen access, improve the quality of teaching, and improve the cost-effectiveness of education.' But 'wise use' will require major organizational and structural change. Bates points out that systematic innovation in teaching often takes place in 'fringe areas' of the university, like distance or extension education. In core areas of the university's programme, however, professors are most likely to innovate on their own. In a competitive environment populated by increasingly sophisticated providers of educational materials, Bates concludes, the university will have to professionalize production in order to ensure quality – not just of content, instructional design and delivery, but also of how materials look and sound.

What kind of university would this be? Bates's proposal for restructuring provides the key. First, this university would have a shared vision for teaching and learning, to help navigate difficult choices about how, when and where to introduce technology-based instruction, and what investment to make in the technology and people needed for its support. Second, to make technology-based instruction a core function of the university, funds would be reallocated to ensure that all professors are encouraged and supported to use technology and that all students have access. Third, to maintain quality and cost-effectiveness, new organizations would be required: teams to develop new courses and teaching modules, a mechanism to set and implement university-wide policies, and alliances with other universities and with commercial firms. Bates recognizes that these strategies entail dangers, but believes that institutions deciding to do little with technology court serious risks as well. Some will fail, and some will find alternative routes to survival. But many universities, he concludes, '*will* protect their core activities by improving the quality of learning and the institution's cost-effectiveness, and will do this through the intelligent use of technology'.

Karl Pister agrees with Bates: universities will have to change in order to stay – in essence – the same. Contemporary US universities evolved through adaptive change to meet the needs of the larger society; now, Pister proposes, they must respond creatively to the challenges of electronic technology and economic globalization if they are to continue to fulfil their historic roles. What are these challenges? The new technology's potential to separate the place and process of learning challenges the university's ability to provide students access to authentic learning communities, while the changing workplace, 'occasioned by economic globalization and the explosive growth of the Internet', values new kinds of knowledge, understanding and skills for students and faculty alike. Pister is cautiously optimistic about the 'faculty's ability to steer an appropriate course through these new, uncharted waters', but notes that their institutions will need to support them by recognizing and rewarding a broad range of scholarly work.

Bruce Johnstone predicts that the university of the future will look quite similar to the university of today. He agrees with Pister that tomorrow's institutions may more fully embrace the 'standard reform agenda' with its long-standing call for more attention to students, teaching and learning, and interdisciplinary knowledge. But he does not believe that this agenda entails consequential change. Although electronic technologies will be used increasingly by faculty and students at universities, Johnstone suggests they will have only a small impact on curriculum and pedagogy. The most 'profound changes, particularly those wrought by technology' will not take place in the universities themselves, he concludes, but in other institutions that will serve less prepared and less motivated students. With decreasing public funding, these 'new' students will have less access to universities with campus environments, and will instead be served by institutions that have been able to use distance education and self-paced learning to lower costs.

Johnstone sees a future of 'ever more diversity in the organizational and institutional forms' of higher education, in which the traditional university will hold 'less hegemony' than it does today.

Which of these futures faces the university? Bates proposes that universities will engineer the major organizational and structural changes necessary to place technology-based teaching at the core. Pister suggests that universities can adapt successfully to the changing technological and economic environment by strengthening their orientation to teaching and interdisciplinarity. Johnstone argues that universities will *not* change significantly, but that their role in higher education will diminish as other institutions, serving a new cadre of students, march forward under technology's bright new flag. These are all futures in which university educators have taken the opportunity to use technology to enhance rather than mass produce instruction. The challenge to us – the *real* authors of the university's future – is to take this opportunity ourselves.

References

Hesse, C. A. (1997) Humanities and the library in the digital age, in A. Kernan (ed.) *What's Happened to the Humanities?* Princeton, NJ: Princeton University Press, 107–21.

James, H. (1875) Preface to *Roderick Hudson.* Cited by K. A. Porter, The days before, reprinted in C. Weglein (ed.) *Tales of Henry James.* A Norton Critical Edition. New York: W. W. Norton and Company, [1984: 391].

Noble, D. (1998) Digital diploma mills: the automation of higher education, *First Monday: Peer-Reviewed Journal on the Internet,* 3(1), 5 January, http://www.firstmonday.dk.issues/issue3_1/noble/index.html

Tolson, J. (1996) The first information revolution: after 13th century Paris scribes began churning out large numbers of portable Bibles, reading and scholarship changed forever, *Civilization,* January/February, 52–7.

16

Restructuring the University for Technological Change

A. W. (Tony) Bates

The challenge for universities

Many universities are making substantial investments in new technologies for teaching purposes. Technologies such as the World Wide Web are becoming increasingly easy to use. They provide the potential for improved presentational and interactive features for teaching. They also provide increased flexibility of access for both students and teachers. As a result many academics are for the first time beginning to make significant use of technology for teaching.

However, although there has been widespread adoption of new technologies for teaching in the last few years, they have yet to bring about major changes in the way teaching is organized and delivered. Without such changes, though, technology-based teaching will remain a marginalized activity, while at the same time leading to increased unit costs.

For technological change to be effective, it usually needs to be accompanied by major structural and organizational changes for its full potential to be realized. This chapter attempts to indicate some of the strategies that universities may need to adopt in order to use technology effectively for teaching and learning.

Why use technology?

Politicians, university presidents, keynote speakers at conferences from government and industry, and teachers themselves offer a number of different reasons to justify the use of technology for teaching and learning.

Here are four of the most frequent reasons given for using technology (there are probably many more):

- to improve access to education and training;
- to improve the quality of learning;
- to reduce the costs of education;
- to improve the cost-effectiveness of education.

Different people in different positions tend to place different emphasis on each of these rationales. For instance, what has really excited many university professors is the possibility of improving the quality of learning through the use of multimedia. The same professor, though, who is a startling innovator in the use of the technology for teaching can at the same time violently oppose any suggestion that more students might be served by the institution through using technology: more means worse – or at least more work for university teachers.

Other professors are fired up by the idea that all the world can access their ideas, their research, their wisdom through the World Wide Web – a passion to widen access to their teaching. This is not always accompanied though by a similar passion to improve the quality of their teaching, as can be witnessed very easily by surfing their Web pages.

Some politicians and business people see technology simply as a replacement for labour, and therefore anticipate that technology when applied properly will reduce the costs of education. Unfortunately, this is to misunderstand the nature of the educational process. While labour costs can be reduced by applying technology, unless done sensitively and carefully it can also lead to a large decline in the quality of learning, which in turn will eventually lead to a less skilled workforce.

Lastly, others look to technology to improve the cost-effectiveness of education. This is not the same as reducing costs. The argument is that for the same dollar expenditure, learning effectiveness can be increased, or more students can be taught to the same standard for the same level of investment.

While technology is unlikely to reduce substantially the costs of education without a parallel loss in quality, the wise use of technology can simultaneously widen access, improve the quality of teaching, and improve the cost-effectiveness of education. These are not bad goals to strive for.

This chapter does not challenge the core functions of a university: teaching, research and public service. Nor does it assume that universities should convert to becoming businesses, using technology to become financially independent of government. The chapter assumes that public universities still have important social and public goals to serve.

However, those core values need to be served in a rapidly changing world. Part of this change is the central role that technologies now play in everyone's life. Using technology for teaching can help universities serve the public more cost-effectively and, more importantly, can help prepare students better for a technologically based society. There are also many things that are valuable in education, as in life, that technology cannot do, and we need to recognize that, but that is another topic. Given then that technology has an increasingly important role in teaching and learning, what do universities need to do to ensure that it is used to greatest effect?

Universities in transition

The ease of use or 'transparency' of technologies, such as the World Wide Web and video-conferencing, makes it much easier than in the past for university teachers to develop technology-based learning materials and course delivery.

The World Wide Web for instance allows a teacher easily to adapt materials created for lecture or classroom use and present them as attractive colour graphics and text. Once the materials are created as Web pages, it is a simple matter to make them available for off-campus as well as on-campus students. This means that innovation in teaching, which has traditionally been associated with more fringe areas of the university, such as the distance education units or specialist R and D educational technology units, is now coming from the 'core': original and exciting technology-based materials initiated and developed by professors themselves, through what I call the Lone Ranger and Tonto approach – the professor with their trusty computer-skilled graduate student, who does the HTML mark-up and scanning.

There are, however, dangers in this approach. In an increasingly competitive environment, and where technology-based teaching is increasingly open to public inspection, the organizations that will survive, as with any of the other new knowledge-based industries, will be those that provide services that the public values, at a better price and quality than the competition.

However, on most Canadian university campuses, amateurism rules in the design and production of educational multimedia. A feature of many Lone Ranger projects is that technology applications end up as a costly supplement to conventional teaching, merely increasing the students' (and academics') workload, and the institution's overall unit costs, because teaching with new technologies is rarely accompanied by the substitution of multimedia for face-to-face teaching. For the extra cost of using technology to be justified, it needs to be accompanied by the reorganization of the teaching process, moving away from fixed, scheduled group instruction to more flexible and individualized modes of learning.

Another common problem with the Lone Ranger approach is that often there is never a final product that can be used on a regular basis in a teaching context. This is because the project drags on, being constantly upgraded or improved, or has to be redesigned as a result of inappropriate technology decisions in the early stages of development. Often the graphics and the interface are poor, compared with commercial games with which students are familiar, and the potential for high-quality learner interaction with the multimedia materials is often missed. Products when finished have limited applicability because they are not of high enough standard in terms of graphics and interface, or sufficient in volume, to become a commercial product. In other words, Lone Ranger materials usually lack quality in the final product.

There are several components of quality in technology-based educational materials. The first is the quality of the content, which is where the status and research capability of an institution becomes critical. Is this unique or valuable teaching material for which there is a need or demand? This is not usually an issue in most research universities.

However, the second component of quality is the standard of media production. Are the graphics clear? Are the screens easy to read? Is the sound and video easy to hear and see? Are the unique features of each medium (video, audio, text, computing) fully exploited? Is the material well assembled? Is the screen designed in such a way that students intuitively understand the range of activities open to them and how to accomplish them (interface design)?

The third component of quality is instructional design. Are the learning objectives clear? Does the material result in the desired learning outcomes? Does it have the appropriate mix of media to achieve the learning outcomes in the most efficient manner? What is the quality of the interaction between student and learning materials? What is the role of the tutor/instructor relative to the technology-based learning? Is the material well structured and well organized? Can the students easily find all the material they need and move around the teaching materials easily?

The fourth is the quality of delivery. Are the materials easy for the student to access? Can learners ask questions or discuss materials with other students? Who gives feedback? What happens if students have technical problems? At what times is help available?

Fifth, there is the issue of project management (see strategy 9). Timelines and budgets need to be established, teams created, meetings organized, materials produced, distributed and maintained, deadlines met.

Lastly, and perhaps critically, there is the question of resourcing and priority. Are there enough resources to do a proper job? Does the professor have enough time, through the reduction of other activities, to produce a good quality set of materials? Is this considered of sufficient priority to get the support needed for the job to be done well?

All these factors contribute to quality in multimedia teaching and learning materials. New technologies are likely to remain marginal, despite high levels of capital investment, and will merely add costs to the system, if we do not at the same time deal with structural changes in our institutions, and in particular if we do not make fundamental changes to the ways we organize teaching.

Twelve organizational strategies for change

If we assume that the intelligent application of technology can improve learning, then what do we have to do to reorganize, restructure or re-engineer the university to ensure that we achieve cost-effectiveness from the application of new technologies to teaching?

From the basis of our experience at the University of British Columbia (UBC), I suggest 12 strategies for change. These are not my strategies; I am merely the chronicler. Some individual strategies have been developed deliberately and thoughtfully by the senior management at UBC. Others have emerged as issues to be addressed. While collectively they reflect an overall strategy for change, they have not been developed or promoted within UBC as a formal plan. Some have not been implemented at all, or where they have been implemented, not on any consistent basis. This list certainly does not represent the full range of possible strategies. Lastly, it is too soon to indicate whether these are in fact useful or validated strategies for change. Nevertheless, they do constitute a useful range of options for consideration by management.

1. A vision for teaching and learning

I use 'vision' in a specific sense: that of creating a concrete description of how teaching should take place in the future, given the current knowledge we have about the goals and purpose of the university, and the potential of new technologies for furthering those goals. 'Vision' describes what we would really like to see or to happen.

It is difficult enough for an individual to identify and describe accurately a personal vision for the future; it is even more difficult to create one for an organization as complex and diverse as a large research university. However, the journey or the process is as important as the goal (Fritz, 1989; Senge, 1990). 'Visioning' is indeed a technique that allows those working in an organization to understand the full range of possibilities for teaching and learning that technology can facilitate, and the possible outcomes, acceptable or otherwise, that might result from its implementation (see Bates, 1995b). It helps people working in an organization to identify and share certain goals. Even more importantly, a shared vision is necessary as a benchmark against which to assess different strategies and actions regarding the development of technology-based teaching.

In particular, an institution needs to define what balance it wants between face-to-face and technology-based teaching. An institution could, for very good reasons, decide not to go down the technology-based teaching route and place special emphasis on face-to-face and personalized teaching. It is likely though to be a very elite and high-cost institution. Alternatively, an institution might wish to vary within its structure the degree of dependency on technology-based teaching, giving more emphasis for instance to face-to-face teaching at the graduate level, and more to technology-based teaching at the undergraduate level. Another institution may make a clear decision to emphasize technology-based learning throughout all its teaching.

Another issue that should be covered in a vision statement is the extent to which an organization sees itself operating on a local, regional, national or international basis, and the implications of that for courses offered and student services. This is important because technology-based teaching does not respect political or geographical boundaries. For instance, regional colleges may need to redefine their role if students are capable of accessing the college's standard courses from other, perhaps more prestigious institutions, anywhere in the world.

In 1996, the Centre for Educational Technology at UBC developed a vision for technology-based teaching (UBC, 1996). The vision included several detailed scenarios of teaching and learning for different types of learners. There were several key features in the vision:

- a mix of teaching models, from programmes delivered entirely in a face-to-face mode to courses available entirely at a distance; it was envisaged though that most students would take a mix of face-to-face and technology-based teaching over the life of a full degree programme;
- an increase in the provision of technology-based non-credit, certificate and diploma programmes, aimed particularly at mature students;
- learning materials developed as discrete modules for multiple uses, i.e. the same CD-ROM might be used for on-campus and distance undergraduate students, as part of a certificate programme, as continuing professional education for individuals, and as a stand-alone CD-ROM for employers/companies;
- more flexible admission and access, particularly for mature students, through the use of technology-based learning, allowing more students to be admitted to the university.

It is clearly a matter of judgement whether to approach the introduction of technology-based teaching on a slow, incremental, ad hoc basis, or whether to have clear long-term objectives and goals driving the use of new technologies. However, what the visioning process does is to bring out into the open some of the real and difficult choices facing universities, and creates a mechanism for engaging a wide range of stakeholders in the process of discussion and decision making.

2. Funding reallocation

The reallocation of funds is another critical strategy. Too often technology implementation is driven by external grant funding or by 'special' funding arrangements. If the university sees the use of technology for teaching as critical for its development, then funds for implementing this must come from the base operating grant. Since most universities in Canada and many other parts of the world are receiving less rather than more government funding on an annual basis, this means reallocating funds.

Figure 16.1 is a theoretical or idealized strategy for funding reallocations at a university-wide level. Between years 2 to 5, despite cuts in overall levels of funding, an increasing proportion of the general operating budget is allocated to the development of technology-based teaching. However, also in year 5 we see a small increase in funding due to a combination of increased enrolments and sales of learning materials as a result of earlier investments in technology-based teaching. This return on earlier investment continues and increases in years 6 and 7, until by year 7 funds are almost back to year 1 levels, despite continued government funding cuts. Also in year 6 the university decides to

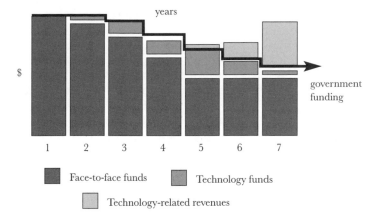

Figure 16.1   A model for reallocating funds to support technology-based teaching

stabilize the level of funding for face-to-face teaching, deciding that any further decrease would be out of balance with its overall teaching goals. (This diagram is not to scale and would in most cases reflect just the top quartile of funding.)

Although this is an idealized strategy, it is not too far from our own reality. In 1994/5 the British Columbian provincial government withheld 1 per cent of all post-secondary institutions' operating budgets, and 0.5 per cent in 1995/6, to be reclaimed by an institution if it came up with proposals for innovative teaching. In UBC's case this came to approximately $4 million over the two years. UBC decided to use half this fund for campus technology infrastructure improvements, and the other half for technology-based teaching applications, with a small amount held back for establishing a small Centre for Educational Technology.

For 1996/7, when the government discontinued its innovation fund strategy, the university itself increased the level of funding for its own Teaching and Learning Enhancement Fund to $2.2 million, to which individual professors could apply.

Eventually, funding reallocation will need to be made at a faculty or even departmental level. The willingness to reallocate funds is not only a necessary strategy if technology-based teaching is to become a core part of a university's operation, it is also a measure of the level of commitment to the concept by different organizational units.

3. Strategies for inclusion

One of the main challenges of making technology-based teaching a core function is to extend its implementation from a relatively small number of enthusiasts and early adopters to the main body of the teaching force. This means introducing a strategy for inclusion, to ensure that all university teachers are encouraged and supported in their use of technology for teaching.

Either deliberately or accidently this is exactly what UBC did with the Innovation Fund and the Teaching and Learning Enhancement Fund. Because initially the funding for innovation was held back from general operating grant, the university applied the same principle as the government: faculties' operating budgets were reduced proportionally, then they were encouraged to put forward ideas as to how to spend 'their' proportion of the operating grant held back by the university for applications of technology. Thus, instead of grants being awarded on a competitive basis across the university, each dean made an assessment of the priority for funding for particular projects within his or her own faculty.

This had two consequences. Innovation grants had relatively weak criteria, in terms of conditions required; and secondly, the money was spread right across the university roughly in proportion to the size of each faculty or department. This meant that between 1994 and the present, a relatively large number of academics in every faculty has had some hands-on experience of developing technology-based materials.

Another strategy that has increased participation in technology and its management was the creation of two sets of committees. The Advisory Committee on Information Technology was established, with the Vice-President, Student and Academic Services (which includes the library and computer and telecommunications services) as chair, with a remit to advise on technology infrastructure and student and staff access issues.

The Media Resources Network (later the Centre for Educational Technology), originally with the Associate Vice-President, Computing and Communications, then later (as CET) with the Dean of Science as the chair, was also established, with a remit to identify academic issues arising from the use of technology for teaching.

Both these committees set up a number of sub-committees, to cover such issues as campus connectivity, student access to computers, copyright, electronic library issues, distributed learning, faculty development, implications for academic research, and evaluation of technology projects. Between them, these committees involve well over 200 academics in addressing issues arising from the use of technology.

4. Technology infrastructure

It is absolutely essential of course to have a strategy for developing the technology infrastructure of a university. Priorities must be set on both the level of investment and the areas of investment.

Large research universities such as UBC may need to spend up to $20 million to develop the necessary campus technology infrastructure: high-speed networks that will link every building and, within every building, every classroom and office. Many universities have old buildings without adequate conduits for wiring, or asbestos fillings within walls that need to be removed before modern cabling can be installed. Many university teachers and staff will not have a computer or know how to use one. Servers will need to be installed within each department and networked to other servers on campus. Internet connections with the outside world will need to be established, and ports and other communications facilities installed to enable students in residences or off-campus to access the main university campus, or satellite campuses and other institutions to be linked.

While such a technology infrastructure strategy is absolutely essential, unfortunately it is often the first – and sometimes the only – strategy adopted by universities: build it and they will come. However, the technology infrastructure plan should be driven, not led, by the university's overall vision and strategy for its teaching.

5. People infrastructure

Just as important as the physical infrastructure are the people required to make the physical infrastructure work.

There are in fact three levels of support required to exploit technology fully. The most obvious is the technical support, the people who make the networks operate and service the computers and telecommunications. At the second level are media production and services, those who produce educational products or supply educational technology services, such as interface designers, graphics designers, video-conferencing managers or graduate students who do HTML mark-up. At the third level are those that provide educational services, such as instructional design, faculty development, project management and evaluation.

The major part of physical infrastructure, such as networks and major equipment purchases, is usually funded from capital budgets and, as such, is less likely to compete for funds (such as general operating budget) that impact directly on teaching. The cost of the human support, though, does compete directly with funds for teaching and research.

Furthermore the human cost of infrastructure support is recurrent (i.e. has to be found each year), whereas physical infrastructure is often seen as a once-only investment, although rapid advances in technology and, hence, the need continually to replace or update networks and equipment make this a dangerous assumption.

Because it is a recurrent cost, and because these costs compete directly with teaching and research funds, the human support side is usually underfunded. Probably the most consistent complaint across universities from those responsible for technology applications is the inadequacy of resources for technical support. Furthermore, the further down the chain, from technological support to educational support, the more difficult it becomes to secure adequate resources. If the network crashes, its impact is obvious; the value of an instructional designer is much harder to sell when funds are tight.

Nevertheless, from a teaching and learning perspective, it is critical that university teachers receive the training and educational support needed; this issue is discussed more fully in strategies 8 and 10.

6. Student computer access

Particularly for distance education students, but also for on-campus students, access to computer technology is a major issue. Approximately 40 per cent of households in Canada have a computer, and about 10 per cent have access to the Internet. Access among university students is higher. A recent IBM survey found that 60 per cent of USA university and college students had convenient computer access. At UBC, 70 per cent of all students have Internet accounts.

However, while access continues to grow, it is strongly related to income, profession (and in many countries) gender – although in Canada, as many women as men are now accessing the Internet, according to a report by Statistics Canada in 1997. Many of those that do have computers have machines that are not suitable for multimedia or Internet access. There is also a chicken-and-egg issue here. If students are not required to have a computer for their studies, they are less likely to purchase one. If students who are thinking of purchasing a computer are not given clear specifications as to what is needed, they are more likely to purchase a less powerful model.

Nevertheless, it would be a reasonable assumption to assume that within five years, at least in North America, most university students, both on- and off-campus, will have convenient access to a computer and the Internet. Universities though will need to put in place strategies to help students acquire the most appropriate kind of computer for their studies, and to help those students who do not have and cannot afford their own computer and/or network access.

There are several strategies that can be used to provide support for student access to computers (see Resmer *et al.*, 1995 for an excellent review). One strategy is to provide computer labs on-campus for students. Once again this is a useful start-up strategy, but in the long run it becomes unsustainable as the primary source of student support. There are several drawbacks to relying on computer labs for access. The first is that as the need to use computers for learning increases, either capital investment costs get out of control, or students' lining up for access reaches unacceptable levels. Second, given the rate of technological change, computers in labs quickly get out of date. More importantly, it requires students to access learning from a specific place, often at a specific time; if they have to book, it thus removes one of the main advantages of using technology: its flexibility.

There will always be a need for specialist computer labs for those subject areas requiring exceptionally high-end or specialized machines and software. There will also always be a need for on-campus access through plug-in ports or drop-in labs for casual use. However, in the long run the most flexible and most cost-effective approach is to encourage students to provide their own computers and Internet access.

Such a policy should not be implemented, though, unless it is clear that students will need a computer, and that means ensuring that there are sufficient courses designed to exploit fully the instructional benefits of using a computer. In particular, it is essential that the use of a computer adds value over and above what students would get from conventional classroom teaching.

If it is decided to require students to have a computer, professors and students will need answers to the following questions. Will access to a computer be compulsory for just some or all courses in a programme? Which courses or programmes should be the first to implement such a policy? Will there be common technical standards for computers for all the courses in a programme requiring the use of a computer? This requires each department to develop a clear strategy for the use (or deliberate non-use) of computers, and this strategy needs to be clearly communicated to staff and potential students. These departmental strategies need to be coordinated at a faculty and institutional level, so that students do not continually have to change machines, operating systems, Internet service providers, etc.

Sonoma State University, California, spent two-and-a-half years preparing for the implementation of a policy requiring all freshmen students to have a computer. They made sure that there were sufficient courses developed in a way that exploited the use of a computer, and therefore made it essential and valuable to use one. This required a major investment in the training of professors to use the technology.

Sonoma State also put in place a whole range of strategies to help students who could not afford a computer: a work-on-campus scheme whereby students could get a computer then work to pay it off. Relatively few students at Sonoma qualified for some form of supplementary state or federal grant that would enable them to purchase a computer, as those eligible for a grant were usually already 'maxed-out', i.e. were already receiving maximum allowable benefit. So, for these students there was a low-cost rental scheme and, for some, free loans of computers from a pool donated by IBM and Apple. There was an additional 'technology fee' imposed on all students. This was used to provide technical help support for students, improving the local area network, providing docking ports for portables, and making available easy access to public computers in public places on campus. Students themselves play a large role in managing this fund and in approving the level of the fee.

Sonoma State found that there was very high compliance with its policy; it was well received by parents and by employers, who praised the university for making higher education more relevant; also most students seemed to be pleased with the policy. The important point here is that it was a total strategy. Implementing only part of it – such as a technology fee when many students clearly do not need to use a computer for their studies – can lead to considerable resistance from students and teachers.

Other strategies to increase the accessibility of computers and networks for learners are the development of government-funded educational networks, through contract leasing or bulk buying of telecommunications services, tax breaks for students on computer purchase, and the development of local community learning centres equipped with advanced technologies.

Lastly, while technology may open up access to some and deny it to others, computer ownership is not the main obstacle to university access at the University of British Columbia. Many more potential students are denied access by restrictive grade point average entrance requirements, arbitrary prerequisites, residency or attendance requirements, and barriers to credit transfer from other institutions. If a primary purpose of introducing technology-based learning is to increase access, these admission policy issues need to be addressed as well.

7. New teaching models

There is a synergistic relationship between different technologies and different approaches to teaching. This is a subject that deserves several books to itself (see, for instance, Laurillard, 1993; Bates, 1995a; Harasim, 1995). However, I want to make three general points that indicate the complexity of this issue.

First, the newer technologies are quite flexible in that they can be used in a variety of different ways for teaching. Second, humans vary enormously between their wish or requirement to follow tried and tested processes, and their ability to be imaginative and inventive. Thus, technologies can be used to replicate traditional forms of teaching; at the same time, they can be used in quite new and different ways, depending on the imagination, skills and resources available to the teacher or learner. Third, media such as video, audio, text and computing are all converging into single multimedia technologies such as the Web or CD-ROM. This is making it increasingly difficult to associate unique educational applications with a particular technology.

Nevertheless, despite this variability, certain trends in the use of technology are evident. It appears that some technologies lend themselves more easily to certain approaches to teaching and learning, while other technologies lend themselves to others (see Bates, 1995a, for a full discussion of this). So far there is no super technology that can meet all teaching and learning requirements, so technologies need to be mixed and matched to the educational purpose.

Thus, we find that instructional television and video-conferencing (one- or two-way television from one site to a class in another site) and certain applications of the World Wide Web (for instance, where information is posted for students to read) tend to be used primarily for information transmission in a didactic style, very close to the classroom lecture model.

Other technologies, such as computer-mediated communication using software such as Soft Arc's First Class, Simon Fraser University's Virtual-U, and Hypernews, allow for more collaborative learning models. These technologies encourage or require a high level of discussion and participation by the learner, and very much resemble the seminar model of classroom teaching.

Although CD-ROM technology is often used merely to replicate a book (i.e. a didactic style), but with better graphics, animation, audio and video, a number of applications that more fully exploit the technology are emerging. Thus CD-ROMs are increasingly being used to simulate human interaction (for language teaching), for representing expert systems (such as forestry management), and for problem-solving approaches based on scientific methodology through, for example, the use of virtual laboratories. These approaches to learning enable students to apply their learning to para-realistic situations, to test their own ideas and use their own experience, and as a result to make and test decisions drawing on their previous learning.

The Web is a particularly interesting technology in the way that it is evolving. It has the ability to combine all these various approaches to learning. For instance, WebCT, designed at the University of British Columbia by Murray Goldberg (see Goldberg *et al.*, 1996), is a Web authoring system that combines didactive and collaborative learning tools, as well as a student learning management system, allowing subject experts without any specialist computer skills to construct their own courses. The limitation of the Web at the moment is lack of band-width and the slow modem speeds of desktop machines, which make it difficult or impossible to run the more powerful applications needed for expert systems, complex simulations and problem solving. However, this will change quite rapidly.

It could be said with some justification that what I have described are not new ways of teaching, merely the application of well-tried teaching methods to delivery by technology. While that may be true, these technologies enable more powerful applications of such teaching methods in more flexible and accessible forms for students, with also the potential for economies of scale. Furthermore, what all these technologies have in common is that, when well designed, they enable learners (irrespective of the subject matter) to develop skills of information navigation, acquisition and analysis, application of knowledge to new situations, new knowledge creation and decision making; all the skills essential for survival in an information society.

In terms of change strategies, these new approaches need to be tested and developed not just in a narrow setting of a particular class or course, but in a system of teaching as a whole; where appropriate, replacing – not adding to – conventional teaching methods. Thus, technology-based teaching needs to be built into mainstream teaching, and not just offered as peripheral or optional learning for students.

The second implication, and one that will be addressed more fully below, is the need for professional development of university teachers, to help them understand not just the technology, but its relationship to teaching and learning.

8. Contract agreements and training

It should be apparent by now that the use of technology needs to be accompanied by some major changes in the way university teachers are trained and rewarded. Teaching with technology is not something that can easily be picked up along the way, as something to be done off the side of the desk while engaged in more important or time-consuming activities such as research.

The most common form of training given to faculty is to show them how to use the technology. This, though, is starting at the wrong place. Many university teachers need to understand why it is important to use technology for teaching in the first place. It has to be related to the changing environment in which universities find themselves, and in particular to the changing needs of learners.

Second, university teachers need a basic understanding of the teaching and learning process, in particular the different kinds of teaching approaches and the goals they are meant to achieve.

Third, faculty need to understand the different roles that technology can play in teaching, and how this alters the way that teaching needs to be organized. Only then does it make much sense to train university teachers in how to use a particular piece of technology.

While this sequence may be logical, it is unlikely to be the most effective way to help university teachers develop skills in using technology; 'show and tell' and hands-on help provided 'just in time', as and when it is needed, are more likely to be acceptable to university teachers than formal programmes (see Holt and Thompson, 1995 for a good discussion of this issue).

University teaching is one of the last craft- or guild-based professions. However, the changing nature and variety of learners, the growing complexity and volume of knowledge, and the impact of technology on teaching now really require that university teachers should have formal training and qualifications in instructional methods. This should eventually become a condition for tenure.

Even more fundamental than the training of university teachers is the need to change their reward system. While many universities have statements that equate teaching with research for tenure and promotion, the reality in most research universities is quite different: the only criterion that really matters is research.

There is really no point in pouring millions of dollars into infrastructure and computers and multimedia unless the reward system is changed. Teaching ability must become, in practice at least, equal to research for promotion and tenure. The good news, though, is that technology-based teaching is usually more public, more observable, and hence more easily evaluated than conventional classroom methods. Furthermore, multimedia technologies provide an excellent means to convert research knowledge directly into teaching and into promotional material for the research itself.

Another way to reward university teachers is to ensure that revenues generated by the use of technology by a department flow back into that department, and do not get swallowed by the central bureaucracy. Innovative mechanisms need to be developed for university teachers (and creative support staff) to share in rights and royalties from the development of generic educational software and learning materials.

Lastly, the very sensitive issue of university teachers' contract agreements needs to be addressed. There are short-term advantages in leaving things loose, but technological innovation will become unsustainable as professors become more experienced in using technology, suffer from increased workloads, and find that they are still unrewarded.

9. *Project management*

It has already been argued that there is a great deal to be learned about how to exploit fully the new technologies for teaching and learning. At the same time there is growing evidence that there is a major difference between 'experimenting' and delivering cost-effective technology-based teaching. The challenge is to encourage professors to be innovative while at the same time maintaining quality control and cost-effectiveness in the delivery of teaching.

However, while new technologies require new applications, a great deal is already known about the process of producing high-quality, cost-effective multimedia learning materials. This knowledge has been developed both in the large autonomous distance teaching universities, and also in private sector multimedia companies in areas such as computer games, advertising, and film and television-programme making.

The process is known as project management. Each course or teaching module is established as a project, with the following elements:

- a fully costed proposal, which identifies
  - the number and type of learners to be targeted (and in particular their likely access to technology)
    clear definition of learning goals or outcomes
  - the choice of technologies
  - a carefully estimated budget (including staff time, copyright clearance, use of media production resources, as well as cash);
- a team approach, involving a combination of the following (depending on the design of the project):
  - subject experts/academics
  - project manager
  - instructional designer
  - graphics designer
  - computer interface designer
  - text editor
  - Internet specialist
  - media producer;
- an unambiguous definition of intellectual property rights and a clear agreement on revenue sharing;
- a plan for integration with or substitution for face-to-face teaching;
- a production schedule with clearly defined 'milestones' or deadlines, and a targeted start date;

- an agreed process for project evaluation and course revision and maintenance;
- a defined length of project before redesign or withdrawal of the course.

In the Distance Education and Technology (DET) unit at UBC, we have a five-stage approach to project definition. Departments or individual professors are invited once a year to submit a short proposal (usually two to four pages) requesting funds or assistance. We provide a short questionnaire to help the process at this stage.

One of our senior managers then works with the lead academic to develop a fully costed proposal. This is a critical stage of the process, where objectives are clarified, alternative modes of delivery are explored, and resources are identified.

The project proposal then goes in competition with all the others to a university-wide committee of academics for adjudication. A set of criteria for selection has been developed, including the number of students to be served, strategic positioning in terms of technology applications, innovativeness, potential for revenue generation, etc.

Following allocation of funds a detailed letter of agreement is drawn up between the academic department and the Distance Education and Technology unit, which clearly sets out responsibilities on both sides, and ties down production schedules, intellectual property, sharing of revenues, etc.

Once the project is funded, DET managers track progress, schedules are rearranged to take account of changing circumstances, budgets are sometimes changed (but more likely rearranged) as a result. This is all done by mutual agreement.

Funds for distance education are allocated differently from the Teaching and Learning Enhancement Fund (TLEF). The differences are really a matter of timing and purpose. To encourage staff who are 'novices' in using technology, and to encourage research and development in the use of new technologies, a 'weak' criteria approach may be best for TLEF. Often professors with little experience of using technology prefer the privacy and control of the Lone Ranger approach. However, as one moves to regular teaching with new technologies, as more experience is gained by professors, and as students become more experienced in using the technology for learning, the more important it becomes to move to a project management model to achieve high-quality materials and teaching.

10. New organizational structures

The challenge with regard to organizational structures is to develop a system that encourages teaching units to be flexible, innovative and able to respond quickly to changes in subject matter, student needs and technology, while at the same time avoiding duplication and conflicting standards and policies.

There has been a long history in universities of setting up large central technology units. In the 1960s and 1970s many universities invested in expensive, centrally managed television studios. More recently universities have established large central computing organizations. Too often these central services have had little impact on the core teaching activities of an institution, and have been considerably underused, partly because faculties have felt that they do not control them. Such units are often subjected to attempts by deans to break them up and reallocate their funding back to the faculties.

Although often dependent on centrally provided networks, new technologies such as the Web are more decentralized. The power is often (or appears to be) on the desktop. This provides considerable empowerment for the individual academic. However, we have seen that high-quality educational multimedia requires a range of specialist skills that go beyond the capability of any single individual. Furthermore, the appearance of decentralization in the new technologies is deceptive. They depend on agreed standards and networks for communication and inter-operation, and they depend on human and technical support infrastructures that require policy making across the university.

The initial strategy at UBC in responding to the challenge of the Innovation Fund was not to centralize all the new technology support services into an existing unit such as Computers and Communications or Media Services, nor to set up a large, new-media centre, as many other universities have done, but to establish a very small coordinating unit, originally called the Media Resources Network and later the Centre for Educational Technology. This had a project director, a multimedia graphics designer, an interface designer and (later) a part-time secretary. It provided services that could be called on by professors to help them if they wished.

UBC has quite a number of separate 'central' units providing technology support with somewhat related or overlapping activities. Each of the directors of these units has different reporting relationships. Lastly, as well as individual academics or departments hiring graduate assistants to provide educational technology support, faculties are now beginning to hire their own directors of multimedia or educational technology.

This sounds like a recipe for chaos, but it can work surprisingly well. For large projects, teams can be called together from across the various groups. Thus, a project to develop a Web-based introductory microbiology programme at UBC has funding from the Faculty of Science, the Teaching and Learning Enhancement Fund, and the Distance Education fund, subject experts and a project manager from science, an instructional developer from Health Sciences, graphics and interface design from CET, media production from Media Services, and an Internet specialist from Distance Education and Technology. Figure 16.2 indicates the kind of arrangement just described. At the other extreme, an individual academic can still work alone, or draw on any one of the services.

Some institutions, especially in Australia (e.g. the University of Wollongong and Griffith University), have integrated their professional development, distance education and media services units into a single multimedia department. The establishment of six cooperative multimedia centres in Australia, with university partners, suggests that multimedia production and services may

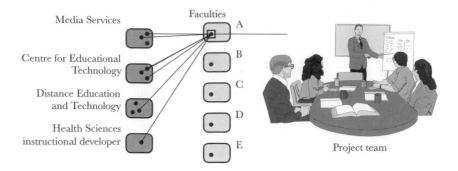

Figure 16.2   A decentralized model of multimedia course design and production

even be shared between several neighbouring universities and private sector organizations.

A major study of managing technology for teaching and administration in Australian higher universities (Australian Graduate School of Management, 1996) classified universities into three different groups: old, divisional and new. The study argued that while centralization of services is appropriate in a new institution with a major commitment to make IT a centre of its vision and strategy, this is less likely to be appropriate for large, well-established 'divisional' universities with a strong faculty structure.

Developing university-wide policy for technology-based teaching and learning is a more difficult issue (see Bates and Mingle, 1997, for a more detailed discussion). In the private sector a number of organizations have recognized the strategic importance of information technology by appointing a single Chief Information Officer at vice-president level, who has a full-time responsibility for information technology policy.

This person is not necessarily someone who has come from a career in computing or communications; in a university environment it would be someone with a strong academic background who has a good understanding of the management and policy issues surrounding information technology, and commands respect and has at least equal status with the other vice-presidents and with deans.

However, many universities have a system of organization that clearly and deliberately separates responsibility for academic and administrative areas. This makes it difficult for a single vice-president in a university to have full responsibility for all aspects of IT policy.

One alternative for setting and coordinating information technology policy is through a committee structure. The difficulty, though, is that committees can allocate resources or recommend policies, but usually an individual has to take responsibility for policy implementation and enforcement.

In short, a conscious effort has to be made to create mechanisms by which university-wide policies and priorities for information technology can be set and implemented throughout the organization. For those institutions that want to make technology a cornerstone of their mission, this means making at least one person at the very highest level of university management responsible for technology policy making and implementation, encompassing both academic and technical issues.

11. Collaboration and consortia

New technologies are resulting in global competition for universities. UBC's competitors are less likely to be our neighbours, such as Simon Fraser or the University of Victoria. There is a good deal of complementarity in programming within British Columbia; UBC offers courses not available from other British Columbian universities, and vice versa. For more than ten years there has been collaboration and coordination in the offering of undergraduate distance education programmes and a system of credit transfer between institutions, through the Open University Planning Council of British Columbia. Where such structures within a state or provincial jurisdiction do not exist, they will be needed to prevent duplication and 'body snatching' (recruiting students from other institutions through distance education programmes).

Our competition is more likely to come from institutions such as the University of Melbourne, Penn State University and the British Open University. Already three Canadian universities (Queens, Western Ontario and Athabasca) are vigorously promoting and offering distance MBAs in British Columbia. In 1995, 43 per cent of all Master's in Education awarded to British Columbian teachers were from institutions in the USA. This competition is going to increase and will be impossible to regulate. Even more of a threat is likely to come from multinational corporations in the areas of telecommunications, entertainment and information technology, such as Microsoft, IBM's Global Networks, and the Disney Corporation, who are all targeting education as a natural growth area for value-added services and products.

As a consequence, we are beginning to see strategic alliances emerging between universities, and between universities and the private sector. UBC is developing a strategic partnership with the Monterrey Institute of Technology in Mexico for staff and student interchange and, more significantly, for the development of joint programmes that can be delivered by technology throughout Latin America and the rest of the world. UBC is already, through this partnership, offering courses at a postgraduate level, with over 300 students per course in 15 different countries.

In addition a number of institutions, such as the California State University system, are entering into partnership agreements with private sector corporations which will provide improved networks and hardware for college campuses, and investment in programme areas critical to the computer and telecommunications industries.

Collaboration and partnerships enable universities to reduce investment risk, share the costs of new developments and reach wider markets for their products and services. They also bring the risk of diverting universities away from their core values, of restricting other forms of development as technology changes, or of putting financial considerations above those of staff or students.

12. Research and evaluation

The need for systematic research and evaluation into the use of new technologies should be obvious. However, it is important that the right kind of research is done. The wrong kind of research is to compare the learning effectiveness of technology-based teaching with the learning effectiveness of classroom-based teaching, using the classroom-based model as the baseline. Many hundreds of thousands of such comparative studies have been made in the past, and the usual result when the comparisons have been done using sound research methodology is that there is no significant difference (see, for instance, Clark, 1983).

As long ago as 1974, Wilbur Schramm pointed to the flaw in this kind of approach: technologies allow the achievement of new or different learning outcomes to those of the classroom lecture method, but if the classroom 'event' is the base, then the new learning outcomes that could be achieved are not usually measured. For instance, if a lecture is used primarily for transmitting information, but a CD-ROM is used for applying that knowledge to solving a problem, then the measure of success for the CD-ROM has to be different from the classroom lecture. The aim then should be to measure the success or otherwise of new technologies in extending the range of learning skills, as well as content acquisition.

Even more important than research into learning outcomes is research into learners' responses to using technologies, and in particular what learners and teachers believe may be lost or gained in using such approaches to learning. These results are likely to vary considerably from individual to individual, so it is important to see whether there are groups or types of learners who benefit more than others from technology-based teaching. This kind of research should also help identify the critical aspects of face-to-face teaching, which are likely to be as much social as instructional.

Another area of research that has so far been neglected concerns the organization of technology-based teaching: which organizational arrangements seem to work best for different kinds of university?

Yet another area where research and development is needed is into new interfaces and applications software that facilitate different kinds of skills. These are generic tools that could be used for the development of a wide range of courses.

Lastly and perhaps most important of all, there is a need for studies into the cost-benefits of technology-based teaching. As well as looking at the costs and benefits of a particular technology, it is also important to look at the social and economic impacts of moving to technology-based teaching (Cukier, 1997).

Conclusions

By this time you may well have asked the question: is it worth it? I must confess that I get tired merely thinking about what needs to be done. The implementation of these strategies will present a major challenge to any university administration. Are they all necessary? If technology is to be used to improve significantly the quality of learning in a cost-effective manner, I believe they are. Indeed, there are probably many other strategies that are also necessary to facilitate the achievement of such a goal.

Furthermore, timing is critical. There is a stage for instance where an institution needs to move from a 'weak' criteria approach to a 'strong' criteria approach to funding. Organizational changes may have to take place later than funding reallocations. Nevertheless these strategies are all interrelated. There is no point in technological investments without a parallel development of a vision of how the institution wishes to teach over the next ten years. 'Build it and they will come' without the other strategies is a very high risk.

Then there is the cost of change. It takes time to design effective learning materials, to put technology systems in place, while at the same time the flow of conventional students and the necessity to conduct research does not stop. What I am suggesting is more like a ten-year strategy than a strategy to be completed within one year.

There is still the option of not going down this road, of having a token or limited use of technology for very specific purposes, of using technology mainly as an additional activity to face-to-face teaching (and being prepared to live with the extra costs of so doing), or deciding to focus entirely on more traditional approaches. However, all these approaches are subject to high risk as well.

The question needs to be asked: can all this be done? It could be argued that the 12 strategies require such fundamental changes within a university that the whole enterprise is unsustainable; it may be 'better' to create new institutions from scratch.

My own view is that this underestimates the ability of some of the most intelligent and well-educated people in the world to learn, to change and to take control of their own destinies. It also underestimates the pressure that is likely to be exerted on universities to change, by governments, by competition and from within. Lastly, I ask sceptical professors: 'Who is having the most fun in teaching: those struggling to serve increasingly large classes within the conventional system, or those who have embraced technology as a possible solution to increasing demands and reduced resources?'

So while I predict that quite a number of universities will not survive, while others will find alternative routes to survival, many will protect their core activities by improving the quality of learning and the institution's cost-effectiveness, and will do this through the intelligent use of technology.

References

Australian Graduate School of Management (1996) *Managing the Introduction of Technology in the Delivery and Administration of Higher Education.* Sydney, Australia: Fujitsu Centre, Australian Graduate School of Management, University of New South Wales.

Bates, A. (1995a) *Technology, Open Learning and Distance Education.* London/New York: Routledge.

Bates, A. (1995b) Creating the future: developing vision in open and distance learning, in F. Lockwood (ed.) *Open and Distance Learning Today.* London: Routledge.

Bates, A. and Mingle, J. (1997) *Distance Education in the University of Maine System: Consultants' Report.* Bangor, ME: Chancellor's Office, University of Maine System.

Clark, R. (1983) Reconsidering research on learning from media, *Review of Educational Research*, 53(4): 445–59.

Cukier, J. (1997) Cost-benefit analysis of telelearning: developing a methodology framework, *Distance Education*, 18(1): 137–52.

Fritz, R. (1989) *The Path of Least Resistance.* New York: Ballantine.

Goldberg, M., Salari, S. and Swoboda, P. (1996) *World Wide Web – Course Tool: An Environment for Building WWW-Based Courses.* Paris, France: Fifth International WWW Conference (url: http://homebrew.cs.ubc.ca/webct/papers).

Harasim, L. (1995) *Learning Networks: A Field Guide to Teaching and Learning Online.* Cambridge, MA: MIT Press.

Holt, D. and Thompson, D. (1995) Responding to the technological imperative: the experience of an open and distance education institution, *Distance Education*, 16(1): 43–64.

Laurillard, D. (1993) *Rethinking University Teaching.* London: Routledge.

Resmer, M., Mingle, J. and Oblinger, D. (1995) *Computers for All Students: A Strategy for Universal Access to Information Resources.* Denver, CO: State Higher Education Executive Officers.

Schramm, W. (1974) *Big Media, Little Media.* San Francisco, CA: Sage.

Senge, P. (1990) *The Fifth Discipline: The Art and Discipline of the Learning Organization.* New York/London: Doubleday Currency.

University of British Columbia (1996) *A Vision Statement for Distributed Learning at UBC.* Vancouver, BC: University of British Columbia, Centre for Educational Technology (http://www.cet.ubc.ca/about/vision.html).

17

The University of the Future –
Place, Process or Paradigm?

Karl S. Pister

In a recent editorial appearing in *Science*, William H. Danforth wrote:

> Even in our sceptical technology-driven era, universities are monuments
> to the hope that through education and deeper understanding we can
> create better lives for ourselves and our children. In this respect they are,
> like the great Gothic cathedrals, symbols of the aspirations of an age.
> Those of us who work in these national treasures have a responsibility to
> understand the requirements of a changing environment and to act so as
> to keep universities alive and well.
>
> (Danforth, 1995: 1651)

An interesting contrast founded in western civilization is noted by Clark
Kerr in the Final Report of the Carnegie Council on Policy Studies in Higher
Education:

> Taking, as a starting point, 1530, when the Lutheran Church was
> founded, some 66 institutions that existed then still exist today in the West-
> ern World in recognizable forms: the Catholic Church, the Lutheran
> Church, the parliaments of Iceland and the Isle of Man, and 62 univer-
> sities. Universities in the past have been remarkable for their historic con-
> tinuity, and we may expect this same characteristic in the future. They
> have experienced wars, revolutions, depressions, and industrial trans-
> formations, and have come out less changed than almost any other seg-
> ment of their societies.
>
> (Carnegie Council on Higher Education, 1980: 9)

Danforth is more tentative as he looks to the future:

> Whether universities adapt successfully to the present environment will, in
> my view, depend on whether individual faculty members correctly read
> the needs of the era and take personal responsibility for the success of their
> institutions. I can think of nothing more important or rewarding than to
> help preserve our research universities for the next generations, so that

they may continue to represent the highest aspirations of the American people.

(Danforth, 1995: 1651)

I certainly concur with Danforth as to both the symbolic and the purposeful position of universities in our society, as well as the essential role of faculty in effecting and sustaining change.

Over the course of history universities have been shaped, and on occasion deformed, by a number of forces: technological, political, cultural and religious, to name but a few. The persistence of universities as vital institutions in society testifies to the ability of faculty to adapt, over time, to the impact of such forces on the academy. Currently the artefacts engendered by the digital electronic revolution – computers, software and the Internet – have the potential to impact the nature and life of our universities in ways that may be as dramatic as the invention of the printing press and the appearance of printed books. (Should one also list the advent of the copy machine here as well?) Both the breadth and force of these technological artefacts of instructional technology present new, unprecedented challenges to faculty to utilize their potential to enhance teaching and learning.

This chapter briefly reviews the evolutionary ecology of universities in the United States, examining what forces have shaped them, in order to attempt to understand how to take responsibility for shaping their continued role in a rapidly, if not dramatically, changing environment – lest, unwittingly, we become dinosaurs while wishing to remain mammals. My examination of these questions will be focused, as the title suggests, on the university as place, as process and as a paradigm for the society in which it is embedded and to which it bears responsibility and accountability.

The evolution of American universities

For the past four to five decades higher education in the United States has been shaped primarily by its research universities. This class of institutions evolved through some two centuries of mutation to adapt to the changing nature and objectives of American society. To emphasize this extraordinary evolution, I quote Charles W. Eliot, who, in 1869 as newly appointed president of Harvard College, declared that 'the prime business of American professors . . . must be regular and assiduous class teaching' (1969: 27). These words hardly describe a contemporary research university.

This quotation must also be understood in the context that the colonial colleges were established to educate young men and prepare candidates for the ministry. Suffice it to say here that institutions were entirely 'people-focused'. The end of the nineteenth century saw the addition of new components to institutional mission. The introduction of research and graduate work appeared at Johns Hopkins and Chicago, following the German university model. Dramatic changes were to follow from the passage of the first and second Morrill

Acts (1862 and 1890) establishing land-grant colleges devoted to agriculture and 'the mechanic arts', the Hatch Act (1887) establishing agricultural experiment stations at these land-grant institutions, and the Smith-Lever Act (1914) authorizing these colleges to create cooperative extension programmes in agriculture. These congressional acts were powerful change agents, adding service to the teaching and research mission (see Simsek and Heydinger, 1993: 22–4).

World War II provided the stimulus for dramatic change in the role of the federal government in universities, as well as in the role of universities in supporting a national purpose. Arising out of the successful partnerships forged during the war and spurred on by Vannevar Bush's 1945 report, *Science – The Endless Frontier*, new agents of change emerged. Among them were the National Science Foundation, which took over the support of basic research from the Office of Naval Research, the beginnings of the National Institutes of Health and last, but surely not least, the newly created Department of Defense. In passing, note that as late as 1952, 43 per cent of the total of federal investment in research and development was concentrated in but ten institutions. By 1987 that figure had dropped to 22 per cent – an indication that the species called 'research university' was increasing and multiplying (see Pister, 1995). It was the beginning of what Clark Kerr once termed 'The Great Transformation' of American universities. Yet another event not attributable to any federal strategy added momentum to the already increasing kinetic energy of change in our universities. The appearance of Sputnik heralded the 'Golden Age' – a renewed commitment to space, science and education of unprecedented intensity. From 1958 to 1968 federal funds for research rose from $178 million to $1.251 billion annually. A concomitant was a substantial strengthening of the infrastructure of academic research and an increase in the number of research universities. Within institutions there emerged a growing dominance of the disciplinary paradigm for faculty effort, with its resultant shift in emphasis in the faculty reward system both in research universities and among the many aspirants to that group of institutions. The decade of the 1980s witnessed a new phenomenon: the rapid growth of research support from private industry, along with the appearance of university–industry consortia, some of which was a result of the National Science Foundation and some industry initiated. Consequently, the federal government no longer held captive the research agenda of universities.

A century after the second Morrill Act (1890), more than 200 universities were calling themselves 'research universities' to reflect their acquired missions and the concomitant work of their faculties. To put it bluntly, the pursuit of knowledge (particularly if acquired through extramurally funded sources that paid for students, bought equipment, provided faculty salary, and contributed indirect cost recovery) became the dominant feature of these universities. Although the focus on students did not disappear, attention paid to undergraduate education has surely diminished when compared to the Harvard days of Eliot, or my own undergraduate days some 50 years ago, for that matter.

To recapitulate, American universities have evolved from teaching colleges, first by the addition of research and graduate studies, followed by service both to private and public sectors. Research universities frequently understand their mission as that of creating and disseminating knowledge through teaching, research and service. What is implicit in the statement and taken for granted is that the mission has historically been implemented at a campus, i.e. a place that brings together faculty, students and staff into a community (of sorts), or more accurately, a group of communities. Unstated in the mission is the critical role that campuses have played in the socialization of cohorts of students and the diverse kinds of networks that are created and that typically follow one through a lifetime.

To this observation must be added consideration of the impact of dramatic changes occurring in the world. The appearance of terms such as global economy, post-industrial society and information age, to name but a few, suggest probable sources of change to which universities must be sensitive if they are to continue to meet the needs of society.

The university as place and process

The concept of the university as a place, or campus, has a long history indeed. It provides facilities for faculty, students and staff through which implementation of the mission of the institution is carried out. Through its academic and often residential structures, it is furthermore a catalyst for the creation of communities, whether disciplinary, social or political in nature. Two significant rites of passage have been associated with campuses: matriculation, at which time many students are away from home for the first time, and commencement, marking entry into the world of work. Both of these events have an important value beyond that held by the institution or the individual. Indeed, both the quality of life as well as the stability of society are benefited thereby for the entire society. This traditional model has never fitted all institutions completely and has been evolving steadily since the end of World War II. Such factors as the changing nature of the student body, numbers of students who are commuters, increasing numbers of transfer students from community colleges, etc. have altered the nature of the university as a place where the educational process occurred. The use of correspondence courses, followed by televised instruction, clearly altered the meaning of a university as a place, but not in a fundamental way. I believe much more profound changes are to be found in the changing character of the workplace caused by economic globalization and the explosive growth of the Internet, with attendant consequences for both business as well as education. Let me give examples. A recent study by Syverson describes the 'new American graduate student' in the following terms:

> [these] . . . influences described above – market segmentation, changing demographics, and changing demand from employers for individuals with advanced degrees – have contributed to a profound change in the graduate student population. Two-thirds of all master's degree students, and nearly one-half of all doctoral students, attend school on a part-time basis.

Women make up more than 50 per cent of master's and 38 per cent of doctoral students. Moreover, the average age of graduate students stands at 33, with about one-fifth of students over the age of 40. More than one-half are married, and many have dependents. And nearly 90 per cent of master's students and 75 per cent of doctoral students work more than thirty hours per week. These developments have important implications for the type of degree programs and fields of study that will appeal to and meet the needs of adult students, as well as the delivery systems used for those programs.

(Syverson, 1996: 23)

What kinds of knowledge, understanding and skills will be needed for such students in the future? In her book *Critical Transitions: Human Capacity Development Across the Lifespan*, Beryl Levinger writes:

In the emerging work-place, the attainment of higher-order skills is a *sine qua non* for long-term employment prospects. Fluidity of workers and jobs is logically the by-product of a technology revolution that places all planet dwellers within close proximity of one another. Computers, communications, satellites and mass transport facilitate an endless flow of information among individuals and groups. Our definition of community is expanded to embrace 'virtual groupings' of like-minded, culturally diverse yet compatible individuals working together to pursue common interests and goals. No matter that they are physically far flung and unlikely to ever meet face to face.

(Levinger, 1996: 9)

Levenger identifies the skills that will be needed in light of these trends:

- collaborativeness and teamwork – no one has all the knowledge;
- flexibility – in a constantly changing environment;
- adaptability – old solutions won't work in the new environment;
- metacognition – learn how to learn over a lifetime;
- ability to solve novel problems – new technologies, globalization and rapid change create unprecedented challenges.

What kinds of faculty qualities will be needed for the teachers of these students? I do not find them present in large numbers in today's universities. In 1944 in his *Mission of the University*, the Spanish philosopher, Jose Ortega y Gasset, wrote:

The need to create sound syntheses and systemizations of knowledge . . . will call out a kind of scientific genius which hitherto has existed only as an aberration: the genius for integration. Of necessity this means specialization, as all creative effort inevitably does, but this time, the [person] will be specializing in the construction of the whole. The momentum which impels investigation to dissociate indefinitely into particular problems, the pulverization of research, makes necessary a compensative control – as in any healthy organism – which is to be furnished by a force pulling in the opposite direction, constraining centrifugal science into a wholesome organization. [Persons] endowed with this genius come nearer being good professors than those who are submerged in their research . . . The selection of professors will depend not on their rank as investigators but on their talent for synthesis and their gift for teaching.

(Ortega y Gasset, 1944: 80–1)

I submit that faculty with such qualifications, as well as interests, are few indeed in our research universities today.

Nor does the issue remain only with the faculty and the content of knowledge and skills to be developed by the student. In a paper, 'Universities in the digital age' (1996), Brown and Duguid propose that there are three essentials that an institution needs to provide to a learner:

- access to authentic communities of learning, exploration and knowledge creation;
- resources to help them work in both distal and local communities; and
- widely accepted representations for work done.

To these essentials are added three other crucial components: faculty (drawn from communities of practice), facilities, and an institution able to provide formal, accepted representation of work done. Clearly, at this stage of the process of evolution, no dominant lifeform has emerged to replace the dominant species – the campus – where place and process are co-located. That is not to say, of course, that models such as the Open University in Britain and newly emerging virtual universities in the United States and elsewhere are not taking more of a role in defining the separation of place and process. Further, the explosive growth of Internet-based audio and video modes of communication, together with curricular materials, has fostered new kinds of learning communities. Whether such communities will or can replace traditional learning communities remains an open question. Based only upon personal experience, I would hesitate to go further than to say that communities that are formed by face-to-face contact can be sustained through electronic media, yet I have found it difficult to create such a community *ab initio* via the Internet.

Accordingly, the challenge of providing learners access to authentic communities of learning, exploration and knowledge creation – to use the words of Brown and Duguid (1996) – remains an unfinished challenge, while the development of resources to help them work in both distal and local communities continues unabated. Similarly, providing widely accepted representations for work done faces formidable obstacles. In my experience it is difficult indeed to achieve such measures at the level of a single college or school, let alone among faculty from separate and separated institutions. Perhaps the experience with the external degree in Britain may be a helpful guide.

The university as paradigm

At least two significant factors lead me to think of American universities as a paradigm for society: the fact that they are energized by the idealism of the youth of the country, on the one hand, and that they provide the academic freedom for their pursuits by virtue of tradition and the faculty tenure system. The motto of the founding college at the University of California, Santa Cruz is 'The pursuit of truth in the company of friends.' While not overlooking the present distance between the ideal and the reality of this goal in everyday life in our nation, its challenge ought to remain alive on our campuses and thereby inform society more broadly.

To broaden the idea, I will turn to the Harvard University President, Derek Bok, who, in an annual report to the Board of Overseers, began by citing a series of accomplishments of faculty and students during the past academic year, accomplishments that one would expect from a very distinguished research university. He then opined that the way of life portrayed by those vignettes is not forever guaranteed. Indeed, he wrote:

> It persists because most people believe that a university so conceived is likely to yield important benefits to society through education and research. The freedom and independence these institutions enjoy and the tolerance and support they receive have the greatest chance of surviving if all of their actions and policies seem consistent with achieving the highest attainable level of teaching and scholarly inquiry. This is so for the obvious reason that education and research are the primary functions of a university and its principal contributions to society.
>
> (Bok, 1991: 4)

Bok went on to say that: 'when universities act in ways inconsistent with the pursuit of education and research, they do not merely compromise their mission; they threaten reservoirs of confidence and trust on which their welfare ultimately depends' (1991: 4).

Before turning to what he considered to be the most pressing problems facing American research universities today, Bok observed that every compromise with the academic mission of universities threatens the integrity of the university, the commitment of faculty and students, and the confidence of the public. And what are Bok's three problems, which in my opinion are still facing us today? They are:

- The politicized university, i.e. using the university for political objectives or imposing political orthodoxy.
- The over-extended university, i.e. broadening the mission of the university beyond a reasonable bound of activities and services.
- The commercialized university, i.e. putting profits before pedagogy and prophecy.

If we are to see our universities as a paradigm for society, and I hold that we must do so, we would be well advised not to forget Bok's problems nor his basic principles in our attempts to respond to the forces of change that are reshaping our institutions. In the Carnegie Foundation for the Advancement of Teaching report, *Campus Life: In Search of Community* (1990), the epilogue concludes with the statement:

> In the end, building a vital community is a challenge confronting not just higher learning, but the whole society. In our hard-edged competitive world, more humane, more integrative purposes must be defined. And perhaps it is not too much to hope that as colleges and universities affirm a new vision of community on campus, they may also promote the common good in the neighborhood, the nation, and the world.
> (The Carnegie Foundation for the Advancement of Teaching, 1990: 67)

This is a paradigm worth striving for in our institutions if we are to serve society well in the coming millennium.

What kind of university?

Let me speculate now as to the future. As noted earlier, American universities underwent a major change in their understanding of themselves following World War II – Kerr called it 'The Great Transformation'. In answer to the question posed in the title of my chapter I submit that universities will continue to represent all three attributes of place, process and paradigm. Society will continue to place pressure on the academy to deal with the purposes and goals of higher education, driven by concerns about the cost of education, productivity of faculty and assessment of educational outcomes for graduates. The rapid expansion of the Internet, with its concomitant facilitation of access to information, will certainly continue to shape both content and style of traditional instruction, not to mention access to education. How institutions respond to these forces is very largely dependent upon the willingness and ability of faculty to be open and creative in accepting and acting upon the changing circumstances. These new circumstances will not be productively examined and acted upon by faculty whose motivation and administrative encouragement and reward is narrowly focused only on the discovery of new, discipline-centred knowledge, i.e. research, as it is commonly understood in the academy. The need for exercise of collegiality and academic citizenship is great indeed.

In contrast to the uncertainty engendered by the forces of change at work today there are clear principles that can guide American universities in shaping higher education. The first of these is recognition of the proposition that the work of faculty ought to support the full scope of institutional mission and that the faculty reward system, both *de jure* and *de facto*, should display the same congruence. This issue of continuing importance has been addressed in the report of the Carnegie Foundation for the Advancement of Teaching, *Scholarship Assessed*: 'The academy must confront the central question of evaluation, or it will not be able to renew the vitality of college learning because scholarship will remain too narrowly defined' (Glassick *et al.*, 1997: ix). There is considerable evidence to show that if the academy is unable to confront this question in an honest, constructive manner, other interests will take on that responsibility for us.

Furthermore, the continuing cry for academic freedom often rings hollow in the public ear in the absence of a concomitant exercise of professional responsibility by faculty and academic administrators. In much the same spirit as Bok's concerns with the interface of trust between the academy and society, Donald Kennedy's book, *Academic Duty* (1997), makes a compelling case for recognizing and respecting the symmetry between freedom and responsibility in the daily life of the academy.

Finally, present and coming generations of students increasingly are accustomed to different learning styles; their access to sources of information on the Internet creates an unprecedented challenge, as well as an unprecedented opportunity for faculty to examine new styles of teaching and learning. Was there not a similar challenge to faculty at the time of the invention of the printing press? Reflecting upon the history of our institutions and their persistence over millennia, I have confidence in the faculty's ability to steer an appropriate course through these new, uncharted waters.

References

Bok, D. (1991) *The President's Report to the Board of Overseers, Harvard University, 1989–1990*. Cambridge, MA: Harvard University.

Brown, J. S. and Duguid, P. (1996) Universities in the digital age, *Change: The Magazine of Higher Learning*, 28(4): 10–19.

Bush, V. [1945] *Science – The Endless Frontier*. Reprint. Washington, DC: The National Science Foundation, 1980.

Carnegie Council on Higher Education (1980) Three thousand futures: the next twenty years for higher education, in *Final Report of the Carnegie Council on Policy Studies in Higher Education*. San Francisco, CA: Jossey-Bass.

Carnegie Foundation for the Advancement of Teaching (1990) *Campus Life: In Search of Community*. Princeton, NJ: The Carnegie Foundation for the Advancement of Teaching.

Danforth, W. H. (1995) Universities are our responsibility, *Science*, 269, 1651.

Eliot, C. W. (1969) *Educational Reform*. Reprint. New York: Arno Press and New York Times.

Glassick, C. E, Huber, M. T. and Maeroff, G. I. (1997) *Scholarship Assessed: Evaluation of the Professorate*. San Francisco, CA: Jossey-Bass.

Kennedy, D. (1997) *Academic Duty*. Cambridge, MA: Harvard University Press.

Levinger, B. (1996) *Critical Transitions: Human Capacity Development Across the Lifespan*. Newton, MA: Education Development Centre and New York: United Nations Development Programme.

Ortega y Gasset, J. (1944) *Mission of the University*. New York: W. W. Norton.

Pister, K. S. (1995) The American research university – quo vadis? in *Reinventing the Research University*, proceedings of a Symposium held at UCLA, 22–23 June 1994. Los Angeles: UCLA Publication Design Services.

Simsek, H. and Heydinger, R. (1993) An analysis of the paradigmatic evolution of U.S.

higher education and implications for the year 2000, in J. Smart (ed.) *Higher Education: Handbook of Theory and Research*, vol. IX. New York: Agathon Press.

Syverson, P. D. (1996) Assessing demand for graduate and professional programmes, in J. G. Haworth (ed.) *Assessing Graduate and Professional Education: Current Realities, Future Prospects*. San Francisco, CA: Jossey-Bass.

18

The Future of the University: Reasonable Predictions, Hoped-for Reforms, or Technological Possibilities?

D. Bruce Johnstone

Projecting the university of the future – say, ten to twenty years out – is a favourite occupation of higher educational leaders, planners and pundits. It is not clear what difference is made by one projection or another, or even who takes such projections, or predictions, seriously. But the exercise is still worthwhile, if only because it causes us (or should cause us) to contemplate the forces that will determine this future and how that future might be purposefully affected.

Forces for change

The university of the future will be a function of many factors or forces. Some of these vary greatly by country; some seem quite universal. Some are predictable, others not at all. In attempting a prediction, it can be useful to view the university as the consequence of three exogenous, or external, forces:

- growth, or the pressure for expansion;
- the changing availability of (especially public) resources; and
- changes in the need or demand for teaching and scholarship.

To these forces, we must add three conditions:

- the standing reform agenda;
- that which is technologically possible; and
- that which is and has been: tradition, or the force of inertia.

Growth, or the pressure for expansion

The first exogenous force is the pressure for expansion, itself a product of three factors:

1. the growth in the number of 18- to 24-year-olds, or the future potential university population (a function mainly of birth rates);
2. the current participation rate and the implied expansionary potential therein (i.e. the smaller the current participation rate the greater the expansionary potential even with a stable population); and
3. the ideological and political pressures to accommodate this potential university population (a function of history and culture and of the answerability of the government to the will of the people).

In the US, there is very little net national pressure for expansion due to a near saturation of potential demand, an apparent diminution of political concern for the very poor or the otherwise educationally bypassed, and a slow growth in the college-going age cohort (for almost 20 years the age cohort nationally has actually declined). There are, however, significant regional pockets of very considerable population growth: California, Texas, Florida, and most of the still sparsely populated, but fast growing, states of the Southwest. But were higher education to be a responsibility of the national government, as it is in almost all other nations (Germany and Canada being notable exceptions), the United States would feel virtually no significant, or at least no problematic, expansionary pressure upon its higher education system. In most European countries, similarly, the sheer force of massification, or expansion of the university-going population, is largely behind them (although the absence of non-university sectors in many countries continues to put significant pressure on their universities).

However, in much of the rest of the world – including the population giants of China, India, Indonesia, Brazil, Bangladesh, Pakistan and Nigeria, as well as most of the rest of the so-called developing world – the combination of population growth and very small current university participation rates will make pressure for expansion one of the significant forces acting upon universities for the foreseeable future.

The changing availability of (especially public) resources

Even in the affluent nations of Europe, North America, Japan and Australia/New Zealand, and much more so in Russia and the new nations of the former Soviet Union, as well as in virtually all of the developing world, the most pervasive force – that is, the force of greatest consequence to the future of the university – is austerity, mainly attributable to the loss of public revenues.[1] Some of this is due to the stagnation, or even collapse, of underlying economies. But even robust economies are suffering from a lack of public revenues. This problem partly comes from the increasing ability of potentially taxable resources (both businesses and persons) to escape or otherwise avoid taxation – itself a function of the increased globalization of both production and finance. Another part of the problem is a growing unwillingness of electorates to bear taxes, a problem compounded by the increasing difficulty of raising public revenues without taxation – that is, through borrowing and deficit financing (another consequence of globalization and the need to maintain the strength of national currencies). Still another source of insufficient public revenues is the increasing competition for what limited public dollars there are: from elementary and secondary education, public infrastructure, environmental protection and clean-up, and the growing burden of retirees on public pensions.

In any case, in almost all universities in all countries, but especially in universities in poorer and/or developing countries – and even more so where the austerity is matched by unrelenting pressures to accommodate more students – in the future, universities will be consumed with the twin tasks of coping with the continuing lack of public revenues and the need to supplement these shrinking funds with revenues from students, parents, corporations and entrepreneurial activities.

Changes in the need or demand for teaching and scholarship

Such curricular changes largely originate from outside any particular university. The origin may be the changing frontiers of the disciplines themselves, especially in basic and applied science, to which universities and their faculty must respond. The force for new subject matter may also lie in the changing needs of business and industry. These changes are felt especially in the more market-sensitive sectors of post-secondary education such as short-cycle, vocational education and other non-university sectors. The wrenching changes in what faculty actually do has been especially traumatic in the universities of the once highly centralized, regimented economies of the former Soviet Union, eastern Europe and China – to which, along with all of the other forces for change (in addition to the diminution of public revenues) must be added the obsolescence and/or irrelevance of many of the academic programmes and faculty, together with much of the physical plant.

Conditions affecting change

To these three forces must be added three conditions to complete the stew from which the future university will emerge.

The standing reform agenda

The first of these is the standing reform agenda, originating from students, politicians, administrators, and even from many of the faculty (even though faculty are the objects, or targets, of much of the agenda). In the case of universities in Europe, North America and other nations that draw on a combination of the classical Humboldtian tradition of scholarship and the newer emphases on access, service and attention to undergraduates, there is a long-standing and rather consistent reform agenda. This agenda urges:

- more attention to students and especially to undergraduate, or first degree, students;
- more attention to, and better performance in, the craft of teaching;
- more attention, ultimately, to student learning;
- more faculty allegiance to institutional mission, as opposed to the more personal goals of individual scholarly recognition;
- more recognition of the need to produce efficiently whatever this mission calls for;
- less disciplinary and/or departmental hegemony, and more interdisciplinary teaching and scholarship; and
- more useful service to corporations, government agencies, and to society generally.

In fact, this long-standing, conventional, reform agenda is actually not a particularly good predictor of the future, precisely because it has been the reform agenda, more or less, for the better part of half a century or more – which ought to suggest to the prognosticators that there must be reasons why institutions and faculty, and perhaps even students, *do not, in the end, sufficiently want it* (Johnstone, 1991). Or perhaps they merely want other goals and more rewards (such as prestige or stability or the absence of political conflict), which necessarily divert attention and resources away from increased attention to teaching or interdisciplinary ventures.

However, this conventional reform agenda is like a spring that will continue to push in the direction of greater attention to first degree students and to the craft of teaching even if the opposing forces continue, for some time, to be strong enough to resist any real movement. But if other things should lessen this resistance – such as new ideologies, or technological possibilities – then the reform agenda gives a good clue as to the likely direction of change.

That which is technologically possible

The second condition, also sometimes confused with a real prediction, is that which is now, or soon will be, technologically possible. University leaders and faculty get especially excited about the new information technologies and their possible application to instruction:

- digital information transmission, and the almost unlimited capacity of broad-band optical fibre connectivity;
- sophisticated interactive software in connection with affordable (at least to upper middle class Europeans and North Americans) personal computers; and
- ubiquitous televisions and video-cassette players.

All of this, of course, gives rise to thrilling possibilities: full multi-way interactive video capability for synchronous distance teaching and learning; synchronous, asynchronous, and near-synchronous Internet connectivity;

video-cassettes and video- and audio-enhanced computer software for self-paced, asynchronous, instruction. But what of all this will actually be adopted, where, and for whom depends not simply on the pedagogical potentialities, nor even on the costs and benefits, of such technologically enhanced teaching and learning. The likelihood of adoption depends on why faculty and universities behave as they do, and why students behave as they do – which may, but more likely will not, lead to the maximum application of all that instructional technology has to offer.

That which is and has been: tradition, or the force of inertia

The final condition that matters (possibly more than any other) is the force of inertia, or what the university is and has been. The university we have today is no accident; rather, it is a product of history, culture, and public and private demand. For example, the American elite private colleges and universities are largely insulated from changes in student demand by a large and affluent applicant pool that will study just about whatever is offered. Similarly, they are largely cushioned from the vagaries of public finance by their large endowments and relatively inelastic demand, which in turn permits a high private tuition fee. In short, while these universities will continue to change, in some respects profoundly, these changes are likely to be mainly *faculty-initiated* and *continuous*, as opposed to *wrenching* and *discontinuous*.

However, where universities and other forms of post-secondary institutions are more vulnerable to exogenous forces – be these changing student demands or declining revenues – and where they have been permitted to respond, many have changed profoundly, albeit still more deliberately than businesses or industries under similarly challenging external forces. The American private regional colleges and the former British polytechnics are examples of such institutions being forced – but also being allowed – to change. In contrast, the universities of the former Soviet Union are examples of institutions buffeted by the most wrenching external forces – particularly in public revenues and in student demand – but being very constrained in the kind and extent of the changes they are allowed to make in response, and therefore, at least arguably, becoming more dysfunctional.

The arenas of change

So some change is likely, even if the magnitude and speed of this change is often overestimated. But if there is to be change, what is it to be? And what are the policy stakes?

There are three possible arenas of 'big change' in the university. First, what is to be taught and learned, or what is the future curriculum? Second, how is that curriculum to be taught and learned, or how will pedagogy or instructional production function in the future? Third, who is to be taught, and for how long, and/or at what public expense; or, what is the future of accessibility? Let us consider each.

What is to be taught?

The first arena of possible change – the curriculum – has been the object of much political scrutiny, at least in the US, but is probably not, as a policy matter, worth the time or the energy so consumed. In spite of the ferocity that the American press and a handful of largely polemical books[2] have ascribed to the battles supposedly fought over that part of the undergraduate curriculum that is common (or 'core'), most students at most colleges and universities will continue to take a mixture of that which is required, which changes slowly because it is in the interest of the faculty that it does so, and what they think will enhance their access to good jobs and social standing, which changes only a little less slowly.

How is it to be taught?

The second arena – how the curriculum is to be taught, or pedagogy, or the process of teaching and learning – has received the lion's share of attention, speculation and prediction. The dimensions of teaching and learning – and thus, the dimensions of possible change – seem to be three, and I shall present them in the form of questions.

First, will teaching and learning continue to be largely didactic and passive – that is, in which the teacher teaches and the student learns (or fails to learn)? Or will the future bring more genuinely active and participatory learning?

Second, will learning time continue to be mainly a constant, and university-determined, as in fixed terms or semesters? Or will that which is to be learned become the constant, and the time required to learn it be made to vary, as in self-paced learning?

Third, will the teacher and learner continue to be proximate in time and space? Or will more teachers and learners be physically separated, as in synchronous distance learning, or separated also in time, as in asynchronous, self-paced learning?

Different combinations of answers to these three questions provide the ingredients for most of the pedagogical variations today. For example:

- It has become fashionable, at least in the US, almost to belittle the didactic, fixed-term, proximate instruction, although such instruction, for many or even most traditional students, may be particularly cost-effective.
- Distance instruction can be (and often is) still didactic and teacher-paced – as in the all-too-common 'talking heads' of broadcast television.
- With video-tapes and inexpensive video-cassette recorders to break the limitations of broadcasting, instruction can finally become more genuinely self-

paced – and perhaps more *accessible* – but it will be *less costly* only to the degree that fewer faculty and staff teach more students without loss of effectiveness.

- With the addition of personal computers, the right kind of software and ubiquitous access to the Internet, instruction can be more active *and* distant *and* self-paced – and thus, at least potentially, more productive by virtue of both lower costs and enhanced learning.

For the present, however, strong forces will hold much of higher education – and particularly the traditional university – in largely conventional pedagogy. Financially, most technology has thus far not been employed to substitute for faculty, which is the traditional source of productivity gains in industry. It has been an additional expense, perhaps bringing additional output, and thus additional productivity, but not offering diminished unit costs – in the way costs are calculated in the academy.[3]

A second conservative force is the substantial autonomy of the professorate, coupled with what has been described as the 'loose technology' of the higher education production process. A widespread and affordable technological revolution in university instruction would take a kind of institutional authority and imposed teaching style that is almost incompatible with the university as we know it.

Third, in so far as universities, largely through the actions of individual faculty, develop new instructional technologies – and they will, increasingly – the spread of these technologies is limited by a kind of mercantilism. Institutions and individual faculty mainly want to be providers, or exporters, of their new developments, not users or importers.

Finally, the consumer demand that drives the successful incorporation of much cost-reducing and benefit-enhancing technology in the rest of the economy is only marginally present in traditional university education. This is not merely because of demand-distorting subsidies, as is often charged (mainly by those looking for further excuses to reduce public revenues to universities), but to the nature of the traditional student demand itself. The traditional-age, well-prepared, and well-motivated student goes to a university, alas, only in part to learn. He or she also goes in very large part for the pleasant socialization provided by a collegiate experience that is shared by large numbers of like-minded young adults. He or she goes for the prestige and the 'career positioning' provided by the university. These goals are perfectly compatible with all sorts of expensive instructional technology, *as long as these forms do not separate the student from other students or from the campus environment.* In other words, as long as the technology does not replace more-or-less regular classes, attended with other students, and presided over by a professor. But this is not the Brave New World of distance education or the virtual university.

Do the virtual university, distance education and self-paced learning have a place in higher education? Decidedly. But not, I would submit, to revolutionize the traditional university, which will continue to be the dominant provider to the traditional-age, well-prepared and academically ambitious young adult. Rather, the enormous potential of technology as well as new organizational forms of higher education delivery are likely to take place more on the important and growing peripheries of traditional university education.

In countries that have not yet achieved mass higher education, this periphery may include those of traditional university age whose parents cannot afford tuition and living expenses and whose governments are unwilling to provide grants of subsidies – but who, with sufficient motivation, may be able to learn via distance modalities. For more educationally advanced and wealthier countries, distance education and other forms of technologically mediated instruction are more likely to supplement and enrich traditional university education, but may also come to dominate the growing and potentially vast arenas of corporate training, continuing professional education, and further education for recreation and personal enrichment.

Who is to be taught, and for how long, and/or at what public expense?

The most potentially significant big change lies in the realm of access: who is to be taught, and for how long, and/or at what public expense? Higher education is costly. The per-student costs of research universities, with low teaching loads, expensive technology, supported graduate and post-doctoral students, and internationally competitive salaries, are especially high. Most of the nations of Europe are well beyond what Martin Trow (1974) once labelled 'mass higher education', signalled by a high percentage of secondary school leavers seeking university access – often, on the European continent, as a constitutional right to all holders of the academic secondary leaving certificate. However, the number of new entrants continues to rise. Furthermore, the amount of higher education partaken by each entering student has also been rising, through the prolongation of study and the accretion of degrees and credentialism.

At the same time, and as discussed above, governments everywhere are besieged by competing claims on public revenues and constrained in the accumulation of those revenues by the increasingly easy exodus of taxable enterprises and by new limits on deficit spending. There is not enough money from public treasuries. The solutions to the new austerity of higher education will be some combination of:

- less spending per student in the traditional universities, mainly meaning fewer regular, fully credentialed faculty per student;
- more students shunted off to lower-cost, short-cycle forms of tertiary education;
- more rigorous standards, including more stages or levels, even within the first degree, at which point students deemed to be insufficiently performing can be turned out of the university system, thereby lowering overall enrolments (and costs);
- a greater share of the costs formerly borne by the taxpayer (whether costs of

instruction or the costs of student living) being borne instead by parents or the students themselves;

- governments encouraging the formation of private universities and colleges – in some cases (Latin America and East Asia in particular) avowedly as institutions to absorb the burgeoning demand for higher education at minimal cost to the taxpayer; and
- governments rushing to embrace new technology-based forms of tertiary education, less for the added access or the added learning that these forms make possible, but for the lower costs that they are thought to promise.

These trends are not diminishing. Most nations have developed non-university alternatives to lessen the hegemony of the research university model. Thus, the American community college (indeed, most American four-year colleges, public and private), the German *Fachhochschulen*, the Dutch HBO, the French Institutes Universitaires Technologies, and at one time the British polytechnics were all created to provide what was thought to be 'more appropriate' forms of tertiary education for more students at lower public costs.

Universities everywhere are increasingly turning to non-public, or non-tax originated, revenues. In 1997, even China declared tuition fees to be fully consistent with their latest version of Marxist-Leninist-Mao Zedong-Deng Xiaoping thought. Private institutions, often fragile and of uneven quality, are springing up all over the former Soviet Union and east Europe. Chile's higher education system, substantially privatized, sufficient in capacity, and evidently stable, is the model held up to developing nations by the World Bank (1994). Only Europe clings to the sanctity of tuition fee-free mass higher education, and cracks are appearing in this principle.

What is at stake is not the accessibility of publicly supported higher education for the well prepared and academically ambitious, to which all nations are committed, to the limits of their capabilities. What is at stake is the access that nations have attempted to provide for those who are only marginally prepared for, or even only marginally interested in, the academic challenges of the traditional western university.

These are the students who now begin, but often do not complete, a true university first degree. But these are also students, many of whom will come from less privileged family and peer backgrounds, some of whom will succeed, and those only because they were given opportunities, either financial or academic, that are now being called into question.

These are also students who almost certainly are gaining personal benefits from their higher education experiences (in addition to some public benefits that accrue to us all), even if they do not graduate, and even if it could be said, albeit only in retrospect, that they would have been better suited to a shorter cycle higher education to begin with.

Finally, these are the students that some governments are saying need not be accommodated at public expense, at least at the traditional university. The public pay-off is thought to be insufficient. And a combination of diminishing financial assistance, rising tuition fees, more rigorous entry and even second-stage examinations, and more rigorous academic criteria for the continuation of financial assistance, will lower their numbers in the universities.

So the question is whether the newer forms of higher education opportunities will accommodate these students with the equivalent access to jobs, careers, social standing and personal fulfilment as the traditional universities might – but probably would not – have.

Likely changes: the future university

Such a scenario, then, projects a future higher education in most countries that features:

- Ever more diversity in the organizational and institutional forms through which higher, or tertiary, or post-secondary teaching, learning and scholarship take place, with much growth outside of, or at least peripheral to, the traditional university.
- The traditional universities – those holding to established forms and principles of research, advanced education and first degrees primarily for the academically well prepared and motivated – will look and operate much as they do today, with curriculum, instructional methodology and scholarship determined mainly by the permanent faculty.
- The traditional reform agenda will continue to be a beacon for, but will not substantially alter the substance of, either the traditional Humboldtian research university or the non-university forms that emulate the main features of this model.
- The use of technology will increase greatly, particularly in the processing, storage and transmission of information among both faculty and students. Technologically mediated instruction – distance education – will dominate the expansion of higher education in those countries that are still below the threshold of mass higher education. In the more developed world, with more resources and where the expansionary pressure is minimal, technology will impact the curriculum and pedagogy of the traditional universities only minimally, and mainly as 'add-ons', at additional cost.
- True labour- and cost-saving technology, however, will profoundly change the method and timing of both teaching and learning in those deliverers at the periphery of the traditional university: short course vocational training, corporate education, professional in-service education, and all forms of continuing and recreational post-secondary education.
- The traditional university will hold less hegemony over these alternative forms of higher learning, research and service.
- Accessibility, at least as we have known it in America, will be diminished at the traditional university for those who are less prepared and less motivated.
- The costs of all forms of higher and post-secondary education will continue to shift away from the taxpayer and more to the student and parent, placing

a premium on need-based financial assistance, student loans, and traditions of parental savings and financial help to their children.

In short, I see a future university that will be much like the present one, at least in curriculum and pedagogy. I do not see the end of the university as we have come to know it. I believe there will be significant changes that are largely foreseeable, and other changes – perhaps dramatic ones – that are quite unforeseeable. But I do not believe that the university is on any more of a 'cusp of radical change', at least in the US, than it was in the decade of explosive growth in the 1960s, or the decades of explosive federal research expansion in the 1950s and 1960s, or the decades of political turmoil of the 1960s and 1970s – or for that matter the wrenching challenges of the Great Depression years of the 1930s, or of World War II in the 1940s.

In so far as profound changes are very possible, I only hope that the most likely – a significant lowering of access and participation – does not come to pass.

And in the larger arena of what we in America have come to term 'post-secondary education' – that is, on the periphery of traditional university education – there may be profound changes, particularly those wrought by technology. In these changes lie great opportunities.

Notes

1. See Johnstone (1988). For austerity in the developing countries, see Ziderman and Albrecht (1995).
2. For example, Bloom (1987), Smith (1990), Anderson (1992), D'Souza (1991), and many others.
3. See Massy and Zemsky (1996) and Twigg (1996). For a comprehensive treatment of the economics of distance and open learning in a comparative context, see Rumble (1997).

References

Anderson, M. (1992) *Imposters in the Temple.* New York: Simon and Schuster.

Bloom, A. (1987) *The Closing of the American Mind.* New York: Simon and Schuster.

D'Souza, D. (1991) *Illiberal Education: The Politics of Race and Sex on Campus.* New York: Free Press.

Johnstone, D. B. (1988) Financing higher education: who should pay and other issues, in P. G. Altbach, R. O. Berdahl and P. J. Gumport (eds) *American Higher Education in the 21st Century: Social, Political, and Economic Challenges.* Baltimore, MD: Johns Hopkins University Press.

Johnstone, D. B. (1991) Higher education in the year 2000, *Prospects*, 21(3): 430–42. [Reprinted in Z. Morsy and P. Altbach (eds) (1996) *Higher Education in International Perspective: Toward the 21st Century.* New York: Garland Publishing.]

Massy, W. F. and Zemsky, R. (1996) Information technology and academic productivity, *EDUCOM Review*, 31: 12–15.

Rumble, G. (1997) *The Costs and Economics of Open and Distance Learning*. London: Kogan Page.

Smith, P. (1990) *Killing the Spirit: Higher Education in America*. New York: Penguin Books.

Trow, M. (1974) *Problems in the Transition from Elite to Mass Higher Education*. OECD, Policies for Higher Education. Paris: Organization for Economic Cooperation and Development.

Twigg, C. (1996) *Academic Productivity: The Case for Instructional Software*. Washington, DC: EDUCOM.

The World Bank (1994) *Higher Education: The Lessons of Experience*. Washington, DC: The World Bank.

Ziderman, A. and Albrecht, D. (1995) *Financing Universities in Developing Countries*. Washington, DC: The Falmer Press.

Index

The Society for Research into Higher Education

The Society for Research into Higher Education exists to stimulate and coordinate research into all aspects of higher education. It aims to improve the quality of higher education through the encouragement of debate and publication on issues of policy, on the organization and management of higher education institutions, and on the curriculum and teaching methods.

The Society's income is derived from subscriptions, sales of its books and journals, conference fees and grants. It receives no subsidies, and is wholly independent. Its individual members include teachers, researchers, managers and students. Its corporate members are institutions of higher education, research institutes, professional, industrial and governmental bodies. Members are not only from the UK, but from elsewhere in Europe, from America, Canada and Australasia, and it regards its international work as among its most important activities.

Under the imprint *SRHE & Open University Press*, the Society is a specialist publisher of research, having over 70 titles in print. The Editorial Board of the Society's Imprint seeks authoritative research or study in the above fields. It offers competitive royalties, a highly recognizable format in both hardback and paperback and the worldwide reputation of the Open University Press.

The Society also publishes *Studies in Higher Education* (three times a year), which is mainly concerned with academic issues, *Higher Education Quarterly* (formerly *Universities Quarterly*), mainly concerned with policy issues, *Research into Higher Education Abstracts* (three times a year), and *SRHE News* (four times a year).

The Society holds a major annual conference in December, jointly with an institution of higher education. In 1996 the topic was 'Working in Higher Education' at University of Wales, Cardiff. In 1997, it was 'Beyond the First Degree' at the University of Warwick; and in 1998 it was 'The Globalization of Higher Education' at the University of Lancaster. The 1999 conference will be on the topic of higher education and its communities at UMIST.

The Society's committees, study groups and networks are run by the members. The networks at present include:

Access	Mentoring
Curriculum Development	Vocational Qualifications
Disability	Postgraduate Issues
Eastern European	Quality
Funding	Quantitative Studies
Legal Education	Student Development

Benefits to Members

Individual

Individual members receive:

- *SRHE News*, the Society's publications list, conference details and other material included in mailings.
- Greatly reduced rates for *Studies in Higher Education* and *Higher Education Quarterly*.
- A 35 per cent discount on all SRHE & Open University Press publications.
- Free copies of the Proceedings – commissioned papers on the theme of the Annual Conference.
- Free copies of *Research into Higher Education Abstracts*.
- Reduced rates for the annual conference.
- Extensive contacts and scope for facilitating initiatives.
- Free copies of the *Register of Members' Research Interests*.
- Membership of the Society's networks.

Corporate

Corporate members receive:

- Benefits of individual members, plus:
- Free copies of *Studies in Higher Education*.
- Unlimited copies of the Society's publications at reduced rates.
- Reduced rates for the annual conference.
- The right to submit applications for the Society's research grants.
- The right to use the Society's facility for supplying statistical HESA data for purposes of research.

Membership details: SRHE, 3 Devonshire Street, London
W1N 2BA, UK. Tel: 0171 637 2766. Fax: 0171 637 2781.
email: srhe@mailbox.ulcc.ac.uk
World Wide Web: http://www.srhe.ac.uk./srhe/
Catalogue: SRHE & Open University Press, Celtic Court,
22 Ballmoor, Buckingham MK18 1XW. Tel: 01280 823388.
Fax: 01280 823233. email: enquiries@openup.co.uk